LORENZA'S ITALIAN SEASONS

LORENZA DE'MEDICI

LORENZA'S ITALIAN SEASONS

200 RECIPES FOR FAMILY AND FRIENDS

PAVILION

Many thanks to John Meis for his assistance

All eggs used in the recipes are large (US extra large) and all sugar is granulated (granular) unless otherwise specified.

First published in Great Britain in 2001 by
Pavilion Books Limited
London House, Great Eastern Wharf
Parkgate Road, London SW11 4NQ
www.pavilionbooks.co.uk

Text © Lorenza de' Medici 2001
Photographs © Gus Filgate 2001
Design and layout © Pavilion Books Ltd. 2001
All other illustrations courtesy of Mary Evans & Fotomas

The moral right of the author and illustrator has been asserted

Art direction and design by David Costa and Fiona Andreanelli at Wherefore Art?

A CIP catalogue record for this book is available from the British Library

ISBN 1 86205 354 5

Printed and bound in Italy by Conti-Tipocolor

2 4 6 8 10 9 7 5 3 1

This book may be ordered by post direct from the publisher. Please contact the Marketing Department.
But try your bookshop first.

CONTENTS

FOREWORD

Surely one of life's most satisfying pleasures—simple and sensual—is seasonal change, the transition from winter to spring and summer to autumn. I especially look forward to the fresh variety it brings to the market and table—spring greens, bright and crisp, summer vegetables, warm in colour and taste, a rich abundance of autumn harvests and comforting winter fare. Happily, Italy's geographic position favours four distinct seasons, none of them extreme, and the climate nurtures agriculture along the peninsula from tip to toe all year round. Italy's diverse topography—mountains, plains, valleys and foothills, surrounded by seas—creates a series of microclimates which encourage the most varied harvests of fruits, vegetables, fish and meat.

For most of my life I have lived between Milan, Italy's most cosmopolitan city, and Tuscany, the most highly agricultural region of the country. Perhaps it is the sharp contrast between these two environments that has shaped my appreciation for seasonal change. In any case, my experience of the seasons is Tuscan. I enjoy nature, plant my garden, go to market, cook and eat mostly in Tuscany. My Tuscan perspective is reflected especially in the seasonal introductions of this book, although I include recipes from other regions as well as many improvised dishes of my own.

Traditional, regional Italian cooking reflects seasonal change. This is still true today, notwithstanding the standardisation that is creeping in due to mass-produced food and the wide availability of 'out of season' produce. Most home cooks and many restaurant chefs go first to the garden or to the market before they decide what to prepare. One aim of this book is to encourage the reader to do the same. Another goal in my cookery books and classes has always been to inspire rather than instruct. Cooking according to the season encourages improvisation. One cannot help but be inspired by the variety, beauty and freshness of local, seasonal foods. The appeal of their lively and honest flavours is immediate. My hope is that this book will encourage you to make a habit of going to the market to choose the finest and freshest ingredients you can find and then to the recipes for inspiration on how to use them to make a wonderful dish. I can promise you both experiences will be immensely gratifying.

The annual cycle of feasts surrounding Christmas, Easter, summer holidays and autumn harvests traditionally features seasonal foods. I have included menus for these festive occasions, which I hope will provide inspiration in the kitchen and pleasure at the table for your celebrations with family and friends.

INTRODUCTION

Spring in Italy is definitely a moveable feast. In Agrigento, on the southern coast of the island of Sicily, just a few miles over the Mediterranean from North Africa, the almond blossom festival welcoming the season is held on the first Sunday of February. Further up the Italian peninsula in the southern region of Campania, whose capital city is Naples, bougainvillea, wisteria, oleander and dozens of other plants and flowers are abloom in March. In northern Tuscany, where I live, it still looks and feels as if we are in the dead of winter. The landscape is naked and the branches of the trees are bare. We have to wait several more weeks before the first violets and daffodils add a little cheer to the countryside. Nor is it at all unusual to eat Easter lunch by the fire. The traditional time to move our potted lemons out into the garden is Easter, but if it comes early, there is still the risk of frost or even snow. Finally by May the season's exuberance begins to unfold. The fields are full of wild flowers and the woods are in bright green leaf.

In local markets a plenitude of produce fills the stalls, sometimes to overflowing. What to choose first? One of the earliest arrivals are *fave*, broad (fava) beans, heaps of them. While they are still small and bright green, they are so sweet and tender they can be eaten raw. As an *antipasto* they are often combined with fresh pecorino (Romano) cheese, made from sheep's milk (see below). Dressed with extra virgin olive oil, they can be prepared as a tasty salad or as a topping for a *crostone*, a large piece of grilled country bread rubbed with garlic.

For an informal gathering, I place a big bowl of broad (fava) beans in their pods in the centre of the table with some salt on the side and let my friends do the work. They should be washed down with generous draughts of white wine. When they are still young, you can cook them quickly like fresh peas. They make a perfect accompaniment to fish dishes. As the season progresses the thin skin that covers each bean should be peeled, as it develops an unpleasant bitterness. This is labour intensive and it helps if you have some willing children at hand. Mature broad beans are delicious stewed with diced pancetta or used as a base for soups and sauces.

Not long after the first broad (fava) beans arrive at the market, I eagerly await the arrival of another delicious legume. This one grows in my garden. I rate the simple, fresh, tiny garden pea a great gastronomic delight. It is an almost ineffable experience to eat fresh peas from the garden—and I *mean* straight from the garden and directly into the pot to cook for not more than a minute or two. Their flavour is incomparable. They are so tender and sweet you can even toss them raw or swiftly blanched into a salad. Unfortunately, once off the vine peas lose their flavour very quickly, in a matter not of days but hours. Fortunately they freeze very well. An American friend of mine says that Italian frozen peas taste better than 'fresh' peas at home. This is because Italian frozen peas have been picked at their peak and frozen at once.

The classic Italian way to prepare peas is to cook them with Parma ham to make *piselli al prosciutto*. The same ingredients make a tasty topping for pasta. Another good recipe for a first course is potato gnocchi dressed with a pea sauce. Peas and rice are also a perfect combination. I purée peas for soup and flavour the purée with tarragon or mint, two herbs that complement the taste of peas. Peas have the advantage of combining well with any number of other spring vegetables, such as broad (fava) beans, artichokes and asparagus. They are also one of the few vegetables that I serve with fish dishes.

Another vegetable that arrives in abundance is the artichoke. Crates of them with their exuberant leaves fill spring market bins to overflowing. At the height of their season (actually they have two—spring and early winter) you even see trucks parked on the outskirts of cities loaded with artichokes selling for a song. I think of artichokes, *carciofi*, as *the* Italian vegetable. Food historians suspect that they may have their origins here, probably in Sicily. What is certain is that Italian horticulture and gastronomy have developed this vegetable to its full, delicious potential. Today Italy is the world's largest producer and consumer of artichokes.

Botanically speaking, the artichoke is a member of the thistle family and related to the wild cardoon, which is native to the Mediterranean and was popular with the ancient Greeks and Romans. Artichokes are cultivated for their flower head. When this is still a small bud, Italians eat the whole head, both raw and cooked. In other places artichokes seem only to be eaten when the bud is more mature. At that stage its petal-like leaves, called bracts, have become tougher and only their fleshy base is tender enough to eat. In Italy we dip these in extra virgin olive oil, instead of the melted butter served for this purpose elsewhere.

It seems that practically every region or even province of Italy has its native artichoke. There are dozens of varieties. Some grow thorns on the tip of their bracts, some come without—an important difference for the cook as well as the eater. Some can only be found locally, while others have become national varieties. When you are in Venice, look for the *castraure della laguna veneta*, 'castrates', which are tiny and delicious. At Harry's Bar, Arrigo Cipriani serves several of them warm with a pile

of *gamberetti*, baby shrimp. It is a dish fit for a king with a price to match. When you consider the preparation time required to peel both ingredients and, in particular, the divine taste of this heavenly match, you realise that it is worth the big splurge.

The *violetti di Toscana*, 'Tuscan violets', are early spring arrivals in that region. Perhaps the most popular artichoke, common also in North America, is the globe-shaped Romanesco. Romans use it to prepare their most celebrated *antipasto, carciofi alla romana*. All the tough, inedible parts of the artichoke are trimmed away and it is braised whole, together with its tender stem, in a mixture of olive oil, parsley, garlic and mint leaves. One of the glories of Roman Jewish cuisine is *carciofi alla Giudia*. Globe artichokes are deep-fried in such a way that the outer leaves are crisp and the centre turns tender and succulent. Unless you are the kind of cook that loves to spend hours of intensive labour in the kitchen, which I am not, both these specialities are best enjoyed in any number of good Roman *trattorie*.

Another way to enjoy artichokes without the toil involved in cleaning them is to go to a farmers' market in any Italian city and there you will be sure to find vegetable sellers doing the work for you. You can watch them skilfully and swiftly pare away the outer leaves with a small, very sharp knife and drop them into a bucket filled with water and lemon halves, to prevent the finished product from discolouring. Inevitably, however, if you want to enjoy the pleasure of eating artichokes, you have to face the task of cleaning them for yourself. My biggest problem was overcoming guilt at the waste factor, as I was always taught never to waste even a crumb. In this case you simply have to throw caution to the wind and sometimes up to a quarter of the bracts as well, until you come to the pale, edible part. I use my fingers. Others prefer a paring knife. And don't forget the lemon water.

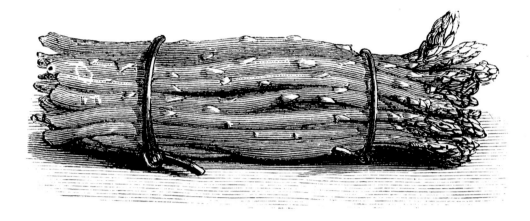

When you visit Italy, be sure to try the tiny, spring variety of artichoke raw, dressed with extra virgin olive oil. And whether you eat artichokes raw or cooked, your dish will be infinitely more tasty if prepared with fine, extra virgin olive oil instead of butter. Artichokes and rice pair well together, either in a risotto or in a rice mould. Each season, I especially look forward to pasta dishes dressed with artichokes, cooked in a tomato sauce or simply sautéed, tender stems and all.

While artichokes arrive in masses, asparagus—the most elegant, in an odd sort of way, of spring vegetables and also the most expensive—makes only a brief and almost furtive visit. One summer, while visiting the Alsatian region of France where asparagus (the white variety) is king, I saw a row of strange-looking plants in a friend's garden. They were about 1.5m/4ft tall, looked like ferns but had bright red berries. 'Asparagus', he said. I was astounded that the tiny spears I was accustomed to would, if left to themselves, grow into such a large and curious plant.

Asparagus officinalis is the botanical name of the plant, which belongs to the lily family. *Asparagi di campo*, wild asparagus, still grow in sandy, marshy places in central Italy. My grandchildren gather them when we go to the sea. Their spears are dark green, very thin, almost wispy, and intensely flavoured. For a brief period they even show up in markets. We sauté them and dress with olive oil, perhaps a squeeze of lemon, salt and pepper. In Rome they add a little anchovy. I like them in a *frittata*, an open-faced omelette, Italian style.

Domestic asparagus is planted in sandy soil and their fresh, bright green spears are harvested just after they start pushing out of the ground, when they are about 15–25cm/6–10in tall and their tips or buds are fully formed but still tightly closed. Some growers, especially in the north-eastern regions of Italy, Friuli and the Veneto in particular, bank up the shoots with earth as they grow, keeping the spears underground. This blanching method produces asparagus that is completely white, except for their tips, which have a violet hue, and yields spears that are fat and smooth. Because of the extra care involved, white asparagus is more expensive than green. It is also more tender but less flavourful, I find. All asparagus cultivation is labour-intensive, as the crop has to be hand-picked. Also it takes three years for the shoots to be thick enough to market, another reason for the high cost.

Cultivation of asparagus in Italy has a long and well-chronicled history. In the first century AD, Pliny the Elder wrote that spears grown in Ravenna came 'three to the pound'. Even leaving room for exaggeration, those were much bigger than the ones we see today. Italians still prefer their asparagus spears big, which are not necessarily better than thinner ones and are just more expensive. They do have the advantage of being easier to handle if you like to eat the spears with your fingers. The vital signs to watch for when buying green asparagus are a compact and firm tip, not open and droopy, and a bright green colour, which is not turning to yellow.

Asparagus is another vegetable that should go directly from the market into the pot, as its flavour diminishes rapidly. I am fortunate to be able to eat it right out of my garden and it is truly wonderful. At the market choose your asparagus as carefully as possible and only during mid-spring, when it is at the height of its season. When you return home you should treat the spears like a bouquet of fresh flowers. Put them, stems down, in a couple of inches of cold water and store in a cool place.

When it comes to preparing asparagus for cooking, remember that all but the woody end of the spear is edible. Just snap or cut that off. Depending on the recipe and the age of the asparagus, you might also want to strip away with a sharp knife the hard outer layer at the base of the stalk. It is also important to soak the spears in a couple of changes of cold water. They inevitably contain a lot of invisible and very unpalatable sand. I usually boil asparagus in a pan of water large enough so they can lie flat. You can also buy a special saucepan that can hold them upright so that the hard ends are under water and the tender tips are cooked by the steam that rises.

The most classically Italian and also the simplest way to prepare asparagus is *alla parmigiana*. You cook the asparagus *al dente*, place them in a baking dish with butter, sprinkle with the freshly grated Parmesan cheese and place under a grill (broiler) until a light golden crust forms on top.

As an *antipasto* or even the main course of a light, spring luncheon, it is hard to beat a platter of cold asparagus, maybe white, dressed with fine, extra virgin olive oil and lemon juice, or served warm with butter. Of course, tender asparagus tips make a perfect main ingredient for risotto and pasta sauce. And I guarantee that the recipe for asparagus croquettes will become a party favourite both for you and your guests.

Another seasonal treat is spring onions (scallions). Of course, the Italian cook could not get along without an onion, *cipolla*, even for a day during the rest of the year. She or he uses large red or yellow ones that have been dried after harvest and are stored in the pantry or bought at market. They are the basis of the *soffritto*, which in turn is the foundation of innumerable recipes. Besides onion, a *soffritto* usually consists of a little finely chopped celery, carrot, garlic, parsley and, depending on the recipe, maybe a piece of pancetta. These are sautéed very gently in extra virgin olive oil (*soffritto* means under-fried).

Spring onions (scallions) or *cipollotti*, are little white bulbs, smaller than a small egg, sometimes elongated and sometimes with a blush of pink and come tied in bunches still attached to their long green stems. Their skin is thin and moist and their flesh is soft and juicy. They are sweet and milder in taste than their big sisters. They are delicious lightly grilled and served as an accompaniment to any

number of dishes. Mostly, however, we eat spring onions (scallions) raw in a salad of spring greens.

Little salad greens are one of the true delights of the season in Italy. They start shooting up in gardens and showing up in markets in the spring and continue into early autumn. Traditionally these greens grew wild. They were really edible weeds. Nowadays they are mostly cultivated. In the country, however, you still see women, often accompanied by their grandchildren, strolling about the hillsides gathering greens. Into their baskets might go the serrated, oval leaves of *salvastrella* (salad burnet), tender *raperonzolo* (rampion), bitter *crescione dei prati*, a kind of watercress that grows out of old stone walls, *terracrepolo*, often called wall-salad and some dandelion greens. Of course, mildly spicy *rucola selvatica*, or wild rocket (arugula), is now widely cultivated, as well as the more peppery domestic variety.

These greens along with many others—mint, purslane and sorrel, together with little lettuces—are mixed to form a *misticanza*. There is a method for composing this mixed salad. It should have quite a balanced combination of flavours and textures, weighted in favour of sweet or bitter greens, according to taste and occasion. The basic Italian recipe for dressing a salad is simple—salt, fine extra-virgin olive oil and quality red wine vinegar, nothing else. The rule-of-thumb is plenty of salt, a generous amount of olive oil and just a little vinegar. The proportion of olive oil to vinegar is usually four to one but it should depend on the greens, with more olive oil and less vinegar when bitter greens are assertive. Using the large tossing spoon for the salad, I dissolve the salt in the vinegar and add it before dressing with olive oil. Otherwise grains of salt will attach to the oiled leaves and not blend.

Giacomo Castelvetro, in his marvellous book, *The Fruit, Herbs and Vegetables of Italy*, written in 1614, gives this recipe for *misticanza*, as fresh and valid today as it was almost four hundred years ago. It deserves to be quoted in full:

'Of all the salads we eat in the spring, the mixed salad is the best and the most wonderful of all. Take young leaves of mint, garden cress, basil, lemon balm, the tips of salad burnet, tarragon, the flowers and the most tender leaves of borage, the flowers of swine cress, the young shoots of fennel, leaves of rocket, of sorrel, rosemary flowers, some sweet violets, and the most tender leaves or the hearts of lettuce. When these precious herbs have been picked clean and washed several times, and dried a little with a clean linen cloth, they are dressed as usual, with oil, salt and vinegar.'

This is the season to enjoy flavouring your dishes with fresh herbs, some of which continue into autumn. Dried herbs are sometimes a necessity in the kitchen but should never be considered a substitute for fresh herbs. No Italian cook could do without them. Even if you don't have a garden, they can be found in most food markets, and everyone can grow a few pots of herbs on their windowsills.

It sometimes seems I can't grow enough Italian flat-leaf parsley, *prezzemolo*, so versatile is its sweet, clean flavour in recipes. I use whole leaves in

salads and roast a roll of deboned lamb filled with a parsley sauce. Sage, *salvia*, is the herb of Tuscany. It is used to flavour bean dishes and roasts, and I coat the large-leaf variety in a light batter and deep-fry for an *antipasto*. Rosemary, *rosmarino*, is a perennial so it can be used fresh all year round, especially with roast lamb and pork and roast potatoes. It should be used sparingly, as its strong flavour can easily overpower a dish. Wild thyme, *timo*, also called *pepolino*, blends well with fish dishes. Oregano and fennel seeds are two herbs that have better aroma and flavour dried rather than fresh.

Besides lamb, which is synonymous with the season (see below), in spring my taste buds turn to poultry, especially chicken, as a main course. After the heavy, slow-cooked meats of winter, chicken is fresh, light and easily prepared. Obviously it is available all year round, but in the spring, local, free-range chickens are back in the butcher's

shop. For a while at Coltibuono I had my own free-range chickens. I even tried raising a couple of turkeys but it was a drama when their time came for the pot. Commercially raised Italian chickens are not bad. (The battery breed, I recently read, is soon to be outlawed altogether.) The best are corn-fed, giving their meat a pale yellow hue, and they are relatively small and lean. Free-range chickens seem best in Tuscany, perhaps because at one time it was a poor region and it has a long tradition of raising this economical food. Their flesh is quite a bit firmer and much more tasty.

Chicken has been a popular dish in Italy since the Renaissance and there are dozens of regional recipes for preparing them. The chicken is usually jointed, which allows the seasonings to impart their flavours more easily. A classic Tuscan recipe is *pollo alla diavola*, chicken cooked in the devil's way, which means that you flatten half a young breast, brush it with olive oil, salt and pepper and grill over a very hot ('hellish') fire until crisp. Perhaps the most traditional way to cook chicken is the hunter's way, *alla cacciatora*. The wife of every hunter I know, since they are the ones who usually do the cooking, has a different recipe for this dish, which generally consists of chicken parts sautéed in olive oil, with tomato, onion, garlic, carrot, celery and wine.

One of my favourite recipes for chicken, as fast as it is flavourful, is to quickly sauté thinly sliced breasts with lemon and sage. For a light, tasty and elegant spring luncheon dish, try the recipe for roasted chicken 'thighs', which are rolled in a mixture of rosemary, sage and garlic and tied with a slice of pancetta.

Many Italian cheeses are best in the spring and some, like pecorino (Romano), sheep's milk cheese, as well as its by-product, ricotta, and the rare *raveggiolo*, are only available fresh during this season and into early summer. In fact, in Tuscany the season's first batch of pecorino (Romano) is called *marzolino*, 'little (or better, delicate) March' cheese. It is made when the sheep are grazing on the first and freshest grasses and herbs sprouting up in the fields.

The art of making pecorino (Romano) is simplicity itself. Fresh ewe's milk is curdled using a rennet. After

about thirty minutes, when the curds have formed, they are lifted from the whey and pressed into large, wide circular forms with perforated bottoms. The remaining whey runs out and is collected in a large container placed beneath the worksurface. This process is repeated until the curds are dry. Then they are rubbed with salt to further draw out any moisture and to impart flavour. The cheese is left in a cool, dark place to age. Care is taken to turn it every so often so that it will dry evenly, which will prevent it from developing mould.

Pecorino (Romano) can be eaten young after a week or so, aged for about three months, or mature at around nine months. When it is fresh it has a milky colour and aroma, a soft, creamy texture and a delicate taste. With age the cheese becomes harder and the taste sharper, or piquant, *piccante*, as we say. Cheeses destined for ageing are rubbed with a mixture of flour and olive oil, which forms a protective crust that enables them to mature gracefully without drying out or cracking. *Pecorino di fossa* is buried in a ditch (*fosso*) and left to age there for the better part of a year. This was an ancient way of maturing cheese, which is currently enjoying a revival among artisan cheese-makers. It confers a very pleasing, distinctive and mellow flavour, with an earthy taste, I suppose you could say, to their product.

In shops these cheeses are usually sold by the wedge. Tuscan pecorino (Romano) is a table cheese, too precious to be used in cooking or grated over food. It is eaten after the meal, maybe with a perfect pear. This is one of those ideal gastronomic marriages between contrasting, yet complementary, textures and tastes—the juicy, sweet pear

and the somewhat dry, piquant pecorino (Romano). In my family we like a slice drizzled with our extra virgin olive oil and a few twists of freshly ground black pepper. With a fresh, green salad and some good bread this makes a completely satisfying light, spring lunch.

Sheep's milk ricotta is made by bringing the whey collected from cheese-making to boiling point. The fat protein remaining in the liquid rises to the surface, is skimmed off and transferred to a perforated mould—and there you have it. Ricotta is an essential ingredient for many Italian recipes. In Tuscany cooks stuff *tortelli*, large ravioli, with a mixture of ricotta and spinach and dress them with butter and fresh sage leaves. It is also used as a filling for sweet and savoury cakes and pies. Real sheep's milk ricotta is hard to find, unless you live in an area with sheep. Cow's milk ricotta, although less flavourful, can be used as a substitute.

Even rarer, but worth knowing about if you should be driving down the Italian peninsula and see sheep grazing, is *raveggiolo*. It is a fresh cheese with the shimmery texture of yoghurt and a very delicate taste. It is made by lifting the curds whole from the whey and pressing them into little moulds. Of course, when curds are used for *raveggiolo*, it means there is none left for making pecorino (Romano). And it is even more perishable than ricotta. Hence its rarity. *Raveggiolo* is normally made to order. It makes a delicious breakfast cheese, eaten with toast and jam. As an *antipasto* it is usually served on a bed of wild herbs and lettuces, seasoned with black pepper.

Cheese, rather than a sweet, is the traditional way to finish off an Italian family meal. When I have guests or am cooking for a special occasion and want to end with a dessert, I can choose from the first fresh fruit of the season to arrive at the market. When I see cherry trees in blossom, I know that spring is here to stay. Their bright red fruit can be sweet or sour. Sweet cherries, like the intensely flavoured Italian *Vignola*, are best for the table. Sour ones, in Italy the *Amarena* and the *Morello*, are better in the kitchen, as their sharp flavour and texture stands up to cooking. The American Bing has a taste that is somewhere inbetween.

Small and aromatic wild berries begin to show up in wooded and mountainous areas of Italy during late spring. These wild varieties are also cultivated and can be found in markets. Early in the season they are a little sour but sweeten in the summer. They are popular in the Italian kitchen, especially for making sauces and syrups as toppings for desserts.

SPRING FEASTS

During my student days, well before the reform of the academic calendar, hardly a week went by without the welcome interruption of a national or religious holiday. The one exception was the period of Lent, between *Carnevale* in late winter and Easter in early spring. Those two months seemed endless, no feasts, no vacations, no relief from routine. The dreary weather made it feel even longer. Happily, about mid-way, on 19 March, we celebrated the feast of San Giuseppe, Saint Joseph, the husband of the Virgin Mary and the foster father of Jesus. Of course, the church still commemorates the day but it is no longer a national nor academic holiday, so the festive spirit has all but disappeared. I doubt whether my grandchildren even notice its passing. I am told it is still a popular feast day in Italian-American communities.

All over Italy the twenty-four-hour suspension, thanks to San Giuseppe, of the Lenten fast and abstinence was celebrated with feasts of special foods. Some of these, in particular the sweets, have survived long after the religious significance of the occasion has been lost. Their names vary from region to region but they are usually made of pastry dough, shaped into rings or buns and then deep-fried. Mostly they are hollow inside but sometimes they are filled. In Milan, where I grew up, they still make sweet *tortelli* on

Saint Joseph's Day, deep-fried pastry dough flavoured with vanilla, sugar, lemon, cinnamon and rum. They come out light and puffy. In Naples *zeppole di San Giuseppe* are fried and sold from street stands. These are doughnut-shaped, filled with pastry cream and sometimes topped with an *Amarena* cherry. In Tuscany where I now live, bakeries make *frittelle di San Giuseppe*, rice fritters flavoured with lemon and orange and covered with granulated sugar. On the island of Sicily, where Saint Joseph and numerous other Saints as well still receive due recognition, they make delicious *sfince di San Giuseppe*, Saint Joseph's cream puffs, filled with local ricotta cheese.

Finally Easter arrives and with it the spirit, at least, of spring, resurrection and rebirth, even if the weather does not always cooperate. In Italy Easter is still welcomed in a festive way as a family celebration. Schools and most businesses close at midday on Good Friday and Easter Monday is a national holiday—unfortunately, Easter Tuesday is no longer. A few days before the actual holidays the parish priest, dressed in black cassock and white linen surplice and accompanied by an acolyte carrying a container with holy water, makes his rounds for the annual blessing of the home. His visit is the occasion for spring-cleaning and in former times, when the faithful abstained from dairy products as well as meat as part of the Lenten

fast, the family would set out eggs and special Easter bread to be blessed along with themselves. This ritual marked the passing (or Passover) from fasting to feasting.

The Paschal Lamb, celebrated in the liturgy of the church, is also the focus of the holiday's gastronomic festivities. Lamb must be one of the most ancient culinary meats—as distinct from the flesh of animals that were eaten for survival—to have been enjoyed by our ancestors. Most religions practised the tradition of sacrificing a lamb to commemorate special occasions, which was roasted on the spit and then the meat was shared among the people in a celebratory meal.

In Italy we eat our spring or Easter lamb very young, ideally while it is still milk-fed. The Latin poet, Juvenal, wrote a rhyme stating that it must have 'milk for blood' and not yet have lost its 'virginity' by eating grass. Usually it is between thirty and sixty days old. Any younger and it would still have too much of its baby fat, and any older it would no longer be perfectly tender. Roasted baby lamb is one of the great gastronomic delights of Rome, where it is called *abbacchio*. I suspect that at least some of the *abbacchio* offered in Roman restaurants is no longer 'virginal' but it is still wonderfully tender and delicious. It is rubbed with lard

or olive oil, pan-roasted with garlic and rosemary and served with new potatoes cooked in the same way. Another Roman lamb dish is lamb chops eaten right off the grill, *scottadito*, meaning 'while still hot enough to burn your fingers'. Of course, you need a pile of them, as there is only a bite or two of flesh on each bone. I have given a variation of this, fried with a coating of finely chopped herbs, thyme, marjoram and mint.

Every region has its preferred way of preparing lamb. The traditional Tuscan method is to cut the lamb into serving pieces without separating them, rub with a mixture of olive oil, garlic and rosemary and roast very, very slowly for at least two hours, moistening with white wine, until the outside becomes crusty and the flesh so tender it practically falls from the bone. In my menu for Easter dinner I prepare my lamb using the same slow-cooking method. The recipe, however, is a little more elaborate. The lamb is deboned, seasoned with a creamy parsley sauce and tied into a roll before being roasted.

For the Easter feast the dishes that accompany spring lamb should feature the fresh, green produce of the new season. I have incorporated several in my menu—broad (fava) beans as an *antipasto* and asparagus and courgettes (zucchini) in the first course. Should you ever be on the Ligurian coast during the holiday season, don't miss the opportunity to taste that region's famous vegetable Easter pie, *torta pasqualina*. It is filled with a rich sauce made of small, tender artichokes, seasoned with borage and marjoram and blended with fresh ricotta, Parmesan cheese and eggs. This mixture is carefully spooned onto innumerable layers of transparently thin pastry dough. Before adding more layers on top, you make twelve (a sacred number in the Christian tradition) little wells in the filling and pour a whole raw egg into each one. As the pie bakes these become hard and when it is sliced their golden yolks add richness of colour as well as flavour to the dish. Needless to say, this is a quite a production. I have actually had the pleasure of eating a home-made *torta pasqualina* at a friend's home, but left to my own devices I would buy the best one I could find at one of the region's fine food shops.

By far the most popular Easter cake nationwide is the *colomba pasquale*, the Paschal Dove, similar to Christmas *panettone* but made in the shape of a dove symbolizing the Holy Spirit, who, according to the Christian scriptures, descended to the faithful on Easter evening. This light, buttery yeast cake is sprinkled with crystallized sugar and studded with toasted almonds. Candied orange is often mixed into the dough and sometimes it is laced with chocolate. It is too difficult to make at home but large industrial bakeries as well as local pastry shops turn them out by the millions during the holiday season.

My favourite Easter cake is the *pastiera* from Naples, a shortcrust-pastry (*pasta frolla*) cake filled with sheep's milk ricotta and chopped candied fruit and seasoned with lemon zest and cinnamon. Two special ingredients give this delicious cake its very distinctive taste and consistency. Grains of soft white wheat berries are first soaked in water and then in milk before being added and the filling is flavoured with orange-flower water. Before baking wide strips of dough are arranged over the filling in a lattice. This is an elaborate and even exotic cake, which recalls the Arab occupation of Naples centuries ago. Every family and every pastry cook has his or her own version of the basic recipe. A few years ago I was in the Naples area the week after Easter and tried several, each different and each more delicious than the other.

Of course, the Easter feast would not be complete without chocolate eggs. Italians, young and old, like theirs big and hollow, with lots of room inside for the surprise, usually some sort of trinket whose value is relative to the price of the egg. Artisan chocolate makers, by special request, will place personalized gifts within their confections, maybe an expensive piece of jewellery or, the most popular 'surprise' last season, a mobile phone—a surprise to me as well, as I would have thought everyone in Italy already has at least one!

May Day, is the last major holiday before summer. It is a national one as well. Usually the weather is fine and if it takes place close to the weekend, everyone makes a 'bridge' between the two, so families have a few days to get away. Lately the most popular destinations have become our own 'cities of art'—Rome, Florence, Venice—before they become crowded with foreign tourists. Traditionally, 1 May is the Feast of the Workers, a holiday brought in by Marxists and later appropriated by the church as the feast of Saint Joseph the Worker. With regards to special food for the occasion, I think of the men I used to see in a popular neighbourhood in Rome where my daughter lived for several years. They celebrated by sitting at outside tables playing cards and eating broad (fava) beans with pecorino (Romano) cheese. The rather dry taste of the beans and the Roman cheese brought on a thirst that they quenched with flasks of Frascati wine from the neighbouring hills. By the end of the evening, these gentlemen were practically up to their knees in broad (fava) bean pods. Luckily they did not have far to go to get to their beds.

THE PANTRY

ACETO DI ROSE

Rose Vinegar

In Italy, we do not usually prepare salads with vinegars other than red wine vinegar, but sometimes a special one as used here gives a pleasant taste to fruit salads or to a roasted chicken or turkey.

480ml/16fl oz/2 cups white wine vinegar
30 rose petals
1 pinch red pepper flakes

Pour the vinegar into a sterilized bottle, add the rose petals and the red pepper and seal with a cork. Store for 1 month in a cool, dark place, shaking the bottle from time to time.
Strain the vinegar and pour into a second sterilized bottle.
Makes 480ml/16fl oz/2 cups

OLIO AL DRAGONCELLO

Tarragon Oil

The perfume of the herbs is particularly concentrated in oils. I especially like tarragon and mint because they flavour the oil better, but any other herb will do.

120g/4oz fresh tarragon
480ml/16fl oz/2 cups extra virgin olive oil

Wash and dry the tarragon leaves on a clean cloth, discarding the stems. Place the leaves in a sterilized bottle, pour in the oil and seal with a cork. Store in a cool, dark place for about 2 weeks.
Strain the oil and discard the leaves. Pour into a clean sterilized bottle. The oil will keep for a long time in a cool, dark place.
You can follow the same method to make tarragon vinegar, using tarragon leaves and white or red wine vinegar. The only difference is that you do not need to remove the leaves—they will stay in the vinegar without becoming mouldy.
You can substitute basil, thyme, parsley or coriander (cilantro) for the tarragon, to make different flavoured oils.
Makes 480ml/16fl oz/2 cups

OLIO ALL'AGLIO
Garlic Oil

Garlic oil is very useful instead of pure garlic, because it is less strong. I often cook a simple pasta, add one vegetable to the cooking water, such as peas, broad (fava) beans or the first string beans of the season then simply flavour with this oil when drained.

5 garlic cloves
1 handful fresh basil leaves
480ml/16fl oz/2 cups extra virgin olive oil

Peel the cloves and mash them with a fork. Put them in a sterilized bottle with the basil and the oil. Cork the bottle and store in a cool, dark place for about 2 weeks.
Strain the oil and pour into a clean sterilized bottle. The oil will keep in a cool, dark place for up to 1 year.

Makes 480ml/16fl oz/2 cups

PESTO ALLA GENOVESE
Genoese Pesto

I never buy pesto sauce because in order to preserve it for selling, lots of chemicals have to be added. I also never keep basil in the freezer, as when added to the pasta it becomes black and is very unpleasant. Instead, take a minute to prepare pesto at home. It is quick to do and keeps in the refrigerator for about one week.

3 handfuls fresh basil leaves
3 tbsp freshly grated Parmesan cheese
3 tbsp freshly grated pecorino (Romano) cheese
3 tbsp pine nuts
2 garlic cloves
120ml/4fl oz/½ cup extra virgin olive oil
Salt

In a blender, combine the basil with salt to taste. Process for a few seconds. Add the cheeses, pine nuts, garlic and olive oil. Process again until a smooth, creamy sauce forms.
Spoon into a bowl, cover with cling film (plastic wrap) and store in the refrigerator. This will keep for about 1 week.
Just before serving with pasta, take 1 ladle of water from the pan in which the pasta is cooking, add it to the pesto, mix well and toss with the pasta when cooked.

Serves 6

COME SECCARE LE ERBE AROMATICHE
How to Dry Aromatic Herbs

Dried herbs give a wonderful touch to lots of dishes: basil, oregano and marjoram for pizza or pasta, a tomato sauce or sautéed *scaloppini*; mint for teas or dessert; thyme for soups; rosemary and sage for fish or meats.

This is the time of year for growing fresh aromatic herbs, such as thyme, mint and parsley. The more you cut them, the better they will grow. Cut the stems as long as possible, then tie the herbs at the stem into a bunch. Hang the bunch with the leaves downwards in an airy, dry place. When the herbs are completely dry—the time it takes will depend on the climate—you can crush the leaves and store them in airtight containers. They will keep for a long time, but after a while they will start to lose their flavour.

APPETIZERS, PASTA AND SOUPS

TORTA DI RICOTTA
Ricotta Cake

Ricotta, when it is the real stuff, is the result of reboiling sheep's milk, and ricotta means 'cooked again'. In fact it is a very non fat cheese and is extremely healthy. Once it was produced only in spring time but it is now possible to buy it all year round and it is often made out of cow's milk.

300g/10oz/1¼ cups fresh ricotta cheese
2 large eggs
2 tbsp chopped fresh flat-leaf parsley
1 garlic clove, chopped
1 tbsp extra virgin olive oil
12 anchovy fillets in oil, drained
12 cherry tomatoes, halved
Salt and pepper

Preheat the oven to 170°C/350°F/Gas 4.
Place the ricotta in a bowl, add the eggs, parsley and garlic and mix until well blended. Add salt and pepper to taste. Grease a 15cm/7in non-stick round cake tin (pan) with the oil and fill with the ricotta mixture. Place in the oven and cook for about 15 minutes. Decorate with the anchovy fillets and the cherry tomatoes and cook for 15 minutes more or until the ricotta is set and slightly golden on top.
Leave to cool before serving.

Serves 6

PALLINE DI PROSCIUTTO
Ham Bites

The difference between ham and prosciutto is that ham is cooked while prosciutto is raw, only cured with salt and pepper. The biggest producer in Italy for prosciutto and ham is Parma, a town in the north that also produces Parmigiano Reggiano, the very best of the Parmesan cheeses.

450g/1lb cooked ham
90g/3oz pistachios, finely chopped
90g/3oz walnuts, finely chopped
2 large egg yolks
3 tbsp double (heavy) cream
1 handful chives, finely chopped

Purée the ham in a blender. Transfer to a bowl, add the pistachios, walnuts, egg yolks and cream and mix together.
Place the chopped chives in a shallow bowl. Form the ham mixture into little balls the size of walnuts and roll in the chives to coat.
Arrange on a serving platter and keep in the refrigerator until ready to serve.

Serves 6

TORTA DI ZUCCHINE

Courgette (Zucchini) Tart

This is not only an elegant starter for lunch or dinner but also a perfect dish for brunch. Instead of courgettes (zucchini), asparagus or peas are nice substitutes.

210g/7oz/1 ¾ cup plain (all-purpose) flour, plus a handful for dusting
120g/4oz/8 tbsp (1 stick) unsalted butter, plus 1 tbsp for greasing the tin (pan)
4 large eggs
600g/1 ¼ lb courgettes (zucchini), thinly sliced
4 tbsp extra virgin olive oil
90g/3oz/6 tbsp freshly grated Parmesan cheese
90ml/3fl oz/6 tbsp double (heavy) cream
1 handful fresh basil leaves
Salt and pepper

Preheat the oven to 200°C/400°F/Gas 6.
In a food processor, mix the flour, butter and 1 egg until a dough is formed. Work the dough briefly with floured hands on a clean worksurface and shape into a ball. Cover with cling film (plastic wrap) and keep in the refrigerator for a maximum of 2 hours.
Sauté the courgettes (zucchini) over a medium heat in the oil, stirring a few times. Add salt and pepper to taste, remove from the heat and add the Parmesan and the cream. Leave to cool and mix with the remaining 3 eggs, stirring with a fork. Add the basil leaves.
Roll out the dough on a floured surface into a circle about 30cm/11in in diameter (large enough to line the base and sides of a 23cm/9in tart tin [pan] with removable base).
Grease the tart tin (pan) with the butter, sprinkle with the flour and line with the pastry.
Fill the lined tin (pan) with the courgette (zucchini) mixture and bake in the oven for about 40 minutes or until golden on top.
Allow to cool slightly. Remove the sides of the tin (pan), transfer the tart to a serving dish and serve immediately.

Serves 6

GNOCCHI DI PATATE AL PURÉ DI FAVE

Potato Gnocchi with Broad (Fava) Bean Purée

The idea of making pasta sauces with purées of various vegetables is fairly new. Before, it was more usual to make a tomato sauce, meat *ragù* or cream and cheese sauces, such as *Fettuccine all' Alfredo*, famous for being served in Rome with a golden fork and spoon.

1kg/2 ¼ lb potatoes for boiling
1 large egg
210g/7oz/1 ¾ cup plain (all-purpose) flour
1kg/2 ¼ lb broad (fava) beans (unshelled weight)
1 handful fresh flat-leaf parsley
A few chives
120ml/4fl oz/½ cup extra virgin olive oil
6 slices pancetta
Salt and pepper

Boil the potatoes in their skins until tender, about 30 minutes, depending on size, then drain and peel. Pass the potatoes through a ricer or food mill while still warm, then add the egg, half the flour, salt to taste and mix well to amalgamate the ingredients.
Using floured hands, divide the mixture into 6 portions and roll each one out on a floured surface until you have 6 long 'sausages' about 3cm/1in in diameter.
Cut into pieces about 1.5cm/¾ in long and, using floured hands, roll them into oval shapes. These can be kept on a floured tray for up to 1 hour.
Shell the broad (fava) beans and boil in salted water for a few minutes. Drain and purée in a blender with the parsley, the chives and oil. Add salt and pepper to taste.
Fry the pancetta slices in a pan over a medium heat until crispy.
Bring a large pan of salted water to the boil, add salt and the gnocchi, a few at a time. Remove them with a slotted spoon as they rise to the surface and transfer to a warmed serving dish.
Add 240ml/8fl oz/1 cup of the cooking water to the purée to thin it and spoon over the gnocchi. Crumble the pancetta on top and serve immediately.

Serves 6

CROCCHETTE DI ASPARAGI

Asparagus Croquettes

People tend to eat the asparagus tip only, discarding the stems, but if they are properly peeled you will be able to eat the whole asparagus. As they are pretty expensive it is worth the work, also because the inner part of the stems is very delicate. However, for convenience I only use the tips in this recipe.

1kg/2 ¼ lb asparagus
2 large eggs
120g/4oz/1 cup fine dry breadcrumbs
4 tbsp freshly grated Parmesan cheese
6 tbsp extra virgin olive oil
90g/3oz/6 tbsp unsalted butter
Salt

Trim the asparagus, discarding the woody ends and keeping only the tender tips.
Bring a pan of salted water to the boil. Add the asparagus and cook for a few minutes, until only just tender. Drain thoroughly and pat the asparagus dry.
Beat the eggs with a little salt in a large bowl.
Mix the breadcrumbs and Parmesan together in a dish. Dip the asparagus tips in the eggs, then dip them in the breadcrumbs to coat well.
Heat the oil and butter in a large pan and fry the asparagus tips until golden, about 5 minutes, over a medium heat, turning them a couple of times.
Drain on absorbent paper. Season with salt to taste, arrange on a warmed serving platter and serve immediately while very hot.

Serves 6

RISO NERO CON PUNTE D'ASPARAGI E GAMBERI

Wild Rice with Asparagus Tips and Prawns (Shrimp)

In recent years, wild, red and long grain rices have been produced increasingly in Italy in the Vercelli and Veneto areas, and they are becoming very popular.

600g/1 ¼ lb/2 ½ cups wild rice (12 handfuls)
600g/1 ¼ lb asparagus
6 tbsp extra virgin olive oil
1 small white onion, finely chopped
300g/10oz prawns (shrimp), peeled and deveined
Salt and pepper

Bring a pan of water to the boil, add salt and the rice and cook over a low heat for about 50 minutes. Trim the asparagus, removing the woody ends and leaving only the tips.
Bring a second pan of water to the boil, add salt and the asparagus tips. Cook for a few minutes or until just tender. Drain and immerse in cold water to stop the cooking process and retain the green colour.
Heat the oil in a pan, add the onion and cook over a low heat until translucent, about 3 minutes. Add the asparagus tips and the prawns (shrimp) and sauté for a couple of minutes. Add pepper to taste.
Drain the rice and transfer to a warmed serving platter. Spoon the asparagus and prawns (shrimp) over the rice and serve immediately.

Serves 6

CREMA DI PISELLI AL DRAGONCELLO
Pea Soup with Tarragon

The combination of peas and tarragon is a winner in pasta, rices and even soups. Tarragon is not very well known in Italy, with the exception of Siena, where every greengrocer and restaurateur uses it.

2kg/4lb peas (unshelled weight)
6 tbsp extra virgin olive oil
1 small white onion, finely chopped
6 slices bacon
6 cups chicken stock
120ml/4fl oz/½ cup double (heavy) cream
1 handful fresh tarragon leaves
Salt and pepper

Shell the peas and boil for about 5 minutes in salted water. Drain.
Heat the oil in a pan, add the onion and bacon and fry over a low heat until the bacon is crisp.
Put the bacon in a blender with the peas and a little of the stock and pulse to a purée. Add the rest of the stock and the cream and cook for about 10 minutes until the flavours are well amalgamated. Add salt and pepper to taste.
Finely chop the tarragon. Transfer the soup to a warmed tureen and serve, sprinkled with the tarragon.

Serves 6

MINESTRONE PRIMAVERA
Minestrone with Spring Vegetables

Minestrone, or a mixture of diced or finely julienned vegetables, is very popular in Italy all the year round, using different vegetables each season. I still remember the attractive smell of minestrone cooking every day in the back of the Milanese *portineria*, in time for lunch. The *portineria* is the Italian version of the doorman's cabin in the United States.

1 lemon, halved
2 artichokes
6 tbsp extra virgin olive oil
1 white onion, finely chopped
300g/10oz peas (unshelled weight)
300g/10oz broad (fava) beans (unshelled weight)
300g/10oz asparagus
120g/4oz beet leaves or spinach, finely sliced
1 courgette (zucchini), sliced
120g/4oz string beans, diced
1 carrot, diced
1 lettuce, finely sliced
2 litres/3½ pints/8 cups water
2 tbsp chopped fresh flat-leaf parsley
2 tbsp chopped chives
Salt and pepper

Fill a bowl with water and place the lemon halves in the water.
Clean the artichokes by discarding the tough outer leaves and the stem. Cut them in half lengthways and remove the inner furry choke with a paring knife. Place the artichokes in the water as you go, to prevent them from discolouring. Drain and pat dry on paper towels.
Heat the oil in a pan and fry the onion over a low heat until translucent, about 3 minutes, stirring constantly. Remove from the heat and set aside.
Shell the peas and beans. Trim the asparagus, discarding the woody ends, and keeping only the tips. Dice the tips.
Place all the vegetables in a large pan, add the onion and return to the heat. Fry for a couple of minutes, stirring. Add the water and bring to the boil. Add salt, and cook for about 1 hour over a low heat, covered. Add the parsley and chives, sprinkle with pepper, transfer to a warmed soup tureen and serve.

Serves 6

TAGLIATELLE AI PISELLI MANGIATUTTO E SALMONE

Tagliatelle with Sugar Snap Peas and Salmon

Peas and snap peas have a very short season. Snap peas in Italy are also called *taccole* and tend to be bigger than the American type but not as sweet. This is the reason why I buy the seeds of this version in the States. The best quality ones are called sugar snaps.

300g/10oz sugar snap peas
450g/1lb dried tagliatelle
210g/7oz smoked salmon, thinly sliced
Grated zest of 1 lemon
60g/2oz/4 tbsp unsalted butter
6 tbsp double (heavy) cream
1 tbsp finely chopped chives
Salt and pepper

Bring a pan of water to the boil, add salt and the sugar snap peas. When the water comes to the boil again, add the tagliatelle and cook until *al dente* (a couple of minutes less than it says on the packet). Meanwhile, cut the salmon slices into fine pieces and put in a pan with the lemon zest, butter and cream. Cook over a low heat without allowing the salmon to fry.
Drain the tagliatelle and sugar snap peas and add to the pan with the salmon. Cook for a couple of minutes, mixing everything together carefully. Transfer to a warmed serving dish, sprinkle with pepper and the chives and serve immediately.

Serves 6

ANELLO DI RISO PRIMAVERA

Rice Ring with Spring Vegetables

This is a very fresh and tasty rice that I like to prepare sometimes in advance and reheat when needed. If I have some cooked rice, I arrange it in the mould and reheat in the oven for about 10 minutes. I then purée the vegetables in order to make a sauce that I reheat in a saucepan and when serving, put in the centre of the ring and around it to serve.

12 asparagus stalks
120ml/4fl oz/½ cup extra virgin olive oil
120g/4oz/¾ cup fresh shelled peas
1 small courgette (zucchini), diced
1 handful string beans, diced
1 carrot, diced
600g/1¼ lb/2½ cups rice
2 tbsp chopped fresh mint
Salt and pepper

Trim the asparagus, removing the woody ends. Dice the asparagus tips.
Heat half the oil in a pan, add the diced asparagus tips, the peas, and the diced courgette (zucchini), beans and carrot. Add 2 tbsp water, cover the pan and cook for a few minutes over a medium heat until *al dente*. Add salt and pepper to taste.
Meanwhile, bring a pan of water to the boil, add salt and the rice and cook for about 15 minutes.
Drain the rice and mix in a bowl with the remaining oil and the mint.
Tip the rice into a 23cm/9in ring mould and press down lightly. Place a serving dish on top of the mould and invert.
Carefully remove the ring mould, fill the centre with the sautéed vegetables and serve.

Serves 6

PIZZOCCHERI CON PATATE NOVELLE

Pizzoccheri with New Potatoes

Pizzoccheri is the name of fresh (or dry, packaged) tagliatelle, made with buckwheat in Valtellina, a region north of Milan and towards St Moritz. We would go skiing there years ago during the weekend. A stop in a little restaurant for *pizzoccheri* was the reward for having skied intensively before returning to Milan.

300g/10oz new potatoes, peeled and diced
300g/10oz string beans, trimmed
600g/1 1/4 lb *Pizzoccheri della Valtellina* or tagliatelle
2 garlic cloves, finely chopped
90g/3oz/6 tbsp unsalted butter
90g/3oz/3/4 cup grated fontina cheese
2 tbsp fresh marjoram leaves
Salt and pepper

Bring a pan of water to the boil. Add salt, the potatoes and the beans and cook for a couple of minutes. Add the *pizzoccheri* and cook for 5 minutes more or until *al dente*.
Meanwhile, fry the garlic in the butter for a few minutes or until golden.
Drain the *pizzoccheri* and transfer to a serving platter. Pour over the garlic and butter and mix well.
Sprinkle with the cheese, the marjoram and pepper to taste, and serve immediately.

Serves 6

PASSATO DI FAVE E CICORIA

Soup with Puréed Broad (Fava) Beans and Chicory (Belgian Endive)

This is a very Neapolitan soup, but is important to use the fresh first green chicory of the year as it becomes bitter after being grown and cut so many times. It is also best when the broad (fava) beans are fresh, but is also delicious with dried beans.

4 tbsp extra virgin olive oil
2 garlic cloves, finely chopped
60g/2oz smoked bacon
2kg/4lb broad (fava) beans (unshelled weight)
2 litres/3 1/2 pints/8 cups light meat stock
300g/10oz green chicory (Belgian endive)
Pinch of hot chilli powder
Salt

Heat half the oil in a pan, add the garlic and bacon and fry over a low heat until the bacon is crisp and slightly golden, stirring occasionally.
Shell the beans and add to the bacon in the pan. Add the stock and bring to the boil. Cook for about 1 hour.
Meanwhile, bring a pan of water to the boil, add the chicory (Belgian endive) and cook for a couple of minutes. Immerse in cold water, then drain and pat dry. Roughly chop the chicory and sauté in a pan with the remaining oil. Add salt to taste, and the chilli powder.
Purée the soup in a blender, pour into a clean pan and bring to the boil. Add the chicory (Belgian endive) and boil for a couple of minutes. Transfer to a warmed soup tureen and serve.

Serves 6

MINESTRA DI PATATE E FINOCCHIO

Potato and Fennel Soup

Fennel is almost at the end of its season in spring, but is still tender, whereas dill is just sprouting in the garden. When I cannot find dill I substitute it with some fresh parsley, the flat Italian kind, which is very tasty. During this season I will also use the tender new leaves whole rather than chop them.

4 fennel bulbs
6 tbsp extra virgin olive oil
4 boiling potatoes, peeled and diced
2 litres/3 ½ pints/8 cups light meat stock
2 tbsp chopped dill
Salt and pepper

Discard the outer leaves from the fennel bulbs, halve them and wash thoroughly. Slice and dice the fennel. Heat the oil in a pan, add the potatoes and fry over a medium heat, stirring constantly, until almost golden. Add the fennel and the stock and bring to the boil. Cook for about 30 minutes over a low heat. Add salt and pepper to taste, pour into a warmed soup tureen, sprinkle with the dill and serve.

Serves 6

FETTUCCINE DI PASTA E ZUCCHINE AL BASILICO

Fettuccine with Courgettes (Zucchini) and Basil

Not only have pasta sauces been changing lately, but the idea of using chopped or sliced vegetables as a complement to the pasta is also new and not very traditional. Usually they are sautéed with a little olive oil so the whole dish is very light.

6 courgettes (zucchini)
600g/1 ¼ lb dried fettuccine
6 tbsp extra virgin olive oil
3 garlic cloves, finely chopped
1 handful fresh basil leaves
6 tbsp freshly grated fontina cheese
Salt and pepper

Peel the courgettes (zucchini), removing any flesh from the peel. Slice the courgettes (zucchini) and peel to the same width as the fettuccine.
Bring a pan of water to the boil, add salt, the courgettes (zucchini) and the fettuccine.
Heat the oil in a pan, add the garlic and fry over a low heat until lightly golden.
Drain the pasta and courgettes (zucchini) and add to the pan. Sauté for a couple of minutes, adding a little of the cooking water and mixing carefully with a wooden spoon.
Transfer to a warmed serving platter and sprinkle with the basil, the cheese and pepper.
Serve immediately while very hot.

Serves 6

LASAGNE ALLA RUCOLA
Rocket (Arugula) Lasagne

Rucola, or rocket (arugula), is very trendy, perhaps too trendy now, on pasta, rice, meats and vegetables. But used carefully and not too often, it is pleasant for a little variety, especially in spring when the vegetable is small and not too strong in flavour.

210g/7oz/1¾ cup plain (all-purpose) flour, plus extra
for dusting
2 large eggs
120g/6oz fresh rocket (arugula)
600g/1¼ lb boiling potatoes
4 tbsp extra virgin olive oil
210g/7oz crescenza (or Camembert) cheese
4 tbsp freshly grated Parmesan cheese
Salt and pepper

First prepare the lasagne.
Place the flour in a mound on a wooden board or work surface. Make a well in the centre and break the eggs into the well. Mix with a fork in a circular motion until the flour has absorbed all the eggs. Knead the mixture with the palm of your hands until you form a smooth, elastic ball of dough.
Using a rolling pin or pasta rolling machine, roll out the dough on a lightly floured worksurface until very thin. Using a pasta cutter, cut out the dough into 9cm/3in squares.
Preheat the oven to 170°C/350°F/Gas 4.
Bring a pan of water to the boil and have a bowl of cold water on the side.
Add salt to the boiling water, then add the lasagne squares. As soon as they come to the surface, remove them with a slotted spoon and transfer to the cold water. Drain immediately and lay them to dry on a clean cloth. Blanch the rocket (arugula) in the same water for 1 minute. Drain the rocket (arugula), squeeze out the water and chop.
Boil the potatoes in their skins until tender. Drain and allow to cool slightly, then peel them and break them up with a fork. Brush an ovenproof dish with a little oil and arrange a layer of lasagne in the base of the dish. Top with the crushed potatoes, the rocket (arugula) and a little olive oil. Crumble the crescenza or Camembert over the top, and sprinkle with half the Parmesan and some pepper. Cover with the remaining lasagne, brush over the rest of the olive oil and sprinkle with the rest of the Parmesan cheese.
Cook in the oven for about 20 minutes and serve immediately while very hot.

Serves 6

MEAT AND FISH

COSCIOTTO D'AGNELLO BRASATO

Braised Lamb Shank

Young lambs are a real delicacy, and not only do we eat the shank and the cutlets but also the kidneys, which are heavenly, the liver or even the head, halved and cooked in the oven. But one of the best parts is the *coratella*, the intestines.

2 lamb shanks weighing 1.5kg/3lb in total
60g/2oz/4 tbsp plain (all-purpose) flour
2 tbsp extra virgin olive oil
1 tbsp unsalted butter
2 carrots, roughly chopped
1 leek, roughly chopped, including the green part
1 fennel bulb, roughly chopped
Handful fresh thyme
½ bottle Chianti wine
Salt and pepper

Preheat the oven to 170°C/350°F/Gas 4.
Dust the shanks with flour and sprinkle them with salt and pepper.
Heat the oil and butter in a large heatproof casserole dish and brown the lamb on the hob over a high heat, for about 10 minutes, until golden all over.
Add the chopped vegetables to the pan with the thyme. Cover the dish and cook in the oven for about 2 hours (3 hours if the meat is older), adding the wine a little at a time.
Lift the lamb shanks out of the dish and transfer to a warmed serving platter. Set aside and keep warm.
Pass the vegetables from the pan through a food mill or fine sieve and return them to the casserole with the cooking juices. Heat the sauce on the hob.
Pour over the lamb and serve immediately.

Serves 6

AGNELLO ARROSTO ALLA TOSCANA

Tuscan-style Roast Lamb

The method of cooking lamb in Tuscany is against all the known rules, but it creates the tastiest result and the most tender and juicy lamb you have ever eaten. You can even try the recipe with the packaged New Zealand lamb. It is important not to cut the lamb through completely so the whole piece remains attached to the bone. When cooked, it is easy to separate the serving pieces.

1.5kg/3½lb 5oz leg of lamb, bone in
3 tbsp finely chopped rosemary
3 tbsp finely chopped garlic cloves
1 tbsp unsalted butter
2 tbsp extra virgin olive oil
120ml/4fl oz/1½ cups dry white wine
Salt and pepper

Preheat the oven to 170°C/350°F/Gas 4.
Divide the lamb into serving pieces by scoring it with a knife but so that the pieces stay together.
In a bowl mix the rosemary with the garlic and add salt and pepper to taste. Coat the lamb with the mixture.
Put the butter and oil in a roasting tin (pan) and place the lamb on top. Cover with foil and cook for about 1 hour. Uncover and cook for 1 more hour.
Cut the lamb into pieces and arrange on a warmed serving platter.
Pour the wine into the roasting tin (pan) and deglaze the cooking juices over a medium heat. Pour the sauce around the lamb and serve immediately.

Serves 6

COSTOLETTE D'AGNELLO IN CROSTA

Lamb Cutlets with a Herb Crust

This is the Italian version of a French recipe, which I find more tasty. The usual way to cook the cutlets in Rome is *scottadito*, or 'until the fingers are burned'. They are sautéed on a very high heat for a few minutes and as they are very small, eaten with the fingers, and they burn!

18 lamb cutlets (not too thick)
240g/8oz/2 cups dry breadcrumbs
60g/4oz/½ cup finely chopped herbs (thyme, marjoram, mint)
150g/5oz blanched almonds, finely chopped
3 large eggs
4 tbsp extra virgin olive oil
2 tbsp unsalted butter
Salt and pepper

Trim the cutlets, removing any fat and nerves.
In a large shallow bowl mix the breadcrumbs with the herbs and chopped almonds. Add salt and pepper to taste. Beat the eggs with a little salt in a deep dish. Dip the cutlets first in the beaten eggs, then in the breadcrumb mixture, pressing the mixture into the meat so it covers the meat completely.
Heat the oil and butter in a non-stick pan, add the cutlets and cook over a medium heat for about 3 minutes on each side (for pink meat).
Drain on absorbent paper and serve immediately.

Serves 6

INVOLTINI DI POLLO ALLA PANCETTA

Chicken Thighs with Pancetta

When I cannot find chicken thighs, I use poussins or Cornish hens instead, halving them and rolling them in pancetta slices. The cooking time is the same and the result can be more elegant.

6 chicken thighs
1 fresh rosemary sprig, finely chopped
6 large fresh sage leaves, finely chopped
6 garlic cloves, finely chopped
6 paper-thin pancetta slices
2 tbsp extra virgin olive oil
1 tbsp unsalted butter
Salt and pepper

Preheat the oven to 170°C/350°F/Gas 4.
Remove the skin from the chicken thighs.
Place the chopped rosemary, sage and garlic in a shallow bowl, add salt and pepper to taste and roll the thighs in the mixture to coat well. Roll each chicken thigh up in a slice of pancetta.
Place in a roasting tin (pan) with the oil and the butter. Cook in the oven for about 1 hour, turning them once halfway through.
Transfer to a warmed serving dish, set aside and keep warm.
Add a little water to the roasting tin (pan) and deglaze the cooking juices over a medium heat. Pour over the chicken thighs and serve.

Serves 6

CARRÉ DI MAIALE AL FINOCCHIO

Pork Loin with Fennel Seeds

The most typical Tuscan way to cook a pork loin is with rosemary, garlic and sage, but this version with fennel seeds is unusual and very tasty. Fennel seeds are also wonderful on roasted potatoes. I usually make this dish with a whole baby suckling pig weighing no more than 4kg/8lb in total, and only available in the spring. Delicious!

2kg/4lb pork loin, bone in
4 tbsp grainy mustard
2 tbsp fennel seeds
1 tbsp unsalted butter
2 tbsp extra virgin olive oil
Salt and pepper

Preheat the oven to 170°C/350°F/Gas 4.
Debone the pork loin, or ask your butcher to do this.
Keep the bones.
Spread the mustard over the meat.
Mix the fennel seeds with the salt and pepper and sprinkle over the mustard-coated meat.
Heat the butter and oil in a roasting tin (pan). Add the loin and the bones and cook over a high heat until browned on all sides, about 10 minutes. Cover with (aluminum) foil and cook in the oven for about 2 hours. Uncover, add a little water to prevent the cooking juices from drying out and cook for 1 more hour or until golden brown.
Discard the bones, and transfer the pork to a warmed serving dish. Add a little water to the cooking juices in the tin (pan) and deglaze over a medium heat. Pour over the pork and serve immediately.

Serves 6

MANZO AL ROSMARINO

Beef Sautéed with Lemon and Rosemary

This is an easier version of a Roman recipe that is made with beef that has been sliced paper-thin. I find that a spring chicken is very juicy and a good substitute.

4 tbsp extra virgin olive oil
3 garlic cloves, sliced
3 rosemary sprigs
600g/1 1/4 lb top round beef
Juice of 1 lemon
Salt and pepper

Heat the oil in a pan, add the garlic and rosemary and cook for a few seconds over a high heat.
Add the beef and cook, stirring a few times, for about 3 minutes.
Squeeze over the lemon juice, add salt and pepper to taste and toss to mix well. Serve immediately.

Serves 6

CONIGLIO AGLI ASPARAGI

Rabbit with Asparagus

Rabbit is very difficult to debone because it is very delicate along the body and the meat tends to break easily. But with patience and a little skill you can do it yourself, starting from the back legs.

1 rabbit, about 1.5kg/3 ½ lb
1kg/2 ¼ lb asparagus
1 potato, peeled and diced
1 large egg
2 tbsp extra virgin olive oil
1 tbsp unsalted butter
Salt and pepper

Debone the rabbit, or have it deboned by the butcher.
Preheat the oven to 170°C/350°F/Gas 4.
Clean and trim the asparagus, discarding the woody ends and keeping only the tender tips.
Bring a pan of water to the boil, add salt, the asparagus and the diced potato and cook for about 5 minutes or until tender. Drain, reserving the cooking water. Set half the asparagus tips aside. Purée the remaining asparagus with the potato. Add a little of the cooking water to thin the purée, until you have a smooth sauce. Add salt and pepper to taste and set aside.
Beat the egg and mix with the reserved asparagus tips.
Flatten the rabbit out on a worksurface and spread the asparagus tips and egg over the centre of the meat.
Roll up the rabbit and secure with kitchen string.
Heat the oil and butter in a roasting tin (pan), add the rabbit and cook over a medium heat until golden all over, about 10 minutes. Cover with (aluminum) foil, place in the oven and cook for 1 hour. Remove the foil and cook for a few more minutes, until golden.
Place the rabbit on a warmed serving platter, set aside and keep warm. Add the asparagus sauce to the roasting pan and deglaze the cooking juices over a low heat.
Pour the sauce around the rabbit and serve.

Serves 6

FILETTI DI SOGLIOLA ALLE ZUCCHINE E DRAGONCELLO

Sole Fillets with Courgettes (Zucchini) and Tarragon

Sometimes sole fillets are frozen and defrosted, which I do not like, so I try not to buy them like this. I usually ask the fishmonger to peel, clean the sole and pull the fillets for me, or I do this myself to be sure that the sole is fresh.

6 chives
6 tbsp extra virgin olive oil
1 garlic clove, finely chopped
3 small courgettes (zucchini), sliced
Handful fresh tarragon leaves, finely chopped
6 sole fillets
1 large potato, unpeeled
90ml/3fl oz/⅓ cup fish stock
Salt and pepper

Blanch the chives for a few seconds in boiling water and drain.
Heat 2 tbsp of the oil in a pan, add the garlic and the courgettes (zucchini) and sauté over a medium heat for about 3 minutes. Add salt and pepper to taste and half the tarragon.
Spread the mixture over the sole fillets, roll them up and tie in place with the chives.
Boil the potato in its skin. Drain, allow to cool slightly, then peel and purée in a blender with the fish stock, 2 tbsp of the oil, the rest of the tarragon and salt and pepper, until you have a smooth sauce.
Heat the remaining oil in a non-stick pan, add the sole fillets and sauté over a medium heat for 2 minutes on one side, then 1 minute on the other, adding a little water if necessary.
Heat the sauce gently. Transfer the sole fillets to a warmed serving dish, pour the sauce around and serve immediately.

Serves 6

PALOMBO AI CIPOLLOTTI E ZAFFERANO

Cod with Spring Onions (Scallions) and Saffron

Saffron comes from crocus threads with only 5 in one flower, and they have to be picked delicately or they lose their powder on top. The best saffron comes from Abruzzo, around the city of Aquila, because it has the best conditions in which to grow, but it is very rare. More common but less good saffron comes from Spain, Morocco or even Kashmir.

1.5kg/3 ½lb cod fillets
1kg/2 ¼ lb spring onions (scallions)
6 tbsp extra virgin olive oil
4 tbsp dry white wine
Large pinch saffron threads
Salt and pepper

Cut the cod into bite-sized pieces.
Clean and trim the spring onions (scallions), discarding the roots but leaving most of the green part.
Heat 4 tbsp of the oil in a pan, add the spring onions (scallions) and sauté for about 3 minutes. Add salt and pepper and the fish. Cover and cook for about 5 minutes. Uncover, add the wine and leave to evaporate.
Transfer the fish and onions to a warmed serving platter, sprinkle with the saffron threads and the remaining oil, and serve immediately.

Serves 6

SCAMPI SALTATI CON SALSA DI ZUCCHINE

Sautéed Prawns (Shrimp) Tails with Courgette (Zucchini) Sauce

When I am in Siena, in my beautiful new house on the Piazza del Campo, I like to cook fish often and the very best is sold in the shop *Romolo*, at Salicotto. But instead of prawns (shrimp) I will buy *mazzancolle*, which are almost alive. I sauté them for a couple of minutes, peel them with my fingers and dip them in the sauce before eating.

6 courgettes (zucchini)
6 tbsp extra virgin olive oil
1 tbsp balsamic vinegar
1 garlic clove
900g/2lb prawns (shrimp), peeled and deveined
Salt and pepper

Peel the courgettes (zucchini), removing any flesh from the peel. Reserve the flesh for another use. Blanch the courgette (zucchini) peel for 1 minute in boiling salted water. Drain, reserving the cooking water, and purée in a blender with 4 tbsp of the oil and enough of the cooking water to make a smooth sauce. Add the balsamic vinegar and mix well.
Heat the rest of the oil in a pan, add the garlic clove, and the prawns (shrimp) and sauté for about 3 minutes over a high heat.
Heat the courgette (zucchini) sauce and season to taste. Remove the garlic and discard. Pour the sauce on to a warmed serving dish, arrange the prawns (shrimp) over the top and serve immediately.

Serves 6

VEGETABLES AND SALADS

INSALATA ALLE ERBE
Salad with Fresh Herbs

Salad for Italians means fresh green leaves with oil, salt and red wine vinegar. Sometimes we will add sliced tomatoes if in season. But in spring, fresh herbs and spring onions (scallions) add a lovely taste.

120g/4oz lamb's lettuce
120g/4oz young, tender lettuce leaves
120g/4oz baby dandelion leaves
1 handful mixed fresh herbs, such as coriander (cilantro), flat-leaf parsley, chervil and mint
3 spring onions (scallions), sliced paper-thin
1 tbsp red wine vinegar
4 tbsp extra virgin olive oil
Salt

Wash the salad leaves and dry in a salad spinner. Repeat with the herbs.
Combine the salad leaves with the herbs in a bowl. Add the sliced spring onions (scallions).
In a cup, mix the vinegar with the salt and stir to dissolve the salt. Add the oil and mix well.
Toss the dressing with the salad.
Serve at once at room temperature.

Serves 6

FAGIOLINI AL PESTO
String Beans with Pesto Sauce

String beans are excellent with just a little oil, salt and maybe a drop of lemon juice, but once in a while I like to add pesto sauce to them, which is a typical dish from Genoa.

1kg/2 1/4 lb string beans
1 handful fresh flat-leaf parsley leaves
1 handful fresh mint leaves
2 tbsp pine nuts
1 tbsp grated Parmesan cheese
1 tbsp grated pecorino (Romano) cheese
6 tbsp extra virgin olive oil
Salt

Clean and trim the beans.
Bring a pan of water to the boil, add the beans and cook for about 5 minutes. Drain, reserving 120ml/4fl oz/1/2 cup of the cooking water. Leave the beans to cool.
In a blender, purée the parsley, mint, pine nuts and the cheeses with the oil and a little salt to taste. Add the reserved cooking water and blend again.
Pour over the beans and serve.

Serves 6

PISELLINI ALLA MENTA
Mint Peas

I think that vegetables should be very simply cooked so as not to lose their flavour, especially when they are freshly picked. Sauces and heavy condiments are usually too much. A few herbs are the best accompaniment.

2kg/4lb fresh peas (unshelled weight)
1 handful fresh mint leaves
4 tbsp extra virgin olive oil
Salt

Shell the peas, reserving the pods for another use—these can be used for a soup.
Bring a pan of water to the boil, add the peas and some salt. Blanch for 1 minute, drain and hold in a sieve or colander under cold running water for 1 minute. Drain and transfer to a serving bowl. Add salt to taste, the mint and the oil.
Mix together and serve.

Serves 6

FRITTATA DI ERBE DI CAMPO
Field Herb Frittata

In the countryside during spring, it is common to see elderly men or women with their nose on the ground, picking up lots of different wild herbs and salads. They are delicious in a *frittata* or used for soups. My grandson Emanuele, who is eleven, likes to go out in the afternoon to pick them and he has a good knowledge of the different types that can be found.

1kg/2¼ lb fresh field herbs (dandelion, wild rocket, chicory, watercress)
3 large eggs
4 tbsp extra virgin olive oil
2 garlic cloves, finely chopped
Salt

Clean and trim the herbs, discarding the roots. Bring a pan of water to the boil and blanch the herbs in the water for 1 minute.
Drain the herbs, squeeze dry and chop finely.
Beat the eggs in a bowl with a little salt. Heat 2 tbsp oil in a pan, add the garlic and sauté for about 3 minutes until translucent. Add the herbs and cook, stirring occasionally, for about 5 minutes, covered.
Remove from the heat and allow to cool.
Mix the herbs with the eggs and add the salt to taste. Heat 1 tbsp of the remaining oil in a non-stick frying pan, add the egg mixture and cook, covered, shaking the pan occasionally until almost set, about 5 minutes.
Slide the *frittata* out of the pan on to a plate, then turn over and slide back into the pan to cook the other side for just a couple of minutes. Transfer to a warmed serving platter and serve immediately.

Serves 6

TIMBALLETTI DI SPINACI
Spinach Timbales

Sometimes I put these little timbales around meat for a main dish, but I also like them as a first course with a little tomato coulis in summertime, when the tomatoes are naturally ripe and tasty.

700g/1½ lb baby spinach
4 large eggs
120ml/4fl oz/½ cup double (heavy) cream
Pinch of grated nutmeg
210g/7oz hazelnuts, finely chopped
1 tbsp unsalted butter
Salt and pepper

Clean the spinach, leaving the stems intact.
Bring a little water to the boil, add the spinach and cook for 1 minute. Drain, squeeze out any excess water and chop finely. Leave to cool completely.
Beat the eggs in a bowl, add the cream, the spinach, nutmeg and salt and pepper to taste. Mix well.
Butter 6 individual ramekins and coat well with the chopped hazelnuts.
Fill with the spinach mixture and cook in a bain-marie (a roasting tin [pan] filled with enough water to come halfway up the sides of the ramekins) for about 30 minutes, or until set and lightly golden on top.
Invert on to individual plates and serve immediately.

Serves 6

ASPARAGI AL SESAMO
Asparagus with Sesame Seeds

Sesame seeds are just beginning to become popular in Italy and I like to use them not only in bread or fish dishes, but on vegetables too, because the taste is not too overhelming.

2kg/4lb asparagus
1 tsp lemon juice
4 tbsp extra virgin olive oil
1 tbsp coriander (cilantro) leaves, finely chopped
Grated zest of 1 organic lemon
2 tbsp sesame seeds
Salt

Clean and trim the asparagus, discarding the woody ends and keeping only the tips.
Bring a pan of water to the boil and cook the asparagus for about 10 minutes.
Drain and transfer to a serving dish.
Add a little salt to the lemon juice, stirring to dissolve.
Add the oil, mix well and pour over the asparagus.
Sprinkle with the coriander (cilantro), lemon zest and sesame seeds.
Serve warm, lukewarm or at room temperature.

Serves 6

CARCIOFI, FAVE E PISELLI SALTATI
Artichokes, Broad (Fava) Beans and Sautéed Peas

In springtime I like to go and visit a friend of mine, Lidia Orsi, owner of a beautiful home near Varese. She also has an apartment in Camogli on the Ligurian coast where the vegetables are at their best, and we like to make simple and delicious dishes with them.

1 lemon, halved
3 artichokes
1kg/2 1/4 lb fresh broad (fava) beans (unshelled weight)
1kg/2 1/4 lb fresh peas (unshelled weight)
6 baby spring onions (scallions)
3 tbsp extra virgin olive oil
Salt and pepper

Fill a bowl with water and place the lemon halves in the water.
Clean the artichokes, and discard the tough outer leaves and the stem. Quarter each artichoke lengthways and remove the furry inner choke with a paring knife. Place the artichokes in the water as you go, to prevent them from discolouring. Drain and pat dry on paper towels.
Shell the beans and peas.
Bring a pan of water to the boil. Blanch the beans and peas in the boiling water for 1 minute.
Drain and hold in a sieve or colander under cold running water for 1 minute.
Clean and trim the spring onions (scallions), slicing the green tips thinly and leaving the white part intact.
Heat the oil in a pan, add the sliced onion tips and sauté for a couple of minutes over a medium heat.
Add the artichokes, mix well, then add the white parts of the onions, the beans and the peas. Sprinkle with salt and pepper and cover. Lower the heat and cook for about 20 minutes, shaking the pan occasionally. If necessary, add a spoonful of water from time to time to prevent the cooking juices from drying out.
Arrange the vegetables on a warmed serving platter and serve.

Serves 6

DESSERTS AND BREADS

CILIEGE AL GRAND MARNIER

Cherries with Grand Marnier

Cherries have a very short season and I usually like them uncooked, especially the type called *Vignola*, which are big and dark and grow in Emilia Romagna. But they are also pleasant when cooked.

1kg/2 1/4 lb fresh cherries
1 tbsp unsalted butter
90g/3oz/1/2 cup granulated sugar
120ml/4fl oz/1/2 cup Grand Marnier
double (heavy) cream, to serve

Stone (pit) the cherries.
Melt the butter in a pan, add the cherries and cook over a low heat, covered, for about 3 minutes.
Add the sugar and cook for 5 minutes more, or until the liquid has become a syrup (if you let a small amount drip on to a cool worksurface or saucer, it should harden immediately).
Add the Grand Marnier—do this carefully, and stand back as you pour, as the syrup will spit.
Cook for 3 more minutes, uncovered, stirring constantly. Allow to cool.
Transfer to a serving dish, whip the cream and serve the cherries with the cream.

Serves 6

FRAGOLINE DI BOSCO ALLO ZABAIONE GRATINATO

Wild Strawberries with Sabayon Gratin

Zabaione is traditionally made with Marsala, but I think this is too powerful, so I prefer to substitute it with Vin Santo or another dessert wine such as Moscato di Pantelleria, which is more delicate for strawberries.

600g/1 1/4 lb wild strawberries
4 large egg yolks
90g/3oz/6 tbsp granulated sugar
180ml/6fl oz/3/4 cup Vin Santo,
or similar dessert wine (not Marsala)
60g/2oz/1/4 cup brown (cane) sugar

Preheat the grill to high.
Clean the strawberries and arrange in an ovenproof dish.
Half fill a pan with water—the pan should be large enough to hold a heatproof bowl without the bowl touching the water. Gently heat the water.
Off the heat, whisk the egg yolks with the sugar in the heatproof bowl for a few minutes, then add the Vin Santo, whisking as you pour it in.
Place the bowl over the water in the pan and whisk constantly over a medium heat until the sabayon starts to thicken.
Pour the sabayon over the strawberries and sprinkle with the brown (cane) sugar.
Put the dish under the grill for a few minutes or until lightly golden. Serve immediately.

Serves 6

UOVA ALLA NEVE CON SALSA DI FRAGOLE
Meringues with Strawberry Sauce

I make this variation of an old recipe that my mother often uses for dinner guests with the first strawberries of the year. I substitute the usual raspberries with strawberries here, and in autumn I use blackberries.

6 large eggs, separated
2 tbsp plain (all-purpose) flour
90g/3oz/6 tbsp granulated sugar
1 litre/1 ¾ pints/4 cups milk
300g/10oz strawberries
120g/4oz/1 cup icing (powdered) sugar

Beat the yolks with the flour in a heatproof bowl, add the granulated sugar and half the milk, a little at a time, whisking between each addition.
Place the bowl over a pan of simmering water—don't let the bowl touch the water—and beat constantly over a medium heat until the mixture starts to boil. Remove the bowl from the heat and allow to cool.
Keep a few strawberries aside for decoration and purée the rest in a blender. Add the purée to the cream mixture, mix to combine, and pour into a serving dish. Place in the refrigerator to cool.
Sprinkle a worksurface with water—you will need to place the meringues on this as they cook.
Bring the rest of the milk to a slow boil in a saucepan. Whisk the whites in a bowl until stiff. Add the icing sugar to the whites, a little at a time, whisking as you do so.
Using a spoon, make oval shapes from the meringue mixture and drop into the boiling milk a few at a time. Cook them for 3 minutes each, turning once carefully. Transfer to the wet surface with a slotted spoon and allow to cool. You will make more meringues than you need, but you will then be able to choose the better ones for this dessert.
Place the meringues on top of the strawberry cream and decorate with the reserved strawberries. Keep in the refrigerator until ready to serve.

Serves 6

TORTA DI LAMPONI
Raspberry Tart

It is not easy to pick raspberries in our garden because as soon as one is ripe it is picked by one of my eight grandchildren. And so although we have many raspberry bushes I sometimes have to buy them.

FOR THE PASTRY:
180g/6oz/1 ½ cups plain (all-purpose) flour
60g/2oz/½ cup semolina
150g/5oz/10 tbsp unsalted butter
60g/2oz/4 tbsp granulated sugar
1 large egg
FOR THE FILLING:
1 whole large egg plus 1 yolk
180g/6oz/¾ cup fresh ricotta cheese
60g/2oz/½ cup icing (powdered) sugar
120ml/4fl oz/½ cup double (heavy) cream
180g/6oz raspberries

Preheat the oven to 170°C/350°F/Gas 4.
In a food processor fitted with metal blades, process the flour, semolina, butter, sugar and egg until a ball is formed. Wrap in cling film (plastic wrap) and put in the refrigerator for about 2 hours.
Butter a 23cm/9in tart tin (pan) with removable bottom. Roll out the dough and line the tart tin (pan).
Bake in the oven until almost golden, about 15 minutes. If the pastry pops up in places during cooking, remove from the oven and flatten with the palm of your hand, protected with a cloth, then return to the oven.
To make the filling, mix the egg and egg yolk with the ricotta and the sugar, until barely stiff. Whip the cream until thickened and fold it into the ricotta mixture.
Fill the pastry shell with the ricotta mixture and dot with the raspberries, pressing them in slightly.
Return to the oven for about 30 minutes or until slightly golden on top.
Leave to cool, then unmould the tart from the tart tin (pan), transfer to a serving platter and serve at room temperature.

Serves 6

PANE ALLE NOCI
Bread with Fresh Walnuts

After 24 June, walnuts start to become hard. They are edible in Coltibuono at least but they will not really be ready until the end of summer. However, I like them when they are very fresh and when the skin is still slightly bitter.

30g/1oz/2 tbsp fresh yeast
240ml/8fl oz/1 cup lukewarm water
360g/12oz/3 cups plain (all-purpose) flour, plus extra for dusting
3 tbsp granulated sugar
300g/10oz fresh walnuts, peeled but not skinned, and chopped into small pieces.
1 tbsp extra virgin olive oil

Preheat the oven to 200°C/400°F/Gas 6.
Dissolve the yeast in the lukewarm water for about 10 minutes.
Sift the flour into a large bowl and add the sugar. Make a well in the centre and gradually add the yeast mixture, stirring in a circular motion with a fork until a dough is formed. Knead the dough on a lightly floured worksurface for a few minutes until smooth, adding the walnuts but trying not to add more flour. Form into a ball and transfer to a lightly floured bowl.
Cover with cling film (plastic wrap) and leave to double in size. The exact time it takes will depend on the temperature of the room.
Brush a 27cm/9in circular tart tin (pan) or baking sheet (cookie tray) with the oil. Punch down the dough on a worksurface and roll into a circle the same size as the tin or sheet. Transfer the dough to the tin (pan) or sheet (tray) and leave to rise again for about 20 minutes.
Bake in the oven for about 30 minutes or until slightly golden on top. Leave to cool on a wire rack and serve.

Serves 6

MACEDONIA DI FRUTTI DI BOSCO ALLA SALSA DI VINO ROSSO
Berries with Red Wine Syrup

This light and very delicious desert is a special spring and early summer treat.

210g/7oz wild strawberries
210g/7oz raspberries
210g/7oz blackcurrant
210g/7oz redcurrants
1 bottle red wine
300g/10oz/1 2/3 cups granulated sugar

Clean the berries and place in a large bowl. Keep in the refrigerator until you are ready to serve.
Bring the wine to the boil in a pan, add the sugar and cook until syrupy for about 20 minutes over a low heat. If you drop a small amount of syrup on to a cold surface, it should stay firm and round. Leave to cool.
Pour half the syrup over the berries and serve.
The rest of the syrup can be kept in a sealed container in a cool, dark place and used for serving with ice-cream.

Serves 6

AN EASTER FEAST

INSALATA DI FAVE E PECORINO

*Salad of Broad (Fava) Beans
and Pecorino (Romano) Cheese*

Broad (fava) beans are plentiful in this season and a good accompaniment to lots of food, but the most typical way of preparing broad beans (fava) and pecorino (Romano), a cheese made from sheep's milk in Tuscany, is with a little oil and pepper. Diced pecorino (Romano) served with the beans is also very good, or sliced on toast with some beans, oil and pepper on top. If the beans are not very fresh, and the pods very big, you will need to peel them as well as shelling them. In this case, you will need to buy an extra 1kg/2¼lb beans.

2kg/4lb fresh broad (fava) beans (unshelled weight)
4 tbsp extra virgin olive oil
2 tbsp chopped fresh flat-leaf parsley
3 tbsp freshly grated pecorino (Romano) cheese
Salt

Shell the beans and place in a serving bowl. Pour the oil over the top, sprinkle with the parsley, the cheese, and the salt to taste. Toss lightly and serve immediately.

Serves 6

RISOTTO CON ASPARAGI E PISELLI

Risotto with Asparagus and Peas

Risotto with asparagus tips and peas is typical in spring, when both these vegetables are in season for a short time. I could eat them every day and they are also excellent combined with fettuccini.

450g/1lb fresh peas (unshelled weight)
450g/1lb asparagus
2 litres/3½ pints/8 cups light chicken stock
½ white onion, finely chopped
60g/2oz/4 tbsp unsalted butter
12 handfuls arborio or vialone nano rice
2 tbsp finely chopped fresh chives
Salt

Shell the peas and trim the asparagus, discarding the woody ends and keeping only the tender tips.
Heat the stock in a pan and boil gently over a low heat.
In a large saucepan fry the onion in half the butter over a medium heat for about 3 minutes or until translucent. Add the rice and cook over a high heat until the rice is very hot, stirring constantly with a wooden spoon.
After about 3 minutes start adding the stock, about 240ml/8fl oz/1 cup at a time, or enough to ensure that the rice is covered with a veil of liquid. Keep adding the stock about once every minute.
Meanwhile, melt the rest of the butter over a very low heat, add the asparagus tips and peas, a little salt and a drop of water. Cover and leave to cook for a couple of minutes, without letting the ingredients sizzle.
About 14 minutes after the rice first started boiling, remove the pan from the heat, add the peas, asparagus and butter, cover and leave to rest for a couple of minutes. The risotto should have a creamy porridge-like consistency.
Add salt to taste, stir well and transfer to a warmed serving dish. Sprinkle with the chives and serve.

Serves 6

GNOCCHI DI PATATE IN SALSA DI ZUCCHINE

Potato Gnocchi with a Courgette (Zucchini) Sauce

We love to eat potato gnocchi for Easter. We do not use the new potatoes that are not starchy enough but ones that have been kept during the winter, otherwise the gnocchi will dissolve in the boiling water. To further avoid this you will have to add a lot of flour which will make the gnocchi as hard as tennis balls.

1.5kg/3lb 5oz boiling potatoes, unpeeled
2 large egg yolks
240g/8oz/2 cups plain (all-purpose) flour
300g/10oz courgettes (zucchini)
120ml/4fl oz/½ cup extra virgin olive oil
1 handful fresh basil leaves
Salt and pepper

Boil the potatoes in their skins until tender, about 30 minutes, then drain and peel. Pass the potatoes through a ricer or food mill while still warm, then add the egg yolks, half the flour and salt to taste and mix well to blend.

Using floured hands, divide the mixture into 6 portions and roll each one out on a floured surface until you have 6 'sausages' about 3cm/1in in diameter. Cut into pieces about 1.5cm/¾in wide and roll them into oval shapes using floured hands. These can be kept on a floured tray for up to 1 hour.

Meanwhile, slice the courgettes (zucchini) and sauté them in a pan with half the oil over a very low heat for about 5 minutes. Purée them in a blender with the basil, then add salt and pepper to taste.

Bring a large pot of water to the boil, add salt and the gnocchi. The gnocchi are ready when they rise to the surface of the water. Meanwhile, reheat the courgette (zucchini) sauce, adding the rest of the oil. Do not allow it to sizzle.

Remove the gnocchi from the water with a slotted spoon, transfer to a warmed serving dish, pour over the sauce and serve immediately.

Serves 6

AGNELLO FARCITO AL PREZZEMOLO

Lamb Stuffed with Parsley

Baby lambs are very small and tender in Italy. This is the typical dish to be served at Easter.

1 leg of lamb, about 1.5kg/3lb, bone in
120g/4oz fresh flat-leaf parsley
300g/10oz chicken breast, roughly diced
2 large egg yolks
60ml/2fl oz/4 tbsp double (heavy) cream
2 tbsp extra virgin olive oil
2 tbsp unsalted butter
½ bottle dry white wine
Salt and pepper

Ask your butcher to bone the lamb.

Preheat the oven to 170°C/350°F/Gas 4. Lay the boned lamb on a worksurface and flatten slightly. Bring a large pan of water to the boil, add the parsley and blanch for 1 minute. Drain the parsley and purée in a blender with the chicken, the egg yolks and salt and pepper, until creamy. Add the cream and mix. Spread the mixture over the centre of the lamb, then roll up the lamb and secure with string.

Put the oil and butter in a roasting tin (pan), add the lamb and cover loosely with (aluminum) foil. Cook in the oven for about 2 hours, adding wine from time to time to prevent the juices from drying out. Uncover and cook for 30 minutes more, or until well browned. Remove the lamb from the tin (pan) and discard the string. Carve into slices, transfer to a warmed serving plate and keep warm.

Deglaze the cooking juices with the rest of the wine over a low heat. Pour over the lamb slices and serve.

Serves 6

FILETTI DI SOGLIOLA ALLE ERBE E FIORI DI ZUCCA

Sole Fillets with Herbs and Courgette (Zucchini) Flowers

When I invite 12 people over I prefer to have dishes served as a buffet, which is why my recipes serve 6, a number that is easy to double or triple. If I made an Easter feast served at the table, I would make one appetizer, one first, one second and a dessert. This dish is nice for Easter, although lamb is usual.

120g/4oz/1 cup fine dry breadcrumbs
2 tbsp mixed fresh herbs, finely chopped (basil, parsley, tarragon, chives)
12 sole fillets
2 tbsp unsalted butter
2 tbsp extra virgin olive oil
300g/10oz courgette (zucchini) flowers
90g/3oz/6 tbsp plain (all-purpose) flour
180ml/6fl oz/³/₄ cup fizzy water
1 litre/1³/₄ pints/4 cups oil, for deep-frying
Salt

Mix the breadcrumbs with the herbs and some salt in a shallow bowl and dip the sole fillets in the breadcrumbs to coat.
Heat the butter and olive oil in a pan over a medium heat, add the fillets and fry for about 3 minutes on each side or until lightly golden. Set aside and keep warm.
Clean the courgette (zucchini) flowers, discarding the inner stamens.
Put the flour in a mixing bowl and add the water, a little at a time, stirring well to avoid lumps. You should end up with a smooth batter. Add a little salt. Heat the oil for deep-frying in a cast-iron pan until it reaches 170°C/350°F. Dip the courgette (zucchini) flowers in the batter and deep-fry a few at a time until golden. Drain on kitchen paper.
Arrange the sole fillets in a warmed serving dish, surround with the courgette (zucchini) flowers and serve immediately.

Serves 6

INSALATA ALLA MELA

Salad with Apples

Slightly acidic apples are good for this recipe.

300g/10oz small salad leaves, such as lamb's lettuce
1 Granny Smith apple
1 tbsp chopped chives
1 tbsp red wine vinegar
4 tbsp extra virgin olive oil
Salt

Wash and dry the salad leaves. Place in a bowl. Peel, core and thinly slice the apple and add to the salad with the chives. Dissolve the salt in the vinegar and pour over. Add the oil and toss. Serve.

Serves 6

TORTA DI CIOCCOLATA E BANANA

Chocolate and Banana Cake

This cake is a perfect ending for an Easter feast.

90g/3oz bitter chocolate
60g/2oz/4 tbsp unsalted butter,
plus 1 tbsp for buttering the tart tin
3 large eggs
90g/3oz/6 tbsp granulated sugar
60g/2oz/¹/₂ cup plain (all-purpose) flour,
plus 2 tbsp for dusting the tart tin
3 bananas
90g/3oz/6 tbsp brown (cane) sugar

Preheat the oven to 170°C/350°F/Gas 4.
Melt the chocolate and butter in a heatproof bowl above a pan of simmering water.
When cool, beat the eggs with the sugar and gently stir into the butter. Fold in the flour a little at a time.
Butter a 23cm/9in round non-stick cake tin (pan) with a removable bottom and dust with the flour. Pour in the mixture and bake for 15 minutes. Remove and leave for a few minutes before turning the cake out on to a wire rack to cool. Preheat the grill to high. Peel and slice the bananas, place on the cake and sprinkle with brown (cane) sugar. Place under the grill for a few minutes to melt the sugar. Serve when cool.

Serves 6

INTRODUCTION

What strikes me most about an Italian summer are the vivid colours, especially in Tuscany, where the relatively moderate climate keeps the flora flourishing throughout the season. In June gardens are full of roses. One of Europe's great rose gardens is just down the road from where I live. At every angle of stone courtyards, on ancient walls and in windows of old farmhouses, multi-coloured geraniums cascade over terracotta pots. The hills are covered with bright yellow bunches of broom and the fields below are carpeted with red poppies. In July poppies give way to gyrating heads of golden brown sunflowers, myriads of them. They are a recent crop in these parts, harvested for their oil-producing seeds. And there are still plenty of wild flowers around. At the height of the season it is possible to gather a bouquet of dozens of different kinds and colours. By August the hot sun brings the grapes on the vines to a deep purple ripeness and creates a climate of lazy stillness. Only lizards and butterflies, it seems, still move around. The evenings, however, are blessedly cool and nature comes back to life with the sound of nightingales and the sight of darting bats and flickering fireflies.

Colours, both bright and deep, characterize the market place as well. Lustrous green, yellow, orange and red peppers, *peperoni*, attract attention first. These are sweet (bell) peppers shaped more like little barrels than bells. The green ones are under-ripe and slightly bitter. As they mature they go through their colour changes and come into full flavour, sweet and mild. If you buy them young, when they are just beginning to take on colour, you can eat them raw in a salad.

Peppers are native to the Americas, from a genus of plant called *capsicum*. They were brought back to Spain by Columbus and soon made their way to the Italian peninsula where they have been popular ever since. Perhaps the simplest way to prepare them and certainly one of the most satisfying, is to peel, grill and dress them with extra virgin olive oil. A very popular southern Italian dish is *peperonata*, (bell) peppers stewed in tomato sauce with onions and garlic. It is delicious with meat dishes. I make a version of this, topped with a fried egg for each person and serve it as a main course. Using these same ingredients but without the eggs and adding anchovies and olives, I layer the ingredients in a casserole, sprinkle with breadcrumbs and bake in the oven. For an elegant summer meal I prepare individual bowls of cream of yellow (bell) pepper soup topped with a little ball of savoury tomato sorbet. It is one of the tastiest summer soups you can imagine.

Related to the (bell) pepper are *peperoncini* or chilli (bell) peppers—small, fire-engine red and so hot that in southern Italy, where they are grown and most used, they are called *diavolilli*, 'little devils.' You will see them in markets tied into strands. Chilli pepper is mostly used dried and added with moderation to give piquancy to many dishes. A very popular pasta sauce is called *all'arrabbiata*, basically a tomato sauce to which you add as much chilli pepper as your taste buds can tolerate. Its name literally means 'angry', as in getting a bit hot under the collar.

Another beautifully coloured vegetable with smooth, shiny skin, which vies for attention in summer market stalls is *melanzane*, aubergines (eggplants). I always wondered why this vegetable was called eggplant in North America, until I saw the white variety for the first time. It is oval-shaped and, with a bit of imagination, could pass for the egg of a very large bird. In Australia I heard a commercial gardener refer to them as 'eggfruit.' He explained that 'botanically' they are fruit and not a vegetable. Aubergines

(eggplants) are thought to have arrived in Europe from India and China via the medieval Italian trade routes. The philosopher-scientist, Albert the Great, teacher of St Thomas Aquinas, mentions them in a thirteenth-century treatise. Italians of that time called any new, exotic fruit or vegetable *mela*, an apple of some sort. Since aubergines (eggplants) were strange and suspiciously regarded, they were thought to be unhealthy, and were called the 'unhealthy apple', *mela-insana* or *melanzana*. It took a couple of hundred years before this prejudice was overcome.

In my travels to the East I have come across aubergines (eggplants) in many colours, shapes and sizes, from large white eggs to huge, purple gourds so deeply coloured they appear black. In Italy we grow mostly the purple variety. The most common is called 'Black Beauty' and is deep purple and oval-shaped with a little green cap. In Florence you will find the *violetta di Firenze*, light purple and globe-shaped with a violet cap. At street markets in Naples you can't miss the *violetta lunga di Napoli*, slender, elongated and, frankly, phallic—a characteristic vendors invariably point out to the customer. The plants are as handsome as their fruit, compact bushes with green-grey leaves and tiny purple flowers. I enjoy them in my garden for their ornamental beauty as well as for their fruit.

Aubergines (eggplants) need a lot of warm sun to fully ripen. For that reason they thrive in southern Italy, where most Italian recipes using them originate. In Italy aubergine (eggplant) is fried, grilled, baked, stuffed and in the south it is even layered with chocolate sauce and served as a dessert. It combines perfectly with all the characteristic Mediterranean flavours: garlic, tomatoes, basil and cheeses. I think the most satisfying dish of all is *parmigiana di melanzane*, Aubergine (Eggplant) Parmesan, layers of slices of fried eggplant topped with cooked tomato and mozzarella, liberally sprinkled with grated Parmesan. This used to be considered a dish too humble to serve in a proper restaurant. Now appreciation for its perfect balance of flavours puts it on prestigious menus. All the ingredients must be fresh and fine to achieve superior results.

For any recipe calling for aubergine (eggplant), it is important to buy ones that are as fresh as possible, shiny and firm and light in weight. Fresh aubergine (eggplant) is tender and sweet. The skin of an over-ripe one is tough and its seeds bitter. When they are fresh, you will not need to go through that process described in many cookbooks of salting them and draining in a colander to draw out excess water. All aubergines (eggplants) absorb olive oil like a sponge. When you grill (broil) *melanzane*, cut them into thick slices and only afterwards dress them with extra virgin olive oil.

Early summer adds its dash of green to the market with one of the most welcome arrivals of the summer, *fagiolini*, tiny, green beans. These are picked early when their pods are still tender and sweet and the seeds inside are minuscule. Green beans should be thin and not more than 9–10cm/3–4in long, easy to snap, and their skin a solid, fresh green. Avoid dull, limp, spotty ones.

I think of green beans as Italian. I know they originally came to Europe from the Americas and that the French have their *haricots verts*. It is just that I find it hard to imagine green beans without fine Italian extra virgin olive oil. These two ingredients alone, with a squeeze of lemon, make a delicious dish. I even serve it as a main course for a light summer lunch, perhaps preceded by a pasta dish. I also like to combine two classic summer tastes, green beans and basil. I dress the beans with pesto sauce enriched with mint and parsley.

When I first started to teach cooking, I had to tell my students not to overcook vegetables in general. Now I need to remind them not to undercook green beans, in particular. They need about five minutes in salted, boiling water to lose their grassy taste and come into full flavour.

Another early summer and popular vegetable in the Italian kitchen is courgettes (zucchini). They begin to arrive at market in late spring, although they do not start to ripen in my garden until midsummer. It is important to buy them when they are young and fresh, a little unripe, in fact, before their seeds develop. They should be small and firm with shiny, pale to dark green, unblemished skin. In local markets they often arrive with their yellow blossoms still attached, which, if they have not yet wilted, is the best sign of freshness. These are not the courgette (zucchini) flowers we fry. The edible flower is the botanical male, which is large, yellowish orange and grows on the stem. The female blossom is what turns into the vegetable. This is why zucchini is *zucchine* (feminine form) in Italian.

The flavour of a good courgette (zucchini) is delicately sweet and tender and congenial to all sorts of seasonings and other ingredients, which is what makes it so popular with cooks. My favourite way to eat them fresh out of the garden is to boil them for several minutes, slice them, dress with extra virgin olive oil and season with chopped fresh tarragon. We also bake, sauté, stuff and fry courgettes (zucchini), and the blossoms as well, of course.

Come midsummer anyone who has a vegetable garden in Italy begins to think of neighbours and friends who don't,

Long Purple Egg-plant (¼ natural size).

because this is the time you start to wonder how in the world you are going to dispose of all those tomatoes that are 'happening' out there on their vines, faster than you can possibly eat them. The only way involves work, canning and preserving, but when winter arrives you will be grateful for the abundance of tomatoes and the work will seem well worth it.

Like Maria Callas, the famous opera singer, tomatoes might not have been born in Italy (they originated in South America) but it is here they first became famous. On the other hand it is not accurate to say that without the tomato there would be no Italian cooking. It took a couple of hundred years after the first tomatoes came to Spain and Italy in the sixteenth century before they caught on in the kitchen. And this happened first in southern Italy. Northern Italian cooking could still get along nicely without the tomato.

The first written recipe that makes use of tomatoes is from a seventeenth-century Neapolitan book and it is for a tomato sauce flavoured with parsley, garlic and onion. It was not until the early nineteenth century, however, that the cultivation and canning of tomatoes began on a large scale, and this took place in Naples and the region of Campania. The United States followed soon afterwards with the industrial production of tomato ketchup.

I have no idea of the names and numbers of all the varieties of tomatoes that are grown in Italy. There must be dozens of them. As always, the best are the local varieties, especially when they are at the height of their season. The first to arrive at market is the little cherry-type tomato, called *pomodorini* or *ciliegini*. It looks like a large cherry and comes in a cluster still attached to the vine. The tomatoes are sweet and full of flavour. Cherry tomatoes are best in salads, sliced in half and dressed with extra virgin olive oil and a few fresh basil leaves. At the end of the season gardeners pull up the entire plant and hang it from the ceiling of a cool and well-ventilated room of the house. The tomatoes will wrinkle a bit but they remain fresh and provide flavour for dishes throughout most of the winter.

The best and most popular tomato for cooking with is the *San Marzano*, a so-called plum variety, because of its thin, elongated shape. It has very firm flesh with fewer seeds and less juice than other types and an intense tomato flavour, both of which qualities make it ideal for sauces.

Another variety of which there are many different regional kinds is called *costoluto* or beef-steak tomato. It is large and ribbed and good to eat when it is greenish orange in colour, not yet fully ripe. This tomato has a good balance of sugar and acid content. I like them sliced raw and dressed with extra virgin olive oil and balsamic vinegar. They are also perfect for stuffing with rice or seafood.

One cannot speak of tomatoes without thinking of the king of herbs, *basilico*. Fresh tomatoes with fresh basil epitomize the sunny Italian summer. Basil is the supremely fragrant herb. This must be why it got its name, which derives from the Greek word meaning 'royal'. And you cannot mention basil in a gastronomic context without thinking of pesto, the essential summer sauce. It is no accident that pesto, oriental in origin, took root in the west in Liguria, the coastal region whose sea air is credited with producing the sweetest, most tender and fragrant basil in all the Mediterranean.

No sauce could be simpler to make than pesto. Nevertheless it is an art to get it just right and according to Ligurians virtually impossible for someone not born and raised in Liguria. Various versions of the classic pesto recipe exist but basically it consists of a bunch of basil leaves, a clove or two of garlic, a pinch of salt, a handful of pine nuts and a bit of pecorino (Romano) cheese. When these have been ground into a fine paste, some olive oil is mixed in until they become a smooth sauce, fresh green in colour. Often Parmesan cheese is added, as are walnuts. The classic technique is to use a marble mortar and a wooden pestle to crush the ingredients but a blender does the job satisfactorily. I have included my pesto recipe in the Spring Pantry section as I recommend making a large enough quantity to have on hand in the refrigerator. It will keep for at least a week and is always welcome as a dressing for pasta, gnocchi or on some cold vegetables, like green beans. A dab or two on sliced or in stuffed tomatoes makes a perfect dish for a light summer lunch.

Along with tomatoes and basil, there is a third ingredient that embodies Italian summer eating, mozzarella cheese. These three combine to make *caprese*, a salad from the Island of Capri, itself an idyllic symbol of sea, sun and summer. Although mozzarella is available all year round, it has such a perfect affinity with summer ingredients that I associate it with the season. Also, when it is too hot to cook, mozzarella provides the substance for a satisfying meal in itself.

Genuine mozzarella is made from fresh, full-fat buffalo milk and now is produced only in a couple of regions in the south, especially in the provinces of Caserta and Salerno, where herds of water buffalo still graze along the coast. Many producers still make it by hand, using a technique of carefully and delicately pulling and tearing the heated curd, gradually forming it into a ball.

For anyone who enjoys food, it is not an exaggeration to say that it is worth a trip to these areas just to taste the mozzarella. Locals say it should be eaten before noon on the day it is made, which is indeed an unforgettable experience, even for those of us who live in the rest of Italy and are used to buying mozzarella that is, at best, a couple of days old. Fresh mozzarella is lively white, soft but solid, still dripping with its own buttermilk. It has a delicate, sweet fragrance and flavour. At home I try to find the freshest buffalo's milk mozzarella possible. If this is not available I use *fior di latte*, the same type of cheese made from cow's milk, which can be delicious in its own right. Great mozzarella is best enjoyed in salads or as a topping for summer pasta dishes.

Towards the end of summer fresh beans begin to arrive at the market. These are the same varieties we eat dried all year around, *cannellini*, *lamon* and *borlotti*. When fresh, they are a tender and delicious seasonal treat. I enjoy them most in salads, combined with onions and tomatoes and seasoned with bay leaves.

Wherever you might be in Italy, you are never far from the sea and its bounty. Excellent fresh fish is available all year round even in large inland cities like Milan and Florence and I have included several seafood recipes in each seasonal section of this book. During the summer months, however, there is a mass exodus from cities and towns to the beaches, and impressive feasts of fish, served up at local restaurants, are a part of the holiday atmosphere. Here, the catch of the day can be found at the market or on the menu. Remember that many fish available in Italy are peculiar to the Mediterranean, although it is often possible to find suitable substitutes from other seas. Remember also that Mediterranean fish names are often different from region to region.

In the main street market of Naples, just down the street from the central train station, you will see a variety and quantity of shellfish that are a marvel to behold. Buckets and basins and tubs are full of mussels (*cozze*), sea-truffles (*tartufo di mare*), razor clams (*cannolicchi*), and numerous others whose names would fill an esoteric catalogue. I remember when all of these could be enjoyed raw with lemon juice but, unfortunately, that is a forbidden pleasure today. Home and restaurant cooks are mostly looking for the freshest *vongole veraci*, carpet shells, a large species of clam, greyish in colour with dark lines. Its flavour is superior to its many cousins also on display. *Vongole veraci* are used in two popular recipes, a soup ladled over grilled bread, *zuppa di vongole*, and as a dressing for *spaghetti alle vongole veraci*. Sometimes they are served in their shells, which is more colourful and fun, and in that case the waiter might offer you an extra large linen napkin to tie around your neck to protect your clothes.

Many stalls feature what my English-speaking grand-children call 'funny fish', several different creatures that belong to the octopus family. The smallest are *seppie*, cuttlefish. They look like little bags with heads and numerous tentacles. Their flesh is more tender than octopus and makes a good sauce for rice and pasta. They secrete an ink which is used to make black rice, *riso nero*, and is now popular for colouring and flavouring dry pasta. The smaller version of the *seppia* is delicious deep-fried. I like them sautéed with potatoes and onions. Ask the fishmonger to clean them for you, as it is tricky to extract their small inner shell and ink sac. Another popular member of this family are *calamari*, squid. These are larger and are very tasty stuffed (*ripieni*) with a mixture of bread-crumbs, garlic, parsley, olives and chilli pepper. Mostly they are stewed or served as part of a *fritto misto*, a mixed fry.

The smaller crustaceans of the prawn and shrimp family are perhaps the most popular seafood on the Italian menu. Various types and sizes of *gamberi*, prawns (shrimp) and *scampi*, shrimps are sautéed, grilled, fried and their tails even stuffed. They go well with all sorts of summer vegetables and for a perfectly delicious summer soup I combine prawns (shrimp) with tomatoes and basil.

The Mediterranean is full of hundreds of varieties of tasty fish (the supply has been decreasing but is reported, happily, to be on the rise), with more flavour, in my opinion, than you will find in any other sea. You will see some that are minuscule by nature and others that are small because they are (illegally) fished before they reach maturity. The anchovy, *acciuga* or *alice*, is the most prevalent of the naturally small species. It is commonly known around the world in its preserved form and used to season many an Italian dish. Less well known outside Mediterranean

countries are fresh anchovies, usually called *alice*, which have a uniquely delicious flavour. They make the perfect summer *antipasto*, simply marinated in lemon and white wine vinegar and dressed with olive oil and parsley. A plate of quickly fried fresh anchovies is not a bad start to a meal, either. Similar to the anchovy, although of a different family, and used in much the same way, is the sardine, *sardina*. Sicily's most celebrated pasta recipe is *pasta con le sarde*—penne or rigatoni baked with a mixture of fresh sardines, golden raisins, pine nuts and flavoured with fennel bulb and seeds. Sardines have an affinity with fennel and I enjoy serving a simple dish featuring these two ingredients, baked with breadcrumbs.

Of the many medium-sized Mediterranean fish, I think my favourite is the silver sea bass, called *branzino* or *spigola*. As with most fish, the less you do to it the better. I bake it in parchment paper and serve with a sauce of anchovies, capers, hardboiled egg and vinegar. This dish is also good served cold. A fish you can't help notice in the market or on display in restaurants is the crimson-coloured *triglia* or red mullet. It takes dedi-cation to clean and eat because of its many tiny bones, but its unique and delicious flavour makes it worth the effort. I bake it with a black olive pesto sauce. Perhaps the most versatile fish in the kitchen is *sogliola*, sole. Its delicate flavour combines well with a host of ingred-ients and seasonings. A good way to incorporate these flavours is to prepare fillets of sole in rolls. I fill them with various mixtures, fennel and orange, or courgettes (zucchini) and tarragon, and secure with a toothpick before cooking.

Two large fish vie for supremacy in our seas and on the Italian table, tuna, *tonno* and swordfish, *pesce spada*. Swordfish are most plentiful off the coast of Sicily, where they are still hunted by harpoon. In the Palermo street market fishmongers proudly display the sword alongside the vanquished fish. You can't better swordfish steaks, simply grilled, dressed with a drop of olive oil and vinegar. Swordfish meat also makes a tasty tartare, flavoured with capers and ginger root, a perfect main course for a summer lunch. Blue-fin tuna has been fished in the Mediterranean since before Greek and Roman times. They are still caught in traps of ancient origin during their breeding migrations.

The best part of their meat is called *ventresca*, the belly, and this is what you should look for when you are buying tuna preserved in oil. The repertoire of Italian recipes using preserved tuna is vast. For something a little unusual, serve your guests tuna and chicken pâté as a summer appetizer.

For me three fruits in particular exude the essence of summer—apricots, peaches and nectarines. It is not only the sunny colours of their skin—warm yellow, glowing orange with a rosy flush—but also their rich fragrance and flavour.

The Persians called apricots 'seeds of the sun', and the ancient Greeks named them 'golden eggs of the sun'. An elegant way to end a summer lunch is with a moulded apricot and yoghurt mousse. It is not difficult to make, is attractive to present (I decorate it with red berries), is rich in flavour but not heavy, and is fresh and cool on the palate.

The easiest way to enjoy a peach at the table is to slice the fruit and add it to a glass of white wine or champagne. Peaches combine well with other fruits and flavours. For a simple dessert I caramelize peach wedges and serve with a sauce flavoured with *amaretti*, macaroons made with sweet and bitter almonds. Nectarines are of the same species as the peach. The only difference is that peach skin is fuzzy and nectarines are smooth. In Italian a nectarine is called *pesca noce*, a walnut-like peach, because without the fuzz it appears harder than a peach. They can be used in the same way as a peach and because of their smooth skin, some prefer nectarines as a table fruit.

I try to steal a little summer from these fruits and hide it away for winter in the form of preserves and jam. Apricots make a tasty chutney, as well.

SUMMER FEASTS

Alfresco is a word that comes from the Italian phrase, *al fresco*, meaning in the fresh or open air, and is an expression that has entered many other languages. It is synonymous with summer eating in Italy, picnics on the grass, at the sea, in the mountains, meals in the garden or out on the terrace of a favourite country restaurant and, most especially, local *feste* held in village and town squares or the *piazze* of city neighbourhoods. Alfresco eating in Italy begins around May, hits a high during the torrid days of mid-July through

to the end of August, and continues into grape harvest time in late September and early October. A friend of mine has worked out that if you planned ahead, you could eat at an outdoor *festa* every night from mid-June to mid-September, and at a cheaper price than it would cost to have dinner at home.

The reason for alfresco meals is the weather, hot days and warm nights and the leisure time the summer provides, vacations from school and job and annual holidays. The real cause is the Italian love of eating and socializing in the company of family, friends and neighbours. The excuse could be the feast day of the local patron saint or a traditional civic gathering. These are events celebrated with special food. Then there is another kind of feast at which a special food itself is celebrated. These are called *sagre*, from the Latin word, *sacer*, meaning sacred. Cultural anthropologists say they got this name because they were originally meals held after a sacred event of some kind.

As the townsfolk both prepare and serve these alfresco meals, you are always assured of good home cooking, if not always the most efficient service—but who cares?—and the price is always right. The typical menu for a village *festa* consists of the kind of food we prepare at home for family celebrations. Recently at one such occasion in Chianti I was served an antipasto of *crostini toscani*, little rounds of crusty bread topped with a spread of chicken livers and *milza*, calf's spleen, cooked in white wine with capers and garlic. The first course was the Tuscan classic, *pappa al pomodoro*, a bread and tomato soup served cold. The main course was mixed grilled and roast meats, beef, guinea hen and pork ribs, accompanied by white beans. At these events, *cocomero*, watermelon, inevitably concludes the meal. After that it's games time for the children and off to the dance floor for the adults.

Sagre, those feasts celebrating the deliciousness of a local speciality, abound throughout the season and their number is growing from year to year. Posters are put up around town to advertise the event. Around the area of Tuscany where I live, between two valleys bordering three ancient regions with very different and distinct culinary traditions (the Valley of the Arno, Florence and Siena), there are *sagre* of everything from soup (*ribollita*, a thick vegetable and bread soup) to nuts (*castagne* or chestnuts). We celebrate such specialities as snails, frogs, hare, wild boar, *porchetta* (roasted piglet), *porcini* mushrooms, olives and pecorino (Romano) cheese, to name but a very few. The general form that *sagre* take is the same as for any other *festa*, except that the fêted food is featured and eaten in abundance. At a recent *sagre della lepre* I attended, the honoured hare was prepared and consumed in a variety of dishes. There was *pappardelle con la lepre*, wide noodles dressed with hare in a rich sauce of red wine seasoned with nutmeg and rosemary. Then as a main course you could have grilled hare or, best of all, *lepre in umido*, hare stewed with tomatoes, onions and various seasonings.

In other regions of Italy you will come across *sagre* of polenta, white asparagus, seafood, melons, tomatoes, gnocchi and maccheroni. In brief, I don't imagine there is an essential food in Italian culinary tradition that does not have its special celebration. Most of these *sagre* are rooted in ancient local custom. Nowadays, however, to attract tourists many towns hold less authentic *sagre*, of *antipasti*, grilled meats, desserts, ice-cream, and so on. Still, the food is good and the alfresco atmosphere of conviviality welcome and enjoyable.

Every year, on 14 August, the evening before the national midsummer holiday, I host an alfresco, torch-lit supper in the Renaissance garden of our family estate, Badia a Coltibuono. It is preceded by a courtyard concert. Recently a chamber group from the Berlin Philharmonic performed. Since the guests number several hundred, I keep the menu simple with a cold buffet featuring various savoury flatbreads and simple Tuscan dishes such as *panzanella*, basically a bread salad to which is added ripe tomatoes, sweet red onion and basil, dressed with the

estate's extra virgin olive oil and red wine vinegar. Another tasty Tuscan dish ideal for large groups is *tonno e fagioli*, a mixture of tuna, white beans and onions. For dessert I serve sweet grapes, the first of the season, and nut bread. All the dishes are accompanied, of course, by Coltibuono's white and red wines. Afterwards the guests return to the courtyard, now transformed into an alfresco disco, to dance until midnight.

Most frequently, however, the alfresco meals I prepare are family picnics with my eight grandchildren by the swimming pool. These occasions qualify as an outing, as the pool is located a long way from the house and kitchen and we must pack our baskets before going down. A proper picnic requires freshly baked bread. One of my family's favourite breads is made with wholemeal (wholewheat) flour and several different cereals, a handful of spelt, barley, sunflower and sesame seeds. It is difficult to satisfy the tastes and appetites of a lot of children of various ages. I have found that the best way is with a variety of cold dishes. Aubergine (eggplant) *parmigiana* is perfect for a picnic. It can be prepared well ahead of time, is delicious cold and easy to serve.

Two family favourites are a dish of sweet red and yellow (bell) peppers, layered with anchovy fillets, tomatoes and black olives, baked with breadcrumbs and served at room temperature; and courgettes (zucchini) filled with chicken and seasoned with marjoram. I also include a couple of seasonal salads, such as wild rice with pesto sauce and short pasta dressed with fresh cherry tomatoes, mozzarella cheese, basil and extra virgin olive oil. A dessert that pleases everyone is *panna cotta*, cooked cream topped with a sauce of strawberries, blueberries, raspberries and cherries. It needs to set in the refrigerator several hours before the picnic but is served at room temperature.

THE PANTRY

MARMELLATA DI PESCHE GIALLE
Yellow Peach Jam

You can use apricots, nectarines or plums in this jam. The apple peel contains pectin, which is the substance that creates the jelly.

2kg/4lb yellow peaches
540g/1lb 7oz/3 cups granulated sugar
Peel of 2 apples

Halve the peaches then peel and stone them. Dice the flesh and place in a pan. Cover and cook over a low heat for about 10 minutes. Drain the pulp through a sieve, reserving the juice. Pass the pulp through a foodmill and reserve.
Place the juice in a pan with the sugar and apple peel and cook for 30 minutes or until syrupy. If you place a drop on a chilled saucer, the surface should wrinkle when you push it with the tip of your finger.
Discard the peel and add the syrup to the peach purée. Mix well, reheat until just boiling and pour into sterilized jars. Seal immediately and place in a cool, dark place. Once opened, the jam must be stored in the refrigerator to prevent it from going off, as there is little sugar to preserve it.

CHUTNEY DI ALBICOCCHE
Apricot Chutney

I like to use any fruit for chutney, including peaches, nectarines, figs or even green (raw) tomatoes.

2kg/4lb apricots
2 litres/4 pints/8 cups red wine vinegar
1kg/2 1/4 lb/5 cups granulated sugar
2 tbsp mustard seeds
1 tsp finely chopped red chilli pepper
300g/10oz ginger, peeled and thinly sliced
300g/10oz raisins
1 garlic clove

Halve and stone the apricots. Place them in a stainless steel pan with half the vinegar and boil for 15 minutes.
Drain the apricots and reserve, discarding the vinegar.
Put the sugar, the remaining vinegar, mustard seeds, chilli, ginger, raisins and garlic clove in a clean stainless steel pan and cook on a slow boil for about 1 hour or until the liquid is syrupy. If you place a drop on a chilled saucer, the surface should wrinkle when you push it with the tip of your finger.
Add the fruit, cook for 5 more minutes and spoon into sterilized jars. Seal tightly and store in a cool, dark place.

CONSERVAZIONE DI BASILICO E PREZZEMOLO
Preserving Basil and Parsley

Basil and parsley can be kept for about 3 months in the freezer. Simply chop them finely and press them into an ice cube tray. Cover with good extra virgin olive oil and store in the freezer. When you want to use them in cooking you can defrost the cubes, adding a little more oil. The parsley will stay green, but the basil will become dark in contact with hot items, although it keeps quite a good flavour.

POMODORI PELATI
Preserved Tomatoes

To preserve fresh tomatoes, plunge them for 30 seconds in boiling water and peel. Pack the peeled tomatoes tightly in clean heatproof jars with some basil leaves. Seal the jars and put them in a large pan filled with water to cover. Bring the water to the boil and boil for 20 minutes. Let the jars cool in the water. The tomatoes can be stored for up to one year in a cool, dark place. You can preserve freshly made tomato sauce in the same way.

NOCINO
Walnut Liqueur

Before the end of June is the perfect season for picking up walnuts, while they are still slightly green and are soft enough to be cut in half.

30 fresh green walnuts
10 cloves
1.5 litres/3 pints/6 cups 95% alcohol, available
at chemists (drugstores)
750g/1lb 10oz/4 cups granulated sugar
1 litre/2 pints/4 cups distilled water
Zest of 1 organic lemon

Quarter the walnuts and place in clean bottles with the cloves, alcohol, sugar, distilled water and lemon zest.
Seal the bottles and leave to stand for a couple of months in a cool, dark place, shaking the bottle once every 2–3 days.
Filter and decant the liquid into clean bottles. Seal and store in a cool, dark place. The liqueur will keep for years.

APPETIZERS, PASTA AND SOUPS

ACCIUGHE SOTT'OLIO
Anchovies in Oil

We can buy these anchovies in many delicatessen shops in Italy, but since they are easy to prepare and they keep in the refrigerator for about one week, it is worth preparing them fresh. Instead of parsley you could use basil or dry oregano.

600g/1 ¼ lb fresh anchovies
Juice of 3 organic lemons and zest of 1 organic lemon
6 tbsp white wine vinegar
4 tbsp extra virgin olive oil
1 tbsp finely chopped flat-leaf parsley
Salt and pepper

Clean the anchovies, discarding the heads and bones, and place them in a deep dish. Pour over the juice of 2 of the lemons, the vinegar and a little salt and pepper. Place in the refrigerator for about 2 hours, mixing once. You can keep them in the refrigerator for longer, but not more than 12 hours.
Drain and arrange on a serving platter. Just before you are ready to serve, sprinkle with the lemon zest, the juice of the remaining lemon, the oil, the parsley and salt and pepper to taste.

Serves 6

SFORMATINI DI POMODORO
Tomato Moulds

I find it easier to prepare something before my friends arrive for dinner, and these tomato moulds are ideal. They are lovely to look at as well as to eat in summertime. Sometimes I prepare a green gelatine made with chopped basil or parsley and I will dice the gelatine around the moulds for decoration.

1kg/2 ¼ lb fresh tomatoes
6 tbsp dry white wine
15g/½ oz gelatine leaves
3 tbsp chopped fresh basil leaves
210g/7oz rocket (arugula), roughly chopped
3 tbsp extra virgin olive oil
Salt and pepper

Bring a pan of water to the boil, add the tomatoes and leave for 30 seconds. Peel and deseed the tomatoes. Process the flesh in a blender to a purée.
Bring the wine to the boil in a pan and simmer until reduced by half. Meanwhile, soften the gelatine leaves in cold water for about 5 minutes. Drain.
Remove the wine from the heat, add the softened gelatine leaves and leave to dissolve.
Mix the gelatine and wine with the tomato purée, add the basil and pour into 6 individual moulds or ramekins. Place in the refrigerator to set for at least 3 hours.
When you are ready to serve, toss the rocket (arugula) with the salt, pepper and the oil. Transfer to a serving platter. Unmould the tomatoes, place on top of the rocket (arugula) and serve.

Serves 6

PETTO D'ANITRA AL RAFANO SU UN LETTO D'INSALATA

*Duck Breast with Horseradish
on a Bed of Salad*

Horseradish is a weed and I have plenty in my garden. I like to prepare it grated in wintertime mixed with a little cream. It keeps for a month. In summertime, it is a little less strong, but still very tasty. For the salad, you can substitute half the baby chicory (Belgian endive) with rocket (rucola) for variety, if you like.

1 duck breast
2 tbsp coarse salt
1 tbsp granulated sugar
300g/10oz baby chicory (Belgian endive)
1 tbsp white wine vinegar
4 tbsp extra virgin olive oil
1 tbsp grated fresh horseradish
Salt and pepper

Slice the duck breast very finely, transfer to a plate and sprinkle with the coarse salt and sugar. Cover and leave to rest in the refrigerator for about 2 hours. Drain the juices from the duck breast and pat dry with absorbent paper.
Finely slice the chicory (Belgian endive) and spread it over the base of a serving dish. Sprinkle with the vinegar, 2 tbsp of the oil and salt and pepper to taste. Arrange the duck breast slices over the top, sprinkle over the horseradish and the remaining oil and serve at room temperature.

Serves 6

CREMA DI PEPERONI GIALLI CON SORBETTO DI POMODORO

*Yellow (Bell) Pepper Cream
with a Tomato Sorbet*

This is the most succsessful and beautiful soup we make in summertime, when the weather is very hot. You will need an ice-cream maker for this recipe.

6 sweet yellow (bell) peppers, halved and deseeded
3 tbsp extra virgin olive oil
2 large potatoes, peeled and diced
1 white onion, thinly sliced
2 litres/4 pints/8 cups vegetable stock
1kg/2 1/4 lb ripe salad tomatoes
1 handful fresh basil leaves
Salt and pepper

Preheat the oven to 170°C/350°F/Gas 4.
Place the (bell) peppers in a roasting tray and cook in the oven for about 40 minutes. Transfer to a paper bag, close the bag and leave for about 10 minutes, then peel.
Heat the oil in a pan, add the potatoes and onion and cook, covered, for about 10 minutes over a low heat. Add the peeled (bell) peppers and stock and cook for another 30 minutes over a low heat.
Purée the contents of the pan in a blender, add salt and pepper and set aside while you make the sorbet.
Bring a pan of water to the boil, add the tomatoes and leave for 30 seconds. Drain, peel and discard the seeds. Purée the tomatoes in a blender with the basil and salt, to taste. Put the tomato purée in an ice-cream maker and make the sorbet according to the manufacturer's instructions.
When you are ready to serve, reheat the soup in a pan. Pour the warm soup into 6 deep individual dishes and, using a small ice-cream scoop, make 6 balls of tomato sorbet and place one on each bowl (or make 3 smaller ones for each bowl). Serve immediately.

Serves 6

SPAGHETTINI AI FIORI DI ZUCCA

Spaghettini with Courgette (Zucchini) Flowers

Courgette (zucchini) plants produce flowers before the vegetable. The edible flowers are male, and are perfect when almost closed. I use them in many recipes and in this recipe they are fried.

300g/10oz courgette (zucchini) flowers
1 small onion, sliced paper-thin
6 tbsp extra virgin olive oil
600g/1¼ lb spaghettini
1 tsp saffron powder, or pinch of saffron threads
Salt and pepper

Clean the courgette (zucchini) flowers, discarding the stems and stamens. Fry the onion in a pan with half the oil over a low heat until translucent, about 3 minutes. Add the courgette (zucchini) flowers and sauté for about 1 minute. Remove the pan from the heat and set aside the flowers on paper towels.
Bring a pan of water to the boil, add salt and the pasta. Cook until very *al dente*. Meanwhile, mix the saffron in a small cup with a ladleful of the pasta cooking water.
Drain the spaghettini, return to the pan and add the courgette (zucchini) flowers, the saffron water and the rest of the oil. Sauté for a couple of minutes. Add pepper to taste, transfer to a warmed serving platter and serve immediately.

Serves 6

SPAGHETTINI AGLIO OLIO E PANGRATTATO

Spaghettini with Garlic Oil and Dry Breadcrumbs

This is a good variation of *spaghetti all'aglio e olio*. The fried breadcrumbs will keep very well for at least a couple of months in a jar.

120g/4oz/½ cup dry fine breadcrumbs
6 tbsp extra virgin olive oil
3 garlic cloves, finely chopped
1 anchovy fillet in oil, drained
1 tbsp dried oregano
1 hot chilli pepper
600g/1¼ lb spaghettini
Salt

Put the breadcrumbs in a non-stick pan with half the oil, the garlic, anchovy fillet, oregano and chilli pepper. Cook over a medium heat, stirring with a wooden spoon, until the breadcrumbs become slightly golden. Do not let them brown too much or they will become bitter. Remove the chilli pepper. The breadcrumbs can be stored in a tightly sealed jar in a cool, dark place for over a month.
Bring a pan of water to the boil, add salt and the spaghettini. Cook until very *al dente*, then drain and mix in a warmed serving bowl with the rest of the oil. Add the breadcrumbs, mix and serve immediately while the breadcrumbs are still crunchy.

Serves 6

RISO ALLE ERBE

Rice with Herbs

Herbs are easy to keep, even if you do not have a garden. Place a pot near the window during summer.

600g/1¼ lb basmati or patna rice
120ml/4fl oz/½ cup extra virgin olive oil
1 tbsp finely chopped fresh rosemary
1 tbsp finely chopped fresh sage
1 tbsp fresh thyme leaves
1 tbsp finely chopped fresh oregano
1 tbsp finely chopped fresh marjoram
2 finely chopped garlic cloves
Salt and pepper

Bring a pan of water to the boil, add salt and the rice. Simmer for about 10 minutes.
Meanwhile heat the oil in a pan, add the herbs and garlic and fry for about 3 minutes, stirring.
Drain the rice, tip into a warmed serving dish and add the oil and herbs. Check the salt, sprinkle with pepper and serve warm or at room temperature.

Serves 6

RISOTTO AL MELONE
Melon Risotto

Mixing risotto with some fruit has become popular in recent years. Strawberries, blueberries, green apples and sometimes pears are added in the last few minutes of cooking for a different taste.

2 litres/3 ½ pints/8 cups vegetable stock
1 white onion, sliced paper-thin
120g/4oz prosciutto (Parma ham), julienned
60g/2oz/4 tbsp unsalted butter
12 handfuls arborio rice
120ml/4fl oz/½ cup dry white wine
1kg/2 ¼ lb melon
1 handful fresh mint leaves
Salt and pepper

Heat the stock in a pan and keep on a slow boil.
In a large saucepan, sauté the onion and the prosciutto in half the butter over a low heat until the onion is translucent and the prosciutto fat has started to melt. Add the rice and cook over a high heat for about 3 minutes or until the rice is very hot, stirring constantly with a wooden spoon.
Start adding the stock to the rice, about 240ml/8fl oz/1 cup at a time, or enough to ensure that the rice is covered with a veil of liquid. Alternate the stock with the wine, always keeping the rice covered with liquid. Don't let it dry out. Stir from time to time.
While the rice is cooking, peel the melon, discard the seeds and dice the pulp. Add the pulp to the risotto during the last 5 minutes of cooking time.
About 14 minutes after the rice first started boiling, remove the pan from the heat. Add the rest of the butter, and salt and pepper to taste. Cover and leave to rest for 2 minutes. The rice should have a creamy, porridge-like consistency.
Pour into a warmed deep serving platter, sprinkle over the mint and serve immediately.

Serves 6

ZUPPA DI GAMBERI
Prawn (Shrimp) Soup

You can prepare the stock by boiling some heads and tails of fish, and of course, if you bought the prawns (shrimp) with head and tails, you could use those too.

1kg/2 ¼ lb raw prawns (shrimp), peeled and deveined
4 tbsp extra virgin olive oil
1 small white onion, finely sliced
2 garlic cloves
1 hot chilli pepper
120ml/4fl oz/½ cup dry white wine
1.5 litres/3 pints/6 cups fish stock
1 handful fresh thyme
6 slices coarse country bread
6 slices ripe salad tomatoes
1 handful fresh basil leaves
Salt

Wash the prawns (shrimp), pat dry and set some aside for decoration.
Heat 3 tbsp of the oil in a pan, add the onion and 1 garlic clove. Sauté over a low heat until translucent, about 3 minutes. Add the prawns (shrimp), raise the heat and sauté for 3 more minutes. Add the chilli, the wine and the stock. Bring to the boil, add the thyme and cook over a low heat for about 20 minutes.
Meanwhile, preheat the grill (broiler). Toast the bread on both sides under the grill (broiler) and rub each side with the remaining garlic clove. Top with the tomato slices and the rest of the oil.
Purée the soup in a blender, transfer to a clean pan and reheat. Season to taste with salt. Pour into 6 warmed deep individual serving dishes, decorate with the reserved prawns (shrimp) and top with the toast and tomatoes.
Place under the hot grill (broiler) for a couple of minutes, decorate with the basil and serve immediately.

Serves 6

ZUPPA D'ORZO
Barley Soup

If you cannot find barley in supermarkets try looking
in health food stores. It is a nice substitution for rice
and has a refreshing taste.

300g/10oz barley
2 litres/4 pints/8 cups vegetable stock
6 red radishes
1 small cucumber
3 ripe salad tomatoes
3 tbsp extra virgin olive oil
1 handful rocket (arugula)
Salt and pepper

Wash the barley thoroughly and place in a pan with
the stock. Cook for about 1 hour over a low heat,
covered. Remove from the heat, add salt and pepper
to taste and leave to cool to room temperature.
Clean and trim the radishes. Peel the cucumber, halve
it and scoop out the seeds.
Bring a pan of water to the boil, add the tomatoes and
leave for 30 seconds. Drain, peel and deseed the
tomatoes, then dice the flesh.
In a blender, purée the radishes with the cucumber,
then add the oil and the rocket (arugula). Add the
purée to the barley stock and mix well. Transfer to a
soup tureen or individual dishes. Sprinkle with the
diced tomatoes and serve.

Serves 6

MINESTRA DI FARRO
ALLA LATTUGA
Spelt Soup with Lettuce

I prefer lettuces when they are young and more
delicate. For a few lira we can buy tiny lettuces for
planting in the garden and so I always have some
fresh salad available.

3 ripe salad tomatoes
2 white onions, sliced paper-thin
1 head of lettuce, sliced crossways
6 tbsp extra virgin olive oil
2 litres/4 pints/8 cups vegetable stock
240g/8oz spelt
Salt and pepper

Bring a pan of water to the boil, add the tomatoes and
leave for 30 seconds. Drain and peel the tomatoes and
discard the seeds, then purée the flesh.
In a large pan, sauté the onions and lettuce with half
the oil for about 3 minutes over a medium heat.
Add the tomato purée, stock and spelt and cook over
a low heat for about 1 hour or until the spelt is soft.
Add salt and pepper to taste, pour into warmed
serving bowls, sprinkle over the remaining oil
and serve.

Serves 6

PENNE CON LE MELANZANE
Penne with Aubergines (Eggplants)

I tend to prefer the long slim aubergines (eggplants) to the round fat ones that have more seeds and are less tasty. I never salt them to drain them—if they are fresh they will be firm and you can use them without this procedure, which will make them mushy and tasteless.

1 small white onion, sliced paper-thin
3 aubergines (eggplants), diced
6 tbsp extra virgin olive oil
90g/3oz black (ripe) olives (Gaeta or Kalamata), pitted
2 tbsp capers in vinegar, drained
2 tbsp pine nuts
600g/1¼ lb penne
2 tbsp fresh flat-leaf parsley
Salt and pepper

Fry the onion and aubergines (eggplant) in the oil over a medium heat for about 10 minutes, shaking the pan often. Don't let them go brown, otherwise they will become bitter. Add the olives, capers, pine nuts and salt and pepper to taste. Set aside and keep warm.
Bring a pan of water to the boil, add salt and the pasta. Cook until very *al dente* (a couple of minutes less than it says on the packet) and drain. Sauté the pasta for a couple of minutes in the pan with the aubergine (eggplant) mixture and a little of the cooking water.
Transfer to a warmed serving dish, sprinkle over the parsley and serve immediately.

Serves 6

FUSILLI CON VERDURE CRUDE
Fusilli with Salad Vegetables

This way of cooking pasta is perfect because it is quick, tasty and very healthy. In fact, it is not pasta that makes you fat but what you put on top. Avoid cream, butter, sausages, cheese and just use plenty of vegetables, sometimes raw or boiled with the pasta in the same pot, and add a little olive oil to create a perfect meal.

3 very ripe salad tomatoes
600g/1¼ lb fusilli
1 handful fresh basil leaves
2 garlic cloves, finely chopped
1 yellow (bell) pepper, diced
Few chives, finely chopped
6 tbsp extra virgin olive oil
Salt and pepper

Bring a large pan of water to the boil and add the tomatoes. Leave for 30 seconds, then lift them out of the water with a slotted spoon and peel them.
Add salt to the water, together with the fusilli. Cook until very *al dente* (a couple of minutes less than it says on the packet). Dice the tomatoes, discarding the seeds. Tear the basil leaves with your hands.
Place the tomatoes, garlic, pepper, chives and basil in a serving dish. Add the oil and salt and pepper to taste. Drain the pasta and tip immediately over the vegetables. Mix together and leave to cool to room temperature. Serve.

Serves 6

PENNE FREDDE ALLA MOZZARELLA

Cold Penne Salad with Mozzarella

Sometimes I will substitute tomato purée for a courgette (zucchini) purée. I will just place the vegetable in a blender, possibly only the peel, and discard the seeds and part of the pulp to make it greener. Then I will add oil and herbs using the same procedure as with the tomatoes used here.

600g/1¼ lb penne
3 ripe salad tomatoes
6 tbsp extra virgin olive oil
1 handful fresh basil leaves
300g/10oz buffalo mozzarella, diced
Salt and pepper

Bring a pan of water to the boil, add salt and the penne. Cook until *al dente* (a couple of minutes less than it says on the packet).
Bring another pan of water to the boil, add the tomatoes and leave for 30 seconds. Drain and peel the tomatoes and discard the seeds. Purée the tomatoes in a blender with 3 tbsp of the oil and the basil.
When the penne are cooked, drain and tip into a serving bowl. Add the remaining oil, mix well and leave to cool to room temperature. Add the tomato and basil purée and the mozzarella. Check the salt, sprinkle with the pepper, mix carefully and serve.

Serves 6

FETTUCCINE AL PECORINO

Fettuccine with Pecorino (Romano) Cheese

For this recipe I recommend a pecorino (Romano) cheese that is not too old, for a more delicate taste. Goats' cheese is a possible substitution.

1 large aubergine (eggplant), oval-shaped if possible
6 tbsp extra virgin olive oil
1 tbsp dried oregano
1 garlic clove
1 handful rocket (arugula)
300g/10oz dry fettuccine
210g/7oz pecorino (Romano) cheese
Salt and pepper

Preheat the oven to 170°C/350°F/Gas 4.
Cook the whole aubergine (eggplant) in the oven for about 50 minutes or until very soft. Leave to cool slightly and peel. Purée the flesh in a blender with the oil, oregano, garlic and rocket (arugula) and reserve.
Bring a pan of water to the boil, add salt and the fettuccine and cook until *al dente*.
Add 120ml/4fl oz/½ cup of the pasta cooking water to the aubergine (eggplant) purée to thin it down, and blend briefly.
Drain the fettuccine and mix well with the aubergine (eggplant) purée.
Slice the cheese paper-thin, sprinkle over the top of the pasta and serve warm or at room temperature.

Serves 6

MEAT AND FISH

AGNELLO RIPIENO AL PROSCIUTTO

Lamb Stuffed with Prosciutto

To debone a leg of lamb you have to make a long vertical cut until you reach the bone, then starting from the thinnest end, carefully carve it delicately along the bone until is completely free. It is not difficult but you may need to try it a few times.

2 legs of lamb, about 1kg/2 ¼ lb each
4 slices prosciutto (Parma ham)
2 fresh rosemary sprigs, finely chopped
1 handful fresh sage leaves, finely chopped
3 garlic cloves, finely chopped
2 tbsp extra virgin olive oil
1 tbsp unsalted butter
About ½ bottle of dry white wine
Salt and pepper

Preheat the oven to 170°C/350°F/Gas 4.
Debone the legs of lamb, or ask your butcher to do it.
Cover each piece of meat with 2 prosciutto slices.
Sprinkle the rosemary, sage and garlic over the prosciutto. Add salt and pepper to taste and roll up the meat to enclose the prosciutto completely. Secure the rolls with string.
Heat the oil and butter in a roasting tin (pan) and place the lamb rolls on top. Cover with (aluminum) foil and cook in the oven for about 2 hours, turning the meat about 4 times. After 1 hour, start adding the wine from time to time to prevent the cooking juices from drying out.
Remove the (aluminum) foil and cook for another 30 minutes or until the meat becomes dark brown.
Slice the meat, transfer to a warmed serving platter and keep warm. Pour away the fat from the roasting tin (pan) and deglaze the cooking juices with a little wine. Pour the sauce over the lamb and serve immediately.

Serves 6

STRACCETTI DI POLLO

Sautéed Chicken Breast

The reason why we are not keen on buying prepared food in Italy is that in a just few minutes we can arrange a meal, since our food is so light and simple to prepare. It is enough to add a salad and some fruit to this dish and you will have the best possible meal.

3 tbsp extra virgin olive oil
1 tbsp unsalted butter
1 handful fresh sage leaves
3 garlic cloves, thinly sliced
3 whole chicken breasts (6 halves), thinly sliced
Juice of 1 lemon
Salt and pepper

Heat the oil and butter in a pan, add the sage and garlic and sauté over a high heat for about 2 minutes, stirring constantly. Add the chicken breasts and continue cooking and stirring for about
3 more minutes.
Add the lemon juice, sauté for 1 more minute and add salt and pepper to taste. Transfer to a warmed serving platter and serve immediately.

Serves 6

PATÉ DI POLLO E TONNO

Chicken and Tuna Pâté

This is a nice fresh summer dish that can be kept for a few days in the refrigerator if well sealed with cling film (plastic wrap). It can also be served on toast as an appetizer.

2 whole chicken breasts (4 halves), about 450g/1lb in total
300g/10oz tuna in oil, drained
250g/8oz/1 cup mayonnaise
3 anchovy fillets in oil, drained
1 tbsp capers in vinegar, drained

Bring a pan of water to the boil, add the chicken and poach for about 20 minutes. Drain and leave to cool. Cut the chicken into large pieces and place in a food processor with the tuna, mayonnaise, anchovies and capers. Process until well blended.
Using your hands, form the mixture into a log shape about 6cm/2in in diameter and roll up in a clean, damp kitchen towel. Place in the refrigerator for a minimum of 3 hours.
Remove the towel, cut into slices and transfer to a serving platter.

Serves 6

TARTARA DI PESCE SPADA

Swordfish Tartare

When some fish is particularly fresh it is excellent raw, as the flavour comes out beautifully. Of course you can substitute the swordfish steak used here with tuna or even sea bass.

1.5kg/3 ½ lb swordfish steak
Juice of 1 lemon
1 tbsp capers in vinegar, drained
1 tbsp grated ginger root
3 tbsp extra virgin olive oil
6 large lettuce leaves
300g/10oz cherry tomatoes
Salt and pepper

Remove the skin from the swordfish, pick out the bones and chop the fish finely with a chef's knife or good sharp kitchen knife.
Place in a bowl and mix with lemon juice, capers, grated ginger and oil. Add salt and pepper to taste and leave to rest for about 20 minutes in the refrigerator.
Arrange the lettuce leaves on a serving platter. Form the swordfish mixture into 6 patties and place on the lettuce leaves. Surround with the tomatoes and serve at room temperature.

Serves 6

TRIGLIE AL PESTO DI OLIVE

Red Mullet with Black Olive Pesto

The best red mullet I have ever eaten were mixed with pasta and served in a restaurant called *Scacciapensieri* in Cecina, a small town south of Livorno, in Tuscany. That part of the coast is particularly beautiful because there are very few hotels to stay in and the beaches are not crowded.

12 red mullet, about 210g/7oz each
180g/6oz black (ripe) olives (Gaeta or Kalamata), pitted
6 tbsp extra virgin olive oil
Zest of 1 organic lemon
2 garlic cloves
3 ripe plum tomatoes
6 large potatoes, peeled and thinly sliced
Salt and pepper

Preheat the oven to 170°C/350°F/Gas 4.
Clean and trim the red mullet, leaving them whole.
Purée the olives in a blender with 75ml/2 ½fl oz/
5 tbsp of the oil, the lemon zest and the garlic.
Bring a pan of water to the boil, add the plum tomatoes and leave for 30 seconds. Drain, peel and thinly slice the tomatoes.
Brush a baking dish with the rest of the oil, then arrange the potato slices over the base, slightly overlapping. Top with the red mullet and place the tomato slices over the top. Sprinkle with salt and pepper, spoon over the olive pesto and cover with (aluminum) foil. Place in the oven and cook for about 10 minutes. Remove the foil, cook for 10 more minutes and serve.

Serves 6

SCAMPI E MELANZANE SALTATE

Sauté of Aubergines (Eggplants) and Prawns (Shrimp)

I usually like to buy prawns (shrimp) whole because they are very easy to peel. I will refrigerate or even freeze the head and tail if they are not used in the recipe to make wonderful fish stocks or fish sauce later on. But it is definitely easier to buy just the tails with the skins on. If you buy them whole, double the weight given below.

6 tbsp extra virgin olive oil
2 garlic cloves
6 small oval aubergines (eggplants), peeled and diced
1kg/2 ¼ lb prawn (shrimp) tails, shell on
4 tbsp dry white wine
1 tbsp finely chopped fresh flat-leaf parsley
Salt and pepper

Heat half the oil with 1 of the garlic cloves in a pan and sauté for about 2 minutes, stirring constantly.
Add the aubergines (eggplants) and sauté, stirring, until lightly golden, about 5 minutes. Reserve.
Make an incision on the top of the prawn (shrimp) tails, but do not remove the shell.
Heat the remaining oil in another pan with the remaining garlic clove for about 2 minutes. Add the prawn (shrimp) tails and sauté, stirring, for about 3 minutes over a high heat. Add the reserved aubergines (eggplants), sprinkle with salt and pepper, mix together and add the wine. Leave to evaporate.
Remove the garlic, transfer to a warmed serving platter, scatter over the parsley and serve immediately.

Serves 6

UOVA CON PEPERONATA

Eggs with (Bell) Peppers

Eggs are very popular in Italy as a second dinner course. We would never have eggs for breakfast, but we like them in other meals.

3 tbsp extra virgin olive oil
3 garlic cloves
2 white onions, sliced
300g/10oz plum tomatoes, peeled
3 red (bell) peppers, seeded and sliced
3 yellow (bell) peppers, seeded and sliced
6 large eggs
Salt and pepper

Heat 2 tbsp of the oil in a pan, add the garlic and the onions and sauté over a medium heat, stirring, until translucent, about 3 minutes.
Bring a pan of water to the boil, add the tomatoes and leave for 30 seconds. Drain and peel. Slice the tomatoes, keeping the seeds. Add the (bell) peppers and tomatoes to the pan with the onions and add salt and pepper to taste. Cover and cook over a low heat for about 30 minutes. If there is too much liquid, uncover and cook until the liquid has completely reduced.
Heat the remaining oil in a large non-stick pan and crack all the eggs into the pan. Cook until the white becomes opaque, about 3 minutes, uncovered.
Transfer the (bell) peppers to a warmed serving platter, top with the eggs and serve.

Serves 6

SARDE AL FINOCCHIETTO SELVATICO

Sardines with Fresh Wild Fennel

There is plenty of wild fennel in the centre and south of Italy and it is easy to pick some. It will last fresh for a few days. Before the autumn comes I will dry some flowers to get the seeds for the winter. Roasted potatoes with fennel seeds are delicious.

1.8kg/3 ½ lb fresh sardines
300g/10oz ripe plum tomatoes
3 garlic cloves
120g/4oz/½ cup fine dry breadcrumbs
1 handful fresh wild fennel (about 3 flowers with the seeds or just the feathery part), finely chopped
3 tbsp extra virgin olive oil
Salt and pepper

Preheat the oven to 200°C/400°F/Gas 6.
Slit open the sardines, remove the bones, keeping the tails intact, and wash under running water.
Bring a pan of water to the boil, add the tomatoes and leave for 30 seconds. Drain and peel. Transfer the whole tomatoes to a blender and purée with the garlic.
Pour the purée into a round ovenproof dish and place the sardines on top in overlapping circles. Sprinkle over the breadcrumbs and the chopped fennel feathers or flowers. Pour over the oil, add salt and pepper to taste and cook in the oven for about 15 minutes. Serve.

Serves 6

INVOLTINI DI ROSBIF E PEPERONI

Roast Beef and (Bell) Pepper Rolls

This is a very good recipe for picnics because the rolls can be eaten almost without a fork. Sometimes for cocktail parties, I will make very small rolls, put them on a toothpick and serve with drinks.

1kg/2 ¼ lb beef, for roasting (lean back cut such as sirloin)
2 tbsp extra virgin olive oil
1 tbsp unsalted butter
3 (bell) peppers (a combination of yellow and red),
halved and seeded
3 tbsp balsamic vinegar
Salt and pepper

Preheat the oven to 200°C/400°F/Gas 6.
Tie the meat carefully.
Heat the oil and butter in a roasting tin (pan), place the meat on top and cook in the oven for about 40 minutes, turning the meat once. Transfer to a wire rack and leave to cool.
Meanwhile place the (bell) peppers in a baking dish and cook in the oven for about 30 minutes. Transfer to a paper bag, close the bag and leave for about 10 minutes. Peel and slice the (bell) peppers. Place in a deep dish, spoon over the balsamic vinegar and add salt and pepper to taste.
When the beef is cold, slice it thinly and place a piece of pepper on each slice. Roll the slice up and secure with a toothpick.
Arrange on a platter and serve at room temperature.

Serves 6

INSALATA DI MANZO

Beef Salad

This salad is great because you will also get a good stock out of it to use in soups when you boil the meat. Remember to keep the stock in the refrigerator for only a few hours, or it is better to freeze it.

1 carrot
1 white onion
1 celery stalk
1 handful fresh flat-leaf parsley, plus 3 tbsp finely chopped
1.2kg/2 ½ lb lean beef for boiling, e.g. boneless brisket
1 anchovy fillet in oil, drained
1 tbsp capers in vinegar, drained
1 handful fresh coarse country bread, crusts removed
3 tbsp red wine vinegar
1 large hard boiled egg, finely chopped
6 tbsp cup extra virgin olive oil
Salt and pepper

Bring a pan of water to the boil, add the whole carrot, onion and celery stalk, the handful of parsley and the meat. Cover and cook for about 3 hours over a low heat. Leave the meat to cool in the liquid, then discard the vegetables.
Place the chopped parsley in a large bowl. Mash the anchovy and capers together with a fork and add to the parsley. Soak the bread in the vinegar, then remove and squeeze well. Add the bread and chopped egg to the parsley mixture with the oil and a little salt and pepper to taste. Mix until well blended.
When the meat is cold, drain, reserving the liquid for a stock, and dice. Transfer to a serving bowl. Pour over the parsley sauce, mix well and serve at room temperature.

Serves 6

VEGETABLES AND SALADS

MELANZANE RIPIENE
Stuffed Aubergines (Eggplants)

Aubergines (eggplants), mozzarella and ripe tomatoes make the best combination for a very Neapolitan recipe. This one was given to me by a little restaurant in Ischia and is from the sister of the sailor who sailed our old boat. She cooked this everytime we passed around the island before going to Capri.

6 aubergines (eggplants)
300g/10oz plum tomatoes
300g/10oz buffalo mozzarella, diced
3 tbsp extra virgin olive oil
1 handful fresh basil leaves
Salt and pepper

Preheat the oven to 170°C/350°F/Gas 4.
Cut the aubergines (eggplants) in half lengthways, scoop out half of the pulp from each piece, cut into dice and reserve.
Bring a pan of water to the boil, add the tomatoes and leave for 30 seconds. Drain and peel the tomatoes and discard the seeds. Dice the flesh.
Mix the reserved aubergine (eggplant) flesh with the mozzarella, diced tomatoes and olive oil. Add salt and pepper to taste and fill the aubergines (eggplants) with the mixture, piling it up in little mounds.
Place in a baking dish, cover with greaseproof (waxed) paper or baking parchment and cook in the oven for about 40 minutes.
Tear the basil with your hands and sprinkle over the aubergines (eggplant). Transfer to a warmed serving platter and serve.

Serves 6

FRITTURA DI FIORI E ZUCCHINE
Deep-fried Courgettes (Zucchini) and Courgette (Zucchini) Flowers

Deep-fried courgettes (zucchini) and their flowers are a must in summertime. I discovered this batter with no eggs and using self-rising flour while on holiday on the beautiful island of Spetses in Greece. The recipe makes the greens far more crispy than the classical Italian version.

450g/1lb courgettes (zucchini)
210g/7oz courgette (zucchini) flowers
120g/4oz/1 cup self-raising flour
240ml/8fl oz/1 cup water
1 litre/1 3/4 pints/4 cups oil, for deep-frying
Salt

Slice the courgettes (zucchini) lengthways into pieces about 0.5cm/1/8 in thick. Pat them dry on absorbent paper. Clean the flowers, discarding the stems and stamens.
Put the flour in a bowl and add the water a little at a time, stirring constantly with a whisk to avoid making lumps. You should obtain a smooth, slightly sticky liquid batter.
Heat the oil in a deep frying pan until it reaches 170°C/350°F on a kitchen thermometer. Dip the flowers and the courgettes (zucchini) in the batter, a few at a time, and place immediately in the hot oil. Fry until lightly golden and pat dry on paper towels. Sprinkle with salt and serve while still very hot and crunchy.

Serves 6

PASTICCIO DI VERDURE ALLA PANCETTA

Greens with Pancetta

When the children where young, we once rented a very simple house on the island of Crete with a friend of mine. We made this dish, obviously substituting fontina with feta cheese, and gave it to the baker to cook in his oven. When we came back after a long day of swimming dinner was ready.

150g/5oz pancetta, sliced paper-thin
300g/10oz plum tomatoes
6 tbsp extra virgin olive oil
2 courgettes (zucchini), sliced lengthwise
2 aubergines (eggplants), sliced lengthwise
1 red (bell) pepper, seeded and sliced
1 yellow (bell) pepper, seeded and sliced
210g/7oz fontina cheese, sliced paper-thin
1 heaped tbsp dried oregano
Salt and pepper

Preheat the oven to 170°C/350°F/Gas 4.
Place the pancetta in a non-stick pan and cook until crunchy and slightly golden. Drain the fat and reserve the pancetta.
Bring a pan of water to the boil, add the tomatoes and leave for 30 seconds. Drain and peel the tomatoes, then slice them crosswise.
Brush an ovenproof dish with a little oil and layer the vegetables in the dish, mixing each layer with some pancetta and fontina and sprinkling with the rest of the oil, the oregano and salt and pepper as you go.
Finish with a layer of tomatoes.
Cover the dish with (aluminum) foil, place in the oven and cook for about 1 hour. Serve hot or at room temperature.

Serves 6

INSALATA DI PECORINO E CROSTONI DI PANE

Salad of Pecorino (Romano) and Croûtons

Raw courgettes (zucchini) are delicious but they have to be very fresh and small otherwise they are bitter. To see if they are fresh feel whether they are very firm to the touch. This is the same for aubergines (eggplants).

120ml/4fl oz/½ cup oil, for frying
6 slices coarse country bread (crusts removed), cubed
210g/7oz watercress
120g/4oz rocket (arugula)
3 small courgettes (zucchini), julienned or finely sliced
4 tbsp extra virgin olive oil
210g/7oz pecorino (Romano) cheese, diced
Salt and pepper

Heat the oil for frying in a pan, add the bread cubes and cook until slightly golden, stirring continuously. Drain on paper towels and reserve.
Wash the watercress and the rocket (arugula) and place in a serving bowl. Add the courgettes (zucchini). Sprinkle with salt and pepper to taste and mix the salad with the oil. Top with the cheese and fried bread cubes and serve.

Serves 6

INSALATA MISTA CON SCAMORZA
Mixed Salad with Scamorza

When grilling (broiling) vegetables, it is better to have a heavy grill that fits on top of the stove. But do not heat it too much otherwise the vegetables will taste bitter. *Scamorza* is a type of cheese from the south of Italy which is available in delicatessens outside Italy.

4 tbsp extra virgin olive oil
1 red (bell) pepper, halved and seeded
1 yellow (bell) pepper, halved and seeded
2 small aubergines (eggplants), sliced lengthwise
2 small courgettes (zucchini), sliced lengthwise
210g/7oz smoked *scamorza*, sliced
210g/7oz baby lettuce leaves
Salt and pepper

Brush a ridged grill pan with a little oil and cook the vegetables over a medium heat, until just tender. Set aside.
Put the grilled (bell) peppers in a paper bag, close it to seal and leave for about 10 minutes. Remove the (bell) peppers, peel them and slice lengthwise.
Place the *scamorza* on the grill pan and cook for a few minutes on each side. Do not let it become too soft. Arrange the lettuce on a serving platter, cover with the vegetables and the *scamorza*, sprinkle with salt and pepper and the rest of the oil and serve while the cheese is still warm.

Serves 6

INSALATA DI FAGIOLI E CIPOLLE
Bean and Onion Salad

This typical Tuscan delicacy, beans and onion salad, is the one dish that never fails to be a success at the buffet held in our courtyard every August after our summer concert, which we have been doing for over twenty years. This is the time to buy fresh beans that are incredibly tender and tasty in comparison to the dried ones.

1kg/2 1/4 lb fresh cannellini beans (unshelled weight)
2 bay leaves
3 ripe salad tomatoes
1 white onion, finely sliced
6 tbsp extra virgin olive oil
Salt and pepper

Shell the beans and discard the pods. Put the beans in a pan, add the bay leaves, cover with water and bring to a slow boil. Cook for about 1 hour or until tender. Drain and reserve, discarding the bay leaves.
Bring a pan of water to the boil, add the tomatoes and leave for 30 seconds. Drain, peel, and seed the tomatoes, then dice the flesh.
Transfer the beans to a serving bowl, mix them gently with the tomatoes and sliced onions and pour in the oil. Add salt and pepper to taste, mix again and serve at room temperature.

Serves 6

INSALATA DI RADICCHIO E RAPANELLI
Green Radicchio and Red Radish Salad

I love green radicchio with its quite bitter taste and I often mix it with slices of ripe tomatoes. But for a more nourishing salad this variation is particularly nice. Use frisée if you cannot find this radicchio.

300g/10oz green radicchio
210g/7oz red radishes
6 large eggs
1 tbsp red wine vinegar
4 tbsp extra virgin olive oil
Salt

Wash the radicchio, dry on paper towels, then twist it with your hands, as you would when wringing out a piece of cloth. Keeping it twisted, cut the radicchio into fine pieces with kitchen scissors, or slice finely with a knife, and transfer to a bowl.
Slice the radishes very finely with a mandoline or sharp knife, and place on top of the radicchio.
Hardboil the eggs and peel them under cold running water. Quarter them and arrange over the salad.
Place the vinegar in a small bowl, add the salt and whisk to dissolve. Add the oil and whisk well. Pour over the salad and serve.

Serves 6

DESSERTS AND BREADS

PESCHE CARAMELLATE CON SALSA D'AMARETTI

Caramelized Peaches with Amaretti Sauce

The best quality amaretti are the ones from Saronno, made by Lazzaroni. It is important to find good ones because some can be either too sweet or have an artificial almond taste. Almond trees usually have white flowers, while the bitter almond ones used for amaretti come from trees with pink flowers.

7 peaches
3 tbsp granulated sugar
2 tbsp unsalted butter
120g/4oz amaretti biscuits (cookies)
120ml/4fl oz/½ cup dessert wine

Peel and stone the peaches. Reserve one and slice the others into wedges.
Heat the sugar with the butter in a pan over a low heat, stirring to dissolve the sugar. Add the peach wedges and cook for about 10 minutes, uncovered, shaking the pan gently and being careful not to break them up.
Transfer the peaches to a warmed serving dish and arrange them so they are slightly overlapping.
Make the sauce by puréeing the amaretti, the reserved peach and the wine in a blender. Pour the sauce around the peach wedges and serve at room temperature.

Serves 6

DOLCE DI FICHI
Fig Mould

Figs have a very short season in summertime and as they grow quite easily we have a lot of them in the garden. When they become ripe, almost all at the same time, I will pick them up to make a very special jam where figs are cooked with lemon slices.

600g/1¼ lb figs
450g/1lb/2 cups ricotta
4 large eggs
240g/8oz/1 cup granulated sugar

Preheat the oven to 170°C/350°F/Gas 4.
Peel the figs and purée in a blender. Add the ricotta, the eggs and 45g/1½oz/1½ tbsp of the sugar. Pulse again until well blended.
Heat the remaining sugar with 2 tbsp water in a heavy-based saucepan until caramelized, but not so dark that it tastes bitter. Pour the caramel into a warmed 1 litre/1¾ pint ring mould and use a pastry brush to coat the sides and base of the mould with the caramel. Leave to cool.
Pour in the fig mixture and place the mould on a baking sheet (cookie tray). Cook in the oven for about 1 hour. If it browns too much on the top during cooking, cover with (aluminum) foil.
Remove from the oven and leave to cool. Invert on to a serving platter and carefully remove the mould.
Leave to cool to room temperature and serve.

Serves 6

GELATO DI PESCHE NOCI

Nectarine Ice-cream

It is not easy to find good peaches and suddenly nectarines are becoming more popular. But of course this ice-cream is also delicious made with peaches. The best peaches are usually the ones with white flesh.

360g/12oz/2 cups granulated sugar
210ml/7fl oz/⁷⁄₈ cup water
1kg/2 ¼ lb nectarines
Juice of 1 lemon

Place the sugar and water in a heavy-based saucepan and bring to the boil. Simmer until syrupy, about 20 minutes. If you place a drop on a chilled saucer, the surface should wrinkle when you push it with the tip of your finger. Remove from the heat and leave to cool.
Peel and stone the nectarines and purée the flesh in a blender. Add the lemon juice and the sugar syrup and blend again. Transfer to an ice-cream maker and make the ice-cream according to the manufacturer's instructions. Alternatively, pour the mixture into a container, place in the freezer and leave for about 4 hours, whisking it at regular intervals, about 3 times in total.

Serves 6

MERINGA DI FRUTTA

Fruit Meringue

There are many methods for cooking meringue, one of which is to bake the meringue for about 2 hours on a lower temperature of about 130°C/250°F.

4 large egg whites
240g/8oz/1 cup granulated sugar
2 peaches
3 apricots
3 figs
240ml/8fl oz/1 cup double (heavy) cream
Pinch of salt

Preheat the oven to 180°C/375°F/Gas 5.
Whisk the whites with the salt in a bowl until stiff.
Add the sugar very gradually, beating continuously between each addition.
Line the base of a 30cm/11in round tart tin (pan) with greaseproof (waxed) paper. Spoon the meringue mixture over the top, smoothing it down with a spatula. Alternatively, form into a 30cm/11in circle on a large lined baking sheet (cookie tray). Place in the heated oven and immediately switch off the heat.
Leave the meringue in the oven until firm and cool.
This will take about 6 hours.
Transfer the meringue to a serving platter. Slice the peaches and apricots and peel and quarter the figs.
Beat the cream until stiff. Pipe it over the meringue or spread it over with a spatula. Arrange the fruit on top and serve.

Serves 6

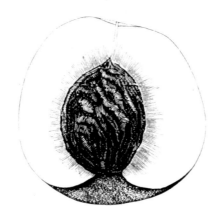

SPUMA DI ALBICOCCHE E YOGURT

Yoghurt and Apricot Mousse

The slightly acidic taste of the yoghurt provides a good balance to this dessert that I sometimes serve with a fresh sauce of puréed apricots and a little Vin Santo, the Tuscan dessert wine made out of dried grapes.

15g/½oz gelatine leaves
600g/1¼ lb ripe apricots, peeled
240ml/8fl oz/1 cup double (heavy) cream
90g/3oz/6 tbsp icing (powdered) sugar
240ml/8fl oz/1 cup yoghurt
A little almond oil
Redcurrants, to garnish

Soak the gelatine leaves in cold water for about 10 minutes. Stone the apricots and purée the flesh in a blender.
Beat half the cream until stiff, fold in the icing (powdered) sugar and reserve.
Heat the remaining cream in a pan but don't let it boil. Remove from the heat. Drain the gelatine leaves, squeeze out any excess water and add to the warm cream, mixing until dissolved. Set aside and leave to cool.
Mix the apricot purée and yoghurt with the cream and gelatine mixture until well blended.
Fold in the beaten cream and icing (powdered) sugar mixture. Brush a 1 litre/1 ¾ pint/4 cup serving dish with the almond oil, pour in the apricot mixture and leave in the refrigerator for at least 4 hours.
Prepare a large pan or bowl of warm water. Unmould the mousse by dipping it in the water for few seconds and inverting it on to a serving platter. Garnish with the redcurrants and serve.

Serves 6

FOCACCIA ALLE ERBE

Herbed Focaccia

Focaccia, or *schiacciata* as the Tuscans call it, is a flatbread usually covered with anything but tomatoes, otherwise it will become a pizza. In fact, in Naples *focaccia* is called *pizza bianca*, or white pizza.

30g/1oz/2 tbsp fresh yeast
240ml/8fl oz/1 cup lukewarm water
360g/12oz/3 cups plain (all-purpose) flour
3 tbsp finely chopped mixed fresh herbs such as rosemary, sage, mint and thyme
3 tbsp extra virgin olive oil
Salt

Preheat the oven to 200°C/400°F/Gas 6.
Place the yeast in a cup with the lukewarm water for about 10 minutes or until it starts to foam.
Sift the flour into a bowl and make a well in the centre. Gradually add the water and yeast mixture, mixing with a fork with a circular motion to form a dough.
Add the herbs and work them into the dough. Transfer to a lightly floured worksurface, working with the palms of your hands for about 3 minutes until smooth. Form the dough into a ball and place in a lightly floured bowl. Cover tightly with cling film (plastic wrap). Leave to rise until doubled in size, for 1 hour or more. The amount of time this takes will depend on how warm the room is.
Brush a 30cm/11in tart tin (pan) or baking sheet with a little oil. Roll out the dough to a 30cm/11in circle and transfer to the tin (pan) or baking sheet (cookie tray). Sprinkle over the salt to taste and the rest of the oil. Leave to rise for another 20 minutes.
Place in the oven and cook for about 30 minutes. Leave to cool and serve.

Serves 6

A MIDSUMMER FEAST

TEGLIA DI PEPERONI ALLE ACCIUGHE
Baked (Bell) peppers with Anchovies

(Bell) peppers are sweet and big and markets are full of them during this season, both red and yellow. They are wonderful in soups, pasta sauces and around meat or fish dishes. As they are also good cold they are perfect for picnics.

3 red (bell) peppers
3 yellow (bell) peppers
12 anchovy fillets in oil, drained
6 garlic cloves, thinly sliced
6 plum tomatoes, peeled but not seeded, halved
1 handful black (ripe) olives (Gaeta or Kalamata), pitted
2 handfuls dry breadcrumbs
3 tbsp extra virgin olive oil
1 handful pine nuts
1 handful fresh basil
Salt

Preheat the oven to 170°C/350°F/Gas 4.
Halve the (bell) peppers, discard the seeds and slice them vertically.
Layer the (bell) peppers in a baking dish, top them with the anchovy fillets, the garlic, the halved tomatoes and the olives. Sprinkle the breadcrumbs over the top, together with the oil and pine nuts and a little salt to taste. Cook in the oven for about 40 minutes.
Leave to cool to room temperature, scatter over the basil and serve.

Serves 6

ZUCCHINE RIPIENE
Stuffed Courgettes (Zucchini)

Courgettes (zucchini) are a lovely ornamental plant, and when we had a big terrace in Milan I planted them all along the walls, to the great admiration of all my friends.

12 medium courgettes (zucchini)
300g/10oz chicken breast
1 small carrot
1 small onion
1 handful fresh marjoram leaves
2 tbsp extra virgin olive oil
1 large egg
3 tbsp freshly grated Parmesan cheese
Salt and pepper

Preheat the oven to 170°C/350°F/Gas 5.
Cut the ends off the courgettes (zucchini) and scoop out the flesh with the appropriate tool (or use a teaspoon or narrow-bladed sharp knife), to make a hollow tube with thin walls. Reserve the flesh and roughly chop.
Put the chicken in a food processor and chop very finely. Remove the chicken from the blender and reserve. Add the courgette (zucchini) flesh to the blender with the carrot, onion and marjoram and pulse until well blended. Add salt and pepper to taste and fry the mixture over a very low heat in 1 tbsp of the oil, for about 10 minutes or until well cooked. Remove from the heat and mix with the chicken, egg and Parmesan.
Fill the hollowed-out courgettes (zucchini) with the mixture. Brush a baking sheet (cookie tray) with the rest of the oil, sprinkle over 2 tbsp water and place the courgettes (zucchini) on top. Cook in the oven for about 40 minutes. Leave to cool to room temperature and serve.

Serves 6

PARMIGIANA DI MELANZANE

Aubergine (Eggplant) Parmigiana

This is one of the most tasty of Neapolitan recipes. For a lighter but not quite as delicious result you could grill (broil) the aubergines (eggplants).

6 small aubergines (eggplants), oval-shaped if possible
1 litre/1 ³/₄ pints/4 cups oil, for deep-frying
1kg/2 ¹/₄ lb plum tomatoes
3 garlic cloves, chopped
2 tbsp extra virgin olive oil
2 tbsp dried oregano
450g/1lb good quality mozzarella cheese, sliced
Salt
FOR THE WHITE SAUCE:
1 tbsp unsalted butter
2 tbsp plain (all-purpose) flour
240ml/8fl oz/1 cup warm milk

Slice the aubergines (eggplants) vertically, discarding the ends.
Heat the oil in a frying pan until it reaches 170°C/350°F on a kitchen thermometer. Add the sliced aubergines (eggplants) a few at a time and cook until lightly golden. Do not let them brown or they will become bitter. Drain on absorbent paper.
Bring a pan of water to the boil, add the tomatoes and blanch for 30 seconds. Drain and peel. Chop, keeping the seeds.
Heat the olive oil in a saucepan, add the garlic and fry over a medium heat until translucent, about 3 minutes. Add the tomatoes, oregano and salt to taste and simmer over a medium heat until thick, about 1 hour.
Make the white sauce. Heat the butter in a pan over a low heat. Add the flour and stir with a wooden spoon for a couple of minutes until well blended. Add the milk a little at a time, stirring, until you have a smooth sauce.
Preheat the oven to 170°C/350°F/Gas 4. Layer half the aubergines (eggplants) in a baking dish, then add half the mozzarella, a few dashes of white sauce and half the tomato sauce. Repeat, finishing with a few more dashes of white sauce, then the tomato sauce.
Cook in the oven for about 40 minutes until bubbling and lightly golden on top. Leave to cool to room temperature before serving.

Serves 6

PANE AI CEREALI

Wholegrain Bread

I often go to Austria and Germany, the best places in the world for good classical music, and I think that they also have the best bread in Europe, which is often dark and very nutritious.

30g/1oz/2 tbsp fresh yeast
240ml/8fl oz/1 cup lukewarm water
360g/12oz/3 cups wholemeal (wholewheat) flour
1 handful spelt
1 handful barley
1 handful sunflower seeds
1 handful sesame seeds
1 tbsp extra virgin olive oil
Salt

Dissolve the yeast in the lukewarm water for about 10 minutes until foamy.
Sift the flour into a mixing bowl, make a well in the centre and gradually add the water, stirring in a circular motion with a fork to form a dough.
Transfer the dough to a lightly floured worksurface and knead with the palms of your hands for a few minutes until smooth. Form into a ball.
Transfer the dough to a lightly floured bowl, cover with cling film (plastic wrap) and leave to rise until doubled in size. The exact time will depend on the temperature of the room.
Meanwhile, place the spelt and barley in a pan of water, bring to the boil and simmer for about 1 hour. Drain.
Knock back (punch down) the dough on a lightly floured worksurface and add the grains and seeds a little at a time to distribute them evenly, working the dough between each addition. Form the dough into a loaf shape and sprinkle with salt.
Brush a baking sheet (cookie tray) with the oil, place the loaf on top and leave to rise for 20 minutes.
Preheat the oven to 200°C/400°F/Gas 6.
Bake for about 40 minutes. Remove to a wire rack and allow to cool to room temperature before serving.

Serves 6

INSALATA DI RISO NERO AL PESTO

Wild Rice Salad with Pesto Sauce

Pesto sauce is nice on more dishes than just pasta. I like it on wild rice, especially now that it is grown in Italy, although it is not yet as popular as in the United States.

450g/1lb wild rice
450g/1lb string beans
120g/4oz/1 cup fresh basil leaves
3 tbsp freshly grated Parmesan cheese
2 tbsp freshly grated pecorino (Romano) cheese
3 tbsp pine nuts
2 garlic cloves
120ml/4fl oz/½ cup extra virgin olive oil
Salt and pepper

Bring a pan of water to the boil, add salt and the rice, cover and simmer over a low heat for 50 minutes. Trim the beans and add to the rice. Cook for 10 minutes more.
Meanwhile put the basil, Parmesan, pecorino (Romano), pine nuts, garlic cloves and oil in a blender with a little salt and pepper. Process until creamy. Add 1 ladle of the rice cooking water to the sauce and process for a few more seconds.
Drain the rice and the beans and mix with the pesto sauce. Leave to cool to room temperature and serve.

Serves 6

PANNA COTTA ALLA FRUTTA

Fruit with Cooked Cream

A fruit dessert is a perfect way to end a lovely picnic, accompanied by a basket of fresh seasonal fruits.

15g/½ oz gelatine leaves
450ml/1 pint/2 cups double (heavy) cream
90g/3oz/½ cup granulated sugar
12 strawberries
120g/4oz blueberries
12 raspberries
12 cherries, stoned (pitted) and halved

Soak the gelatine leaves in cold water until soft, about 5 minutes. Heat half the cream with the sugar in a pan until just boiling. Remove from the heat. Drain the gelatine leaves and squeeze out excess water. Add them to the warm cream, mixing until dissoved.
Allow to cool completely.
Beat the remaining cream to very soft peaks.
Gently fold the beaten cream into the cooled cream and gelatine.
Quarter each strawberry vertically and add to the cream with the blueberries, raspberries and cherries. Mix carefully.
Fill a 1 litre/1¾ pint/4 cup mould with water, drain and fill with the fruit *panna cotta*. Place in the refrigerator until set, about 4 hours. Unmould and serve at room temperature.

Serves 6

INSALATA DI PASTA E PECORINO

Pasta and Pecorino (Romano) Salad

Pasta salads are good if they are kept simple and served at room temperature, never cold. I often buy another cheese such as fontina for this recipe.

300g/10oz short pasta like penne, rigatoni or fusilli
1 handful fresh basil leaves
120ml/4fl oz/½ cup extra virgin olive oil
300g/10oz cherry tomatoes
300g/10oz fresh pecorino (Romano) cheese, diced
Salt and pepper

Bring a pan of water to the boil, add the pasta and cook until *al dente* (a couple of minutes less than it says on the packet).
Tear the basil with your hands. Drain the pasta and tip it into in a serving bowl. Add the oil and mix well. Add the whole tomatoes and leave to cool to room temperature. Add the pecorino (Romano), the basil and salt and pepper to taste, and serve.

Serves 6

INTRODUCTION

Autumn comes late in Chianti, where I live. The sun is still hot in September and hopefully the weather will stay warm and dry into October for the grape harvest. We still enjoy picnics and alfresco luncheons and I notice that everyone, especially autumn visitors from the north, seems to spend more time at the table in gardens, outdoor restaurants and cafés, soaking up the last rays of the sun. By November there is a definite chill in the air and we must make haste to pick our olives, the other major crop in Tuscany, before the first frost. In the vineyards the vine leaves turn yellow and brown and in the woods the chestnut and oak trees begin to show their autumn colours. The days are short and in the evening it is time to light a fire and enjoy the comforting aroma and taste of grilled (broiled) meats for supper.

Besides the cultivated harvests of grapes and olives, autumn provides an abundant wild harvest of mushrooms, chestnuts, figs, berries, even snails and, of course, game, big wild boar and small birds. The season for wild mushrooms begins with the first autumn rains, when the combination of heat and moisture *fa ribollire la terra*, makes the earth boil, and causes these exotic and somewhat mysterious fungi, *funghi* in Italian, to pop up. Sometimes, if the weather conditions are right, late spring produces a small harvest of mushrooms, but it is in autumn that bumper crops appear. Not every year, however. During some seasons there are virtually none due to lack of rain or early frost. At other times there are just a few. Local wisdom has it that a good year for wine is a bad year for mushrooms—a dry, hot autumn favouring the quality of grapes and hindering the growth of mushrooms.

In any case, when the time does come, literally thousands of hopeful Italians set out in their cars for the woods wearing boots and carrying walking sticks and baskets and armed with small knives. 'Authentic' mushrooming baskets are woven from strips of wood and have a hard, thick, arched handle that is used for support while climbing along hillsides and crawling through the undergrowth. They cut the mushrooms from the ground with their knife and the spaces between the strips in the basket allow the spores of the fungus to fall to the ground to reproduce another year. Passionate locals regard Sunday 'city types' carrying plastic bags with disdain.

These 'professionals' each have their secret section of the woods where they hope to strike it rich again. Some are even acknowledged by the others as having a sixth sense for spotting specimens that no one else can see. In fact, it does take a certain type of vision to make out these tiny delicacies in the midst of trees, brush and a deposit of autumn leaves. In my neck of the Tuscan woods the kind of mushroom everyone is most hoping to find is the *Boletus edulis*, the cep. In Italian they are called *porcini*, little pigs, probably because of their fat, squat shape. *Porcini* have a reddish-brown cap that can grow as big as 2–3cm/6–7in across. One of the best ways to enjoy tasty *porcini* is to grill (broil) the cap like a meaty steak or bake it in (aluminum) foil with a few drops of olive oil. There are dozens of Italian recipes using fresh *porcini*, in soups, salads, pasta, risotto, fried and sautéed. I almost always add a sprig of wild catmint (catnip), *nepitella*, or a handful of mint leaves when I prepare *porcini*. Their flavours blend beautifully. Fresh *porcini* can be preserved in olive oil, to which you can

PI. XXXIV.

Bolet comestible. *Com.*
Boletus edulis. Bull.

and egg-coloured volva (the cup-like structure at the top of some mushrooms) that opens later to reveal a beautiful yolk-orange cap. They are usually eaten raw and are exquisite sliced and mixed with shavings of fresh Parmesan dressed with olive oil and lemon. One of the 'highs' of gastronomic pleasure is a combination you might find in a few, fine restaurants in late autumn, during the brief period when mushroom and truffles are available at the same time—a salad of *ovoli* and white truffles. For a dish that is almost divine, dress thinly sliced raw fillet of beef with olive oil and lemon and then cover with shavings of Parmesan, *ovoli* and truffles.

While a somewhat intense and competitive spirit marks 'mushrooming', chestnut-gathering is a more relaxed recreation for a clear, crisp, autumnal family outing. One of the characteristic sounds of autumn in the woods is of chestnuts falling to the ground into a bed of dried leaves. If you are quiet you might hear other sounds, such as those made by a pack of ravenous wild boar trying to get to the chestnuts first. It is their favourite food. You won't see the boar, however, as they are very shy and will scurry away as soon as they scent your proximity.

add a bay leaf, chilli pepper and a clove of garlic. They can also be dried very successfully. Dried *porcini*, even more intense in taste than when fresh, enhance many an Italian sauce. Some of my neighbours, when the year's harvest has been particularly abundant, freeze their *porcini*. First they wipe them clean with a damp cloth and then seal them, whole or sliced, in bags. Before cooking, they need to be partially thawed under running water. Their texture softens in the process but they maintain their aroma and they flavour perfectly.

Of the dozens of types of edible mushrooms that grow along the Italian peninsula, my favourite is the rare and exotic *ovolo* or egg-mushroom, known botanically as *Amanita caesarea*. When they first come up, *ovoli* are completely enclosed in an egg-shaped

These shiny, reddish-brown nuts are the fruit of the chestnut tree and develop inside a prickly burr that opens when they are mature. Several varieties of chestnuts grow in mountainous regions with a temperate climate, in Piedmont and Tuscany especially. Wild chestnut trees are common in the woods surrounding Badia a Coltibuono, where I live, and provide most of the timber in these parts. In past centuries, even as recently as the last World War when food was scarce, peasant farmers in remote areas gathered chestnuts to survive. Because they contain less oil and more starch than other nuts, they can be ground into a fine flour and used for making bread and polenta.

Cultivated chestnuts, on the other hand, have become a luxury food. There are several kinds but *marroni* are the biggest and best. Each burr contains only one plump nut, instead of several small ones. They are shiny and bright in colour and have a thinner shell and inside skin which makes them easier to prepare for eating. Ordinary chestnuts, *castagne*, might be thrown to the pigs, while fresh *marroni* cost almost ten dollars a kilo (2 ¼ lb).

By far the most popular way to enjoy chestnuts is roasted. In cities street vendors roast them in portable braziers and sell them in heavy paper cones. Their aroma warms the atmosphere and they provide a quick energy snack while you do your crrands. At home we roast them over the fire using a round iron pan with a very long handle and holes punched into the bottom. Before roasting the chestnuts you must slit their shell and inner skin with a very sharp knife. This makes peeling them easier once they are done. Then they are placed over hot embers until their shells begin to burn and burst. When chestnuts have been off the tree for a while, they can be boiled in water flavoured with a pinch of fennel seeds.

Chestnuts have that particular taste which adapts both to savoury and sweet dishes. They can be added to risotto or to stuffing for game. In Tuscany a curious semi-sweet cake called *castagnaccio* is made with fresh chestnut flour mixed with water and olive oil and seasoned with raisins, pine nuts, fennel seeds and rosemary and baked in a round, shallow tin (pan). It comes out brown and cracked on top and the inside is paler with the consistency of pudding. Traditionally you buy it by the slice and wash it down with a glass of sweet Vin Santo. Appreciation for *castagnaccio* is definitely an acquired taste, which I admit I have never acquired. For my cooking classes I even tried adding a little unorthodox chocolate but the results still did not enjoy much success either with me or with my students.

On the other hand, *necci*, chestnut flour crêpes, are delicious. At autumn festivals in the countryside around Lucca, they still make them in the traditional way, with an ancient implement called a *testi*, which consists of two iron disks with two long handles that are joined at the end. The batter is spread over one, the *testi* is then closed and placed over hot embers. When the crêpe is formed, it is filled with fresh sheep's milk ricotta or shavings of pecorino (Romano) cheese.

The most delicious dessert using chestnuts, at least for me, is *montebianco*, a spectacular speciality of Piedmont, a region with an abundance of chestnuts and with, for creative culinary inspiration, a view of the white-capped Alpine peak of Mont Blanc, 'the White Mountain', in the distance. Fresh chestnuts are boiled, peeled and simmered in milk and then passed through the large holes of a food mill. You stir in

Pl.297. Châtaignier vulgaire. Castanea vulgaris. Lamk.

cocoa and refrigerate the mixture. When it has been chilled, you form it to look like a mountain peak and top it with whipped cream. When I was a child and stayed with my cousins at their country home in Piedmont, my aunt use to serve it with a bowl of extra cream on the side so we could make our helping 'snow' even more. And by the way, candied chestnuts, the French *marrons glacés*, are not only a speciality of France. A shop in Milan (Giovanni Galli, not far from the Duomo) has been famous for these elegant confections for well over a hundred years.

Certainly the most curious of the autumn foragers are the snail hunters. Both they and the tiny titbits they are rummaging for come out at night after the first autumn rains. The former carry a torch (flashlight) and plastic bag and the latter crawl out of recesses in stone walls to feed on the fresh, wet grass along fields and roadside ditches. Italian snails, *lumache*, the edible wild variety, have a small brownish spiral shell enclosing a tiny and succulent body. The cultivated kind is large and similar to the Burgundian *escargot*. Both have been cooked in Italy since ancient times. The Romans kept breeding-grounds where they developed different colours and sizes and fattened them on special diets. The medieval Catholic Church gave snails a gastronomic advantage as they were not considered meat and therefore could be enjoyed at table during the many days of religious fast and abstinence. And the first Renaissance reference to snail-eating comes not from France but from the region of Lombardy.

Contemporary Tuscan connoisseurs consider the garden variety the tastiest, while in the north of Italy the cultivated types are preferred. Both require a certain amount of dedication to prepare for the table. They have first to be purged for a couple of days in several changes of a solution of water, salt, vinegar and a dusting of bran. In the north they are cooked in a sauce of olive oil, garlic and parsley. Tomato is added in central and southern Italy. I like them stewed in red wine.

In early autumn many Italian men begin to stalk more challenging prey than the lowly snail. Hunting season opens in mid-September. The shoot starts with small game, quail, pheasant, partridge and hare. These all enrich the seasonal variety at the table. I combine game birds with another autumn wild food, fresh *porcini* mushrooms. Many regional recipes exist for hare. *Lepre in salmì* is the classic way to cook hare in northern Italy. *In salmì* is a cooking method which involves marinating the meat in wine and herbs and stewing very slowly. Traditionally it is served with polenta. I prepare hare with a sweet sauce of cherries in syrup. In central Italy they make a delicious dish called *pappardelle con la lepre*, large noodles dressed with pieces of hare in a rich sauce.

In Tuscany where I live, the chase for wild boar, *cinghiale*, begins on 1 November. Tuscany has more hunters per capita than any other region. It also has more wild boar. Like their domestic cousins, boar are prolific, intelligent and have a voracious appetite, especially for ripe grapes. They constitute a major menace to this harvest and so hunters help to control their population through the chase, as well as provide a tasty meat for the table.

The shoot begins shortly after dawn and in the best of Italian traditions starts off with a *merenda*, a hearty snack of bread, salami and grilled sausages, with just enough red wine to warm the system but not put off the aim. The hunters and their dogs form a team, usually about thirty men and fifteen canines, and cordon off the ridge of a valley. Below, a few men and the dogs begin to stalk their prey. There is much hooting and barking to rout the boar out of hiding in the thick undergrowth.

An average boar weighs about 55kg/115lb. The head goes as a trophy to the hunter who brings down the beast. The meat is divided among the team. Back home it will be prepared *alla cacciatora*, 'the hunter's way', stewed

with onions, celery, carrots, tomatoes and herbs. The most famous recipe for wild boar dates from the Renaissance. *Cinghiale in agrodolce* is a dish of wild boar stewed in a sweet-and-sour sauce of red wine vinegar and dark chocolate, seasoned with bay leaves, juniper berries and pine nuts. My recipe calls for marinating the meat in red wine with herbs and spices for two days and is served with a redcurrant sauce or at Thanksgiving (why not?) with cranberries.

At market, summer's cornucopia of produce spills out well into autumn, with several seasonal arrivals adding to the variety. After a summer holiday, spinach makes a comeback. During spring I use its tender, tiny, emerald green bunches in salads, raw or lightly steamed in just the moisture left on its leaves after washing, dressed with olive oil and lemon. In autumn I use it in fillings and as an accompaniment to many main courses, sautéed with a little olive oil and garlic. Beets and leeks and many varieties of cabbage, available practically all year around, seem to taste best as the weather turns cold.

I most look forward to fresh fennel, which is available from autumn to spring. Perhaps second only to the tomato, fennel is characteristic of Italian cuisine. In fact in France it is known as Florence fennel, probably because Caterina de'Medici brought it with her to France along with so many other good things she could not do without, when she married the future King Henry II.

Fennel in Italian is called *finocchio*, meaning 'fine eye'. According to a Renaissance medical text it was so called because eating it improved one's vision. The seventeenth-century Venetian, Giacomo Castelvetro, claims it 'warms a cold stomach, gets rid of wind, aids digestion and sweetens bad breath'. He also adds a more ambiguous effect, namely that it improves the taste of

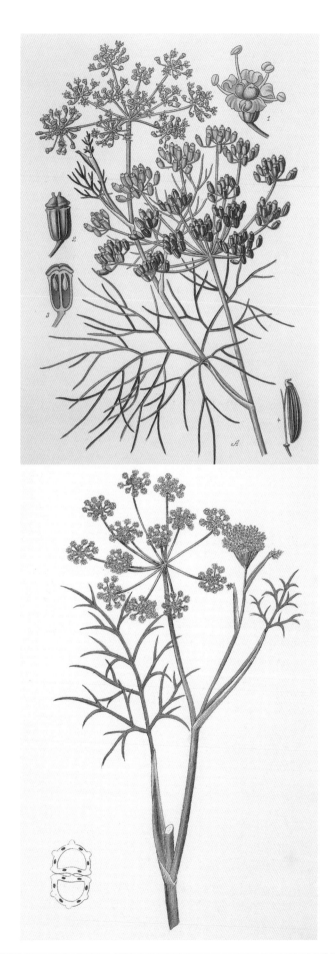

bad wine. He records that, 'villainous Venetian wine-sellers solicitously offer innocent or simple-minded customers a piece of nice fennel to eat with their wine… insisting that otherwise they might do themselves harm by drinking wine on an empty stomach'. This 'deceiving' property of *finocchio* might account for the verb, *infinocchiare*, meaning to bamboozle, to hoodwink, to con. It might also explain why in slang a transvestite or female impersonator is called a *finocchio*.

I have never tried the wine trick but I do know that fennel enhances the flavour of everything with which it is served. This is why it shows up in so many dishes of the traditional Italian meal, *antipasti*, first courses, main courses, vegetable dishes and even desserts. This versatile vegetable can be cooked in dozens of different ways—boiled, braised and baked. In Sicily they combine it with sardines to make the island's most traditional pasta dish, *pasta con le sarde*. In Tuscany it meets its perfect match in *arista*, roast loin of pork. It combines especially well with cheese, boiled and sprinkled with Parmesan or baked with melted cheese on top. It is delicious on its own raw and thinly sliced and dressed with extra virgin olive oil and lemon. I often top *carpaccio* with shavings of raw fennel.

Fennel is used in several different forms. The wild variety, knows as *finocchiella* or *finocchietto*, grows in profusion all over the peninsula. Its celery-like stalks, that reach a height of 40m/6ft, produce a tiny yellow flower that Tuscan women pick and tie into little bouquets to dry and hang in the kitchen. These flowers are crumbled over dishes, especially to flavour pork and fish. Left on the stalk, the flowers develop into seeds, which are also used as seasoning. Cultivated fennel is similar to the wild variety, except that the leaves swell to form pale green to white bulbs, out of which grow stalks with characteristic fronds. You can use this attractive fern-like foliage as a garnish. When you buy fennel, select bulbs that are firm and fresh, not dried out or discoloured and spotted. Peel away and discard the coarser outer layer of the bulb.

The three elemental fruits of the Mediterranean—grapes, olives and figs—all come to maturity in autumn. The fig tree, which probably originated in Asia Minor, yields two crops of fruit annually. In June the previous season's buds, called *fioroni*, produce large and juicy figs, which, however, are almost tasteless. The true fig, fruit of the current season's growth, ripens from late August to October. These figs are small in size but big in flavour, tasting of honey and berry jam.

Botanists have counted hundreds of varieties of figs growing in Italy. They can be divided into two groups according to their basic colour. White figs develop hues ranging from pale green to dark gold. Red figs can vary from a burnished brown to a purple so deep it appears almost black. Inside, figs contain many minute flowers that are really undeveloped fruits, which give them that characteristic crunch. A classic sweet and savoury Italian *antipasto* which takes no preparation at all is figs with prosciutto. Before serving I like to leave the figs out in the sun for a few minutes to warm them. A delicious combination to end a meal is figs with ricotta cheese. You can prepare them in a mould for an elegant luncheon dessert.

In late summer and early autumn the woods surrounding the area where I live in Tuscany are full of wild berries and currants—juicy sloes, which the locals call *susine di macchia*, wild scrub plums, juniper berries, hawthorn berries and, best of all, luscious blackberries. In Italian we have an expression, *andar per more*, which translates as 'to go blackberry-picking' and in September and October that is a favourite pastime for my grandchildren and their friends.

Wild blackberries, really a shiny reddish-black in colour, grow on thorny canes, which makes picking them a challenge but it is worth the inevitable scratches.

They have a more concentrated flavour than the larger and juicier thornless blackberry developed for commercial growing. Each berry is actually an aggregate fruit composed of individual 'drupelets'. The little seeds in each drupelet of the wild blackberry are harder than in the domestic variety but their exposure to the sun and heat of a long summer intensifies their sugar content, so they are also sweeter. During late summer and early autumn you will see displayed in markets and restaurants little boxes of a mixture of wild blackberries, strawberries, blueberries and redcurrants that comprise what is called *sottobosco*, 'wild berries from the wood'. The fruit is served as dessert, eaten as it is or with a little lemon and sugar.

The last fruit to come to market in late autumn is the persimmon, called *caca* in Italian. Its glowing golden colour and luscious orange-red flesh are like the last burst of warm sunshine before the arrival of winter. In north-central Italy persimmons begin to ripen so late in the season that they have to be picked before they are fully mature, then left to ripen off the tree.

A fully ripe persimmon has an almost transparent skin, which often bursts before you get it home from the market. The easiest way to enjoy its deliciously sweet and mildly spicy flavour is simply to cut off the top and scoop out the soft and gelatine-like flesh with a spoon. I find a squeeze of lemon enhances its taste.

HARVEST FESTIVALS

For decades Italy has been the largest producer of wine in Europe and the second largest consumer (the French, I believe, are second and first respectively), so it is no wonder that the grape harvest is celebrated from the tip to the toe of the Italian peninsula by local fairs and festivals, tastings, international conventions and seminars. Actually it would be more accurate to say that the harvest is anticipated by these events. Whereas in former times peasants made merry while stomping on the grapes, today, when wine-making involves considerable financial investment and serious science as well as art, there is no time for play. So September is the month of wine harvest festivities and in October everyone prays for good weather and gets down to work.

When I was growing up in Milan I often spent weekends with my cousins in the region of Piedmont whose vineyards produce some of Italy's finest red wines, Barolo, Barbera and Barbaresco, to mention only three of the most internationally famous. In those days the little village where we lived had a very lively *sagra dell'uva*, grape festival, during harvest time. I remember the doorways and terraces of houses decorated with bunches of grapes and the streets lined with wine barrels. There was even a little parade consisting of the local band, some of the citizenry in folk costume and several floats featuring Bacchus and other picturesque symbols of the harvest. You could sample the new wine straight from the barrels in the street and from vats down in my uncle's cellar.

Today the atmosphere at these wine festivals has changed. They have become less folkloristic and more market orientated. In Tuscany's Chianti region, where our family winery is located, every township holds its *festa dell'uva*. Local producers set up stalls and offer tastings of their various vintages. Critical appraisal is encouraged as well as purchase of the product. Seminars are held on subjects such as wine appreciation and the pairing of wine with food. These occasions, however, have not become all work and no play. Outdoor meals featuring local dishes are served and the evening ends with music and dancing.

All over Tuscany during harvest time bakers make a sweet bread in varying versions featuring the region's noble red grape, the *Sangioveto*. In our town they call it *panello con l'uva*. Grapes, walnuts, mixed ground spices, aniseed and rosemary are added to the dough before kneading and more grapes and walnuts are sprinkled on top before baking. It is turned out in large sheets and you buy it by weight. In Florence bakers make it by placing a bunch of grapes in-between two layers of dough. The grapes remain juicy to the bite. At home I bake *schiacciata con l'uva*, grape flat bread, in a tart tin (pan) and cover the top with purple seedless grapes and sugar. This bread is delicious for breakfast as well as a harvest snack, served with a glass of Tuscany's premium dessert wine, Vin Santo. As the conclusion to an elegant harvest luncheon at our winery I like to serve cups filled with peeled red and white grapes sprinkled with sugar and covered with 'champagne'—Italian *spumante*, of course.

In Tuscany as well as in many other regions of Italy, after all the grapes have been picked and the new wine is fermenting in the cellars, it is time to harvest the olives, the area's second most important crop. These olives are destined for the production of the region's celebrated extra virgin olive oil. They are much too valuable to cure for table olives.

In Upper Chianti where our olive groves are located, the trees are planted on hillsides at altitudes up to 450m/150ft, unusually high for a Mediterranean fruit. The species of olive tree that can survive at these heights produces olives that never fully mature. They remain a lean, reddish ripe. This is what gives the oil its fruity rather than fatty flavour. In warmer climates the glossy black fruit is so heavy with juice it drops from the trees or can easily be shaken off. Here, olives must be picked by hand. The seasonal challenge is to let the olives ripen on the tree for as long as possible, and yet to pick them before they are damaged by the first frost.

Once off the tree the olives are brought to the local *frantoio*, the mill where they will be crushed and pressed for oil. Here the atmosphere is industrious and festive. Since freshly picked olives kept in piles will begin to ferment after only a few days, everyone must move fast to get the crop crushed as quickly as possible. For this important reason the *frantoio* schedules pressings practically twenty-four hours a day during the several weeks of harvest. The place bustles with activity. Farmers arrive with their olives in bulging great sacks and others leave with their new oil in stainless-steel containers. The grower follows his harvest through each step of the milling process, while they are weighed-in, crushed under huge granite stones and finally pressed. Then comes the moment of truth, the first taste of his precious green-gold liquid.

Upon reflection, I have come to the conclusion that it is precisely this moment which makes the olive harvest so satisfying. While one has to wait for at least a year before the results of a grape harvest can really be appreciated at the table, olive oil is immediately delicious. In fact, the taste of olive oil right after it has been pressed is unique. It has a distinctive, fruity flavour all its own, with a pleasingly peppery aftertaste that softens with time. This is a quality characteristic of oil from under-ripe, cold-pressed olives, to which no heat or chemicals were added during the milling process, and indicates a low acidity content, under one per cent, which qualifies the oil as 'extra virgin.'.

Traditionally the season's new oil is celebrated with *la sagra della bruschetta*. In Tuscany a *bruschetta* is often called a *fettunta*. *Fettunta* literally means an 'oiled slice' of bread and *bruschetta* a slice of bread *bruschinato,* 'brushed', with olive oil. In culinary terms it all comes down to the same thing, a thick piece of country-style bread, grilled over the fire, rubbed with a clove of garlic and doused with new oil. This simple dish is the best way to savour new oil. At olive harvest festivals the basic *bruschetta* is often enriched by the addition of other toppings. Some of the most popular are chopped tomatoes flavoured with fresh basil or dried oregano; boiled and sliced cauliflower florets seasoned with salt and pepper and a little red wine vinegar; or dried white beans cooked with a couple of fresh sage leaves. *Bruschetta* can be enjoyed with different seasonal dressings all year around and I have given several variations in the recipe sections. The one essential ingredient is the very best extra virgin olive oil you can find.

Just as the olive harvest gets underway, all of Italy celebrates the last religious and national holiday of the autumn season, All Saints' Day on 1 November, *La Festa di Tutti Santi.* This is an ancient holy day in the calendar of the Catholic Church, honouring believers who have died and gone to heaven. Centuries later an even older, pre-Christian tradition was attached to this celebration on the following day, 2 November, the feast of All Souls, or *I Morti*, which is a remembrance of the dead.

Cemeteries throughout Italy, in large cities as well as in small villages, are full of flowers that relatives, often returning from afar for the occasion, have placed on family graves. In Rome, Naples and Palermo, people visit the city's largest cemetery just to see the sight of these vast 'cities of the dead' abloom, mostly with chrysanthemums, the Italian flower of the dead.

In Tuscany, several days before the holiday, bakeries begin to sell a special sweet bread made from wholemeal (wholewheat) flour, walnuts and raisins. It has a curious name, *pan coi Santi*, literally 'bread with the Saints'. One explanation is that the numerous raisins in the bread represent 'the Saints', the dead, who are hopefully enjoying their heavenly reward. Another more anthropological and fascinating interpretation of the name traces its origin back to the ancient tradition of communicating with the dead by ritually sharing bread with them, often over the grave itself. This bread, then, would seem a fitting culinary conclusion to the cycle of seasons.

THE PANTRY

FUNGHI SECCHI
Dried Mushrooms

In autumn when I am in Coltibuono, I often go to pick *porcini* mushrooms in the woods with my grandchildren. Emanuele, my daughter's son, is the best. He can spot *porcini* from far away. Sometimes we pick so many of them that we dry them for the winter.

lkg/2 ¼ lb fresh *porcini* or other mushrooms

Wipe the mushrooms clean with a cloth—do not wash them.
Slice vertically about 0.5cm/¼ in thick and place close together on trays lined with greaseproof (waxed) paper—try not to overlap the slices.
Put the mushrooms in a well-ventilated room, but not in the sun. Cover with a piece of cheesecloth or muslin so they do not become dusty and leave them, turning them every now and then, until completely dry. The exact time depends on how dry the atmosphere in the room is, but don't leave them for more than 10 days or they will start to go mouldy.
Once the mushrooms are very dry they can be stored in a sealed jar for the whole year.

You will obtain about 90g/3oz dried mushrooms

TARTUFI sotto VINO
Truffles in Wine

I particularly love white truffles and my passion is to eat them in Milan at the restaurant *Paper Moon*, where they serve them on top of polenta and fried eggs, a real delicacy that is much better than serving them on noodles.

The white truffles should be cleaned with a brush. You will need a clean heatproof jar.
Take enough white wine to cover the truffles in your chosen jar, plus a little more, as it will reduce when boiling. Pour into a pan and boil well for a couple of minutes.
Place the truffles in the jar and pour the hot wine over. Seal the jar tightly and place in a large saucepan. Fill the pan with water so it covers the top of the jar and bring to the boil. Simmer for 30 minutes, remove the pan from the heat and let the jar cool in the water. When cold the truffles can be stored in a cool, dark place for up to 3 months.

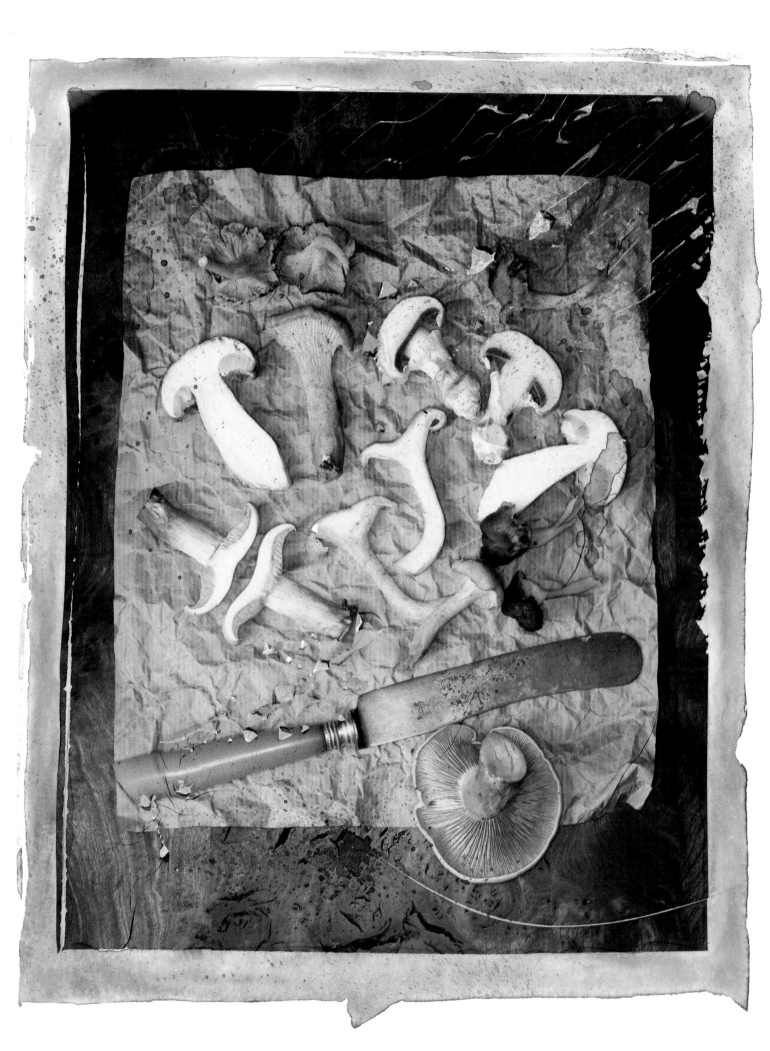

FOGLIE DI VITE SOTTO SALE

Vine Leaves Preserved in Salt

Before the leaves in the vineyards become too red, I pick them for preserving for the winter. I will fill them with rice and raisins, chopped meat or many other different ingredients, as I learned in Greece where I often go for summer holidays.

60 vine leaves
Salt

Make sure the leaves are pesticide-free.
Wash them well.
Bring a large pan of water to the boil, add 2 handfuls of salt and add the vine leaves, a few at a time. Leave to boil for a few seconds and drain them flat on a cloth.
Fill a heatproof jar with the leaves, pressing them in lightly. Close the jar tightly and place in a large saucepan. Fill with water to cover the jars and bring to the boil. Boil for 20 minutes, remove the pan from the heat and leave the jar to cool in the water.
When cold, the vine leaves can be stored in a cool, dark place for up to 2 months.

BURRO AL LIMONE

Lemon Butter

I like to prepare scented butter, which is very handy for perfuming various types of food, pasta, vegetables or meats, or to place on toast. I also prepare butter scented with rosemary, garlic, sage or thyme.

2 organic lemons
240g/8oz/12 tbsp unsalted butter

Wash the lemons carefully and dry well with a cloth.
Grate the zest finely and mix with the butter.
This will keep in the refrigerator in a sealed container for up to 1 month.

POMODORI VERDI IN CONSERVA

Preserved Green Tomatoes

This is a recipe from the south provided by Lina, the person who has helped my daughter to look after her children for many years. It is very useful for using up all the tomatoes that our plants still produce in autumn. The tomatoes are green because the sun is not strong enough at this time of year.

1kg/2¼ lb green tomatoes
300ml/10fl oz/1¼ cups white wine vinegar
6 tbsp water
6 garlic cloves, thinly sliced
2 handfuls fresh basil leaves
240ml/8fl oz/1 cup extra virgin olive oil
Salt

Wash the tomatoes carefully and dry them with a cloth.
Cut the tomatoes in half. Lay them out on a board and sprinkle generously with the salt. Cover the tomatoes with a plate or plates and place a weight on top. Leave for about 12 hours.
Drain the tomatoes and place in a bowl. Pour over the vinegar and the water and mix well. The tomatoes should be completely covered by liquid. Leave for about 4 hours.
Drain the tomatoes and dry thoroughly with a cloth or paper towels. Press them into a sterilized jar, alternating them with the garlic and the basil. Pour over the oil to cover completely, seal the jar and store for up to 3 months in a cool, dark place.

Makes 600g/1¼lb

APPETIZERS, PASTA AND SOUPS

BRUSCHETTA DI PROSCIUTTO E FUNGHI

Porcini Mushroom and Prosciutto Bruschetta

This is a very typical autumn dish that I eat at our favourite restaurant in Badia a Coltibuono if I am too lazy to try to pick up some mushrooms myself. They use a nice ham there that is produced in Chianti from a special breed of pig that is very tasty. Parma ham is easier to find abroad.

300g/10oz fresh *porcini* mushrooms
4 tbsp extra virgin olive oil
3 garlic cloves
1 tbsp chopped fresh flat-leaf parsley
6 large slices coarse country bread
6 paper-thin slices prosciutto (Parma ham)
Salt and pepper

Wipe the mushrooms clean and slice them vertically. Heat 3 tbsp of the oil in a pan, add the garlic cloves and mushrooms and cook over a high heat, stirring often, for about 5 minutes. Add salt and pepper to taste and discard the garlic. Sprinkle the mushrooms with the parsley and keep warm.
Toast or grill (broil) the bread slices lightly until just golden. Brush the toast with the remaining tablespoon of oil and top with the prosciutto, curling it up slightly to fit on the bread. Top with the mushrooms. Serve warm.

Serves 6

COPPETTE DI PASTA AI FUNGHI E GRANTURCO

Mushroom and Sweetcorn Pasta Cups

This offers a different way of eating pasta, when both mushrooms and sweetcorn are fresh. If you do not want to go to the effort of preparing the cups you can just use sweetcorn and mushrooms as a spaghetti or penne sauce.

FOR THE PASTA DOUGH:
300g/10oz/2 ½ cups plain (all-purpose) flour,
plus extra for dusting
3 large eggs
FOR THE FILLING:
300g/10oz fresh *porcini* mushrooms
3 tbsp extra virgin olive oil
6 tbsp double (heavy) cream
300g/10oz cooked sweetcorn
Salt and pepper

Preheat the oven to 200°C/400°F/Gas 6.
Make the pasta dough: sift the flour into a bowl, add the eggs and mix with a fork in a circular motion, until a dough is formed. Transfer to a lightly floured worksurface and work with the palms of your hands until the dough becomes smooth and elastic. Pass through a pasta rolling machine until you have long thin strips, about 9cm/3in wide. Cut the strips into 18 squares.
Flour the outside of 18 moulds or cups (or as many as you have). Shape the pasta squares round the outside of the moulds. Place in the oven and cook until golden, about 5 minutes. Repeat as necessary until you have made 18 cup shapes. Remove the pasta carefully from the moulds, invert the shapes on to a warmed platter so the rims are resting on the platter and keep warm.
Wipe the mushrooms clean. Heat the oil in a pan and sauté the mushrooms for about 5 minutes over a medium heat, stirring constantly. Add the cream, salt and pepper to taste and the sweetcorn. Cook for a few minutes more until the cream has reduced. Fill the pasta cups with the mixture and serve immediately.

Serves 6

SPIEDINI DI CIPOLLINE E UVA

Grape and Baby (Pearl) Onion Skewers

When it's harvest time we get a lot of small and tasty grapes from our vineyards. They are not as big as the ones grown for eating and sometimes the little seed inside can be unpleasant, but the flavour is strong and quite nice and goes very well with the little onions I grow in my garden.

18 baby (pearl) onions
2 tbsp granulated sugar
2 tbsp balsamic vinegar
2 tbsp extra virgin olive oil
18 large black grapes
Salt

Peel the baby (pearl) onions. Heat the sugar in a pan with the vinegar and cook over a low heat until caramelized. Do not let it become too dark or it will be bitter. Add the oil and when hot, the onions. Sauté over a medium heat for a couple of minutes, adding a little water from time to time to prevent the cooking juices from drying out. Shake the pan, but do not stir. Add salt to taste, then continue to cook until tender, about 10 minutes.
Add the grapes and cook for a couple more minutes.
Drain the onions and grapes and thread them alternately on to 6 skewers.
Serve immediately, while still warm.

Serves 6

RISOTTO ALLE CASTAGNE

Chestnut Risotto

We are very lucky to still have lot of chestnuts in our forest and on Sundays we have to be sure to go there early before people from the valley come and pick up all the chestnuts when they are ripe. This recipe was popular in my grandmother's Piedmontese castle when we used to visit her in autumn.

300g/10oz chestnuts
1.5 litres/3 pints/6 cups vegetable stock
1 small white onion, chopped
60g/2oz/4 tbsp unsalted butter
450g/1lb arborio rice
$\frac{1}{2}$ bottle dry white wine
Salt and pepper

Place the chestnuts in a saucepan, cover with water, bring to the boil and cook slowly for about 20 minutes or until soft. Drain the chestnuts, allow to cool slightly, then peel them.
Heat the stock in a pan and keep on a slow boil.
In a large saucepan, fry the onion in half the butter over a low heat for about 3 minutes, or until translucent.
Add the rice and cook over a high heat until the rice is very hot, stirring constantly with a wooden spoon.
Add half the wine and let it evaporate almost completely. Add a ladleful of hot stock or enough to ensure that the rice is covered with a veil of liquid, and a little more wine. Keep adding the stock and wine about once every minute, always making sure the rice is covered. Cook for about 14 minutes from the moment when you first added the wine. After 10 minutes, add the whole chestnuts.
When the risotto is ready, remove from the heat, add the rest of the butter, and salt and pepper to taste. Cover and let stand for a couple of minutes. The rice should have a porridge-like consistency.
Pour into a warmed deep serving dish and serve immediately.

Serves 6

GNOCCHI DI PATATE E BARBABIETOLA

Potato and Beetroot Gnocchi

I usually use the beetroots from the garden which are not particularly big, probably due to dry soil, but I also buy them already cooked, as they are available in Italy, from vegetable shops or supermarkets. However, I carefully avoid the ones pre-cooked and packaged in plastic. Our small vegetable shops sell the ones that have been grown and cooked by the owners.

1kg/2 ¼ lb boiling potatoes
450g/1lb beetroots
210g/7oz/1 ¾ cups plain (all-purpose) flour
1 large egg
60g/2oz/4 tbsp unsalted butter
60g/2oz/4 tbsp freshly grated Parmesan cheese
Salt and pepper

Boil the potatoes and beetroots in separate pans in their skins until tender, then drain and peel. Pass the potatoes through a ricer or food mill while still warm. Repeat with the beetroots. Mix the two purées together in a bowl, add half the flour and the egg. Season to taste with salt and pepper.
Using floured hands roll the mixture out on a lightly floured surface into 'sausages' about 3cm/1in in diameter. Cut into pieces about the size of a walnut then roll into oval shapes. These can be kept on a floured tray for up to 1 hour.
Bring a large pan of water to the boil, add salt and the gnocchi, a few at a time. When they rise to the surface they are ready. While they are cooking, melt the butter in a pan. Remove the gnocchi from the water with a slotted spoon when they are ready, transfer to a warmed serving bowl and pour over the melted butter. Sprinkle with the Parmesan and salt and pepper to taste. Serve immediately.

Serves 6

PENNE ALLA SALSICCIA

Penne with Sausages

This is the best moment to eat sausages because traditionally, during harvest, the pig was killed to provide food for the workmen in the fields. A little drop of vinegar will balance well with the fat.

3 tbsp extra virgin olive oil
120g/4oz/½ cup fine dry breadcrumbs
3 garlic cloves, crushed with a fork
1 hot red chilli pepper
450g/1lb Italian pork sausages
1 tbsp red wine vinegar
600g/1 ¼ lb penne
Salt

Heat the oil in a pan over medium heat, add the breadcrumbs and the garlic and chilli, stirring constantly. Cook for about 3 minutes or until the breadcrumbs are lightly golden. Remove from the heat and set aside.
Split the sausages, remove the meat from the casings and crumble into a pan. Sauté over medium heat, stirring, for about 5 minutes. Add the vinegar and allow to evaporate. Meanwhile, bring a pan of water to the boil, add salt and the penne. Cook until very *al dente*—a couple of minutes less than it says on the packet.
Drain the pasta, toss with the cooked sausage meat in a warmed serving platter, sprinkle with the breadcrumb mixture and serve immediately.

Serves 6

POLENTA CON CREMA DI SEDANO

Polenta (Yellow Cornmeal) with Celery Cream

The best moment to eat polenta (yellow cornmeal) is in autumn when it has recently been ground. I prefer the coarse type, but sometimes I also use the finer, white version, a speciality from Veneto.

600g/1 ¼ lb white celery stalks
120ml/4fl oz/½ cup double (heavy) cream
300g/10oz/2 cups coarse polenta (yellow cornmeal)
White truffle, sliced into shavings (optional but important)
Salt and pepper

Peel the celery stalks, using a vegetable peeler or sharp knife to remove the strings.
Bring some water to the boil in a pan, add the celery stalks and cook until tender, about 10 minutes. Drain and purée in a blender. Add the cream to the purée and salt and pepper to taste and reserve.
Bring 1.5 litres/3 pints/6 cups water to the boil in a heavy based pan, add salt and the polenta (yellow cornmeal) in a steady stream, whisking constantly.
Cover and let cook for about 30 minutes.
Meanwhile reheat the celery cream. Pour the polenta (yellow cornmeal) into a warmed serving dish, cover with the celery cream and top with the truffle shavings, if using.

Serves 6

FETTUCCINE ALLE NOCCIOLE

Hazelnut Fettuccine

I usually buy the dry fettuccine if it is made by a good manufacturer, or I will use a fresh one made by myself. The ones to really avoid are the fresh commercially sold ones because they are far too thick.

300g/10oz hazelnuts (unshelled weight)
6 anchovy fillets in oil, drained
3 garlic cloves, chopped
6 tbsp extra virgin olive oil
2 tbsp fresh flat-leaf parsley, finely chopped
450g/1lb dried fettuccine
6 hard boiled quail's eggs
Salt and pepper

Preheat the oven to 200°C/400°F/Gas 6.
Shell the hazelnuts and toast them in the oven until golden, about 5 minutes. Wrap them in cling film (plastic wrap) and crush them with a pestle or rolling pin.
Mash the anchovies in a pan, add the garlic and oil and sauté over a medium heat for about 3 minutes or until the garlic is lightly golden. Add the parsley and remove from the heat.
Bring a pan of water to the boil, add salt and the fettuccine. Cook until very *al dente* (about 2 minutes less than it says on the packet), drain and transfer to a warmed serving dish. Toss the pasta with the anchovy and parsley oil, sprinkle with the crushed hazelnuts and garnish with the whole quails' eggs.
Serve immediately while very hot.

Serves 6

CREMA DI CIPOLLE E FUNGHI

Cream of Onion and Mushroom Soup

The onions that are planted in this season will be the last in my garden and from now on I will have to buy ones from the market. But some of the red ones will last for about one month if laid out on straw mats and kept in a cool place. White onions start sprouting earlier.

5 tbsp extra virgin olive oil
1kg/2 ¼ lb white onions, sliced
2 litres/3 ½ pints/8 cups vegetable stock
3 handfuls rice
300g/10oz fresh *porcini* mushrooms
1 tbsp finely chopped fresh flat-leaf parsley
Salt and pepper

Heat 3 tbsp of the oil in a pan, add the sliced onions and sauté over medium heat, stirring, for about 5 minutes or until lightly golden. Add the stock and the rice, bring to the boil, cover and simmer for about 2 hours over a very low heat. Check the salt.
Wipe the mushrooms clean. Heat the rest of the oil in a pan, add the mushrooms and sauté over a high heat, stirring, for about 5 minutes. Add salt, remove the mushrooms from the pan and allow to cool slightly.
Chop the mushrooms roughly and set aside.
Pass the onion soup through a foodmill or fine sieve into a clean pan and reheat. Transfer to a warmed soup tureen, add the mushrooms, sprinkle with parsley, add pepper to taste and serve.

Serves 6

MINESTRONE D'AUTUNNO

Autumn Minestrone

Just before the first frosts I like to make minestrone with what is still available in the garden. After that, the garden becomes sad, with only a few greens, cabbages and salad leaves left, although radicchio grows continuously.

3 tbsp extra virgin olive oil
90g/3oz pancetta, chopped
1 onion, diced
2 carrots, diced
1 celery stalk, diced
½ savoy cabbage, finely sliced
1 beetroot, diced
1 celeriac, peeled and diced
1 handful fresh thyme
6 slices coarse country bread
2 garlic cloves
Salt and pepper

Heat 1 tbsp oil in a pan, add the pancetta and sauté over a medium heat until golden.
Add the vegetables to the pan, mix well and sauté for a couple of minutes. Add the thyme and 2 litres/3½ pints/8 cups of water and a little salt. Cover, lower the heat and simmer gently for about 2 hours.
Toast the bread and slice the garlic cloves in half. Rub the toast with the garlic and put 1 slice in each individual soup bowl. Pour over the soup, sprinkle with the rest of the oil and some pepper and serve quite hot.

Serves 6

MINESTRA DI SEMOLINO E SPINACI
Semolina and Spinach Soup

Like cornmeal, semolina is also fresher now than in winter or spring, especially if you buy it from health food stores. Autumn spinach is tender but more flavoursome than the winter varieties.

1kg/2 1/4 lb fresh spinach
6 tbsp semolina
60g/2oz/4 tbsp unsalted butter
4 tbsp freshly grated Parmesan cheese
Salt and pepper

Clean and wash the spinach thoroughly, keeping the stems intact. Place the leaves in a pan with no extra water, cover and cook over a medium heat for about 3 minutes, stirring a couple of times.
Drain the spinach, reserving the liquid given off during cooking. Allow to cool slightly and chop.
Return to the pan with the reserved liquid and 1.5 litres/3 pints/6 cups water. Bring to the boil and add the semolina, whisking constantly. Cook for about 20 minutes.
Add salt and pepper to taste, the butter and the Parmesan cheese. Remove from the heat and mix well to blend the ingredients. Serve immediately.

Serves 6

MINESTRA DI RISO E RADICCHIO ROSSO
Red Radicchio and Rice Soup

With its slight bitterness, this is a nice soup with a different taste due to the smoky bacon. If you can find it, Italian smoked pancetta has less fat than bacon. The rich colour of the radicchio makes this soup one of my favourites.

90g/3oz smoked bacon, chopped
1 red onion, finely chopped
1 tbsp extra virgin olive oil
1kg/2 1/4 lb red radicchio, finely sliced
6 handfuls rice
Salt and pepper

Fry the bacon and onion in a large pan with the oil until the bacon is crispy, about 5 minutes, stirring constantly. Add the radicchio to the pan and cook for a minute.
Add 1.5 litres/3 pints/6 cups water and bring to the boil. Add the rice and cook until *al dente*, about 14 minutes. Add salt and pepper to taste and serve immediately.

Serves 6

MINESTRA DI PORRI E PATATE
Leek and Potato Soup

Sometimes instead of making this soup I place leeks and potatoes layered in a baking dish, covered with milk and lot of grated Parmesan cheese. After an hour of cooking in a medium oven this makes an alternative first course.

3 tbsp unsalted butter
1kg/2 1/4 lb leeks, cleaned and thinly sliced
1kg/2 1/4 lb potatoes, peeled and diced
1.5 litres/3 pints/6 cups vegetable stock
1 tbsp chopped fresh flat-leaf parsley
Salt and pepper

Heat the butter in a pan, add the leeks and sauté over a low heat, stirring often, for about 10 minutes. Add the potatoes and the stock and bring to the boil. Cook until tender, about 10 minutes. Add salt and pepper to taste and the parsley.
Pour into a warmed soup tureen and serve.

Serves 6

ZUPPA DI BIETOLE E FAGIOLI

Beet Leaf and Bean Soup

This is the moment when beets and Swiss chards are at their best. And maybe it is still possible to find some fresh beans to make the soup really perfect, but if not, the dried ones are a good substitute.

300g/10oz cannellini or other beans
1kg/2¼ lb beet leaves
60g/2oz pancetta, chopped
1 tbsp extra virgin olive oil
½ onion, chopped
½ carrot, chopped
½ celery stalk, chopped
1 handful fresh flat-leaf parsley, chopped
1 garlic clove, chopped
Salt and pepper

Place the beans in a pan, cover with plenty of water and bring to a slow boil. Cook for about 2 hours or until tender. Drain the beans and reserve the water. Finely slice the beet leaves and cook in a pan with 480ml/16fl oz/2 cups water for about 2 minutes. Drain the leaves, reserving the water.
Sauté the pancetta in the oil with the onion, carrot, celery, parsley and garlic, stirring often, for about 5 minutes. Add the beans, the beet leaves, half the reserved cooking water from the beans and all the cooking liquid from the beet leaves. Add salt and pepper to taste and simmer for about 10 minutes. The soup should be quite thick. Pour into a warmed soup tureen and serve.

Serves 6

CREMA DI ZUCCA AGLI AMARETTI

Pumpkin and Amaretto Soup

This is very popular in northern Italy, particularly in Mantua. If you like, you could serve this soup in half a pumpkin shell that has been hollowed out and cleaned.

2kg/4lb pumpkin
2 tbsp extra virgin olive oil
1 white onion, finely chopped
2 litres/4 pints/8 cups vegetable stock
6 amaretto biscuits (cookies)
Salt and pepper

Peel the pumpkin, discard the seeds and dice the pulp. Heat the oil in a pan, add the onion and cook over a low heat, stirring constantly until translucent, about 3 minutes. Add the pumpkin and sauté for about 5 minutes over a medium heat. Add the stock, bring to the boil and simmer until the pumpkin is tender, about 20 minutes.
Purée the contents of the pan in a blender. Transfer to a clean saucepan and reheat. The soup should not be too runny—if it is, let it cook for a few more minutes. Add salt and pepper to taste and pour into a warmed soup tureen.
Crush the amaretti and sprinkle over the top. Serve immediately.

Serves 6

MEAT AND FISH

LUMACHE AL VINO ROSSO

Snails with Red Wine

The garden in spring and autumn is full of snails that unfortunately love my vegetables, but as they are a wonderful food in themselves, I do not complain. I just pick them up, purify them for about one week and they are ready to be cooked.

2 tbsp extra virgin olive oil
1 garlic clove, chopped
½ onion, chopped
1 handful fresh flat-leaf parsley, chopped
1.5kg/3¼ lb unshelled snails, prepared for cooking
½ bottle red wine
1 celery stalk
1 carrot
Salt and pepper

Heat the oil in a pan, add the garlic, onion and parsley and sauté over a medium heat, stirring, until translucent, about 3 minutes. Add the snails, mix well and pour in the wine. Add the celery, carrot and salt and pepper to taste. Cover and cook over a low heat for about 2 hours, adding water if necessary to prevent the cooking juices from drying out.
Remove and discard the celery and carrot, transfer the snails and cooking juices to a warmed serving platter and serve.

Serves 6

FILETTI DI SOGLIOLA ALLE BIETOLE

Fillets of Sole with Beet Leaves

Beets are very soft in taste and are a nice complement to sole. Sometimes I will substitute them with the leaves of Swiss chard and use the stems for another dish, unless I still have some of them in my garden that are particularly small and tender, in which case I will also use the white part.

1kg/2¼ lb beet leaves
4 tbsp extra virgin olive oil
6 sole fillets, about 150g/5oz each
90g/3oz/6 tbsp plain (all-purpose) flour
1 tbsp unsalted butter
3 tbsp pine nuts
Salt and pepper

Bring a small amount of water to the boil in a pan. Add the beet leaves and a little salt and cook briefly. Drain the leaves, allow to cool slightly and squeeze out any excess water.
Heat 2 tbsp of the oil in a pan and sauté the leaves for a couple of minutes. Add salt and pepper to taste, set aside and keep warm.
Coat the sole fillets in the flour. Heat the remaining oil with the butter in a pan and sauté the fillets for 2 minutes on each side. Add salt and pepper to taste. Arrange the beet leaves on a warmed serving platter. Place the fillets over the leaves, sprinkle with the pine nuts and serve immediately.

Serves 6

SARDINE RIPIENE
Stuffed Sardines

Sardines are one of my favourite types of fish. I
remember when my children were small and we used
to have a sailing boat in Porto Ercole, the fishermen
would grill sardines, their first catch from the night,
offering them to us on a piece of bread early in the
morning. This was the best breakfast from times
forever lost as there is now a large harbour there.

60g/2oz dried *porcini* mushrooms
60g/2oz fresh soft breadcrumbs
1 large egg
4 tbsp freshly grated Parmesan cheese
1 tbsp dried oregano
1.5kg/3lb fresh sardines
3 tbsp extra virgin olive oil
30g/1oz/2 tbsp fine dry breadcrumbs
Salt and pepper

Preheat the oven to 200°C/400°F/Gas 6.
Soak the *porcini* in water for about 30 minutes or until
soft. Drain, filter the soaking water and reserve for a
stock or risotto. Squeeze out any excess water from
the mushrooms and chop. Place in a
mixing bowl.
Soak the fresh breadcrumbs in water for about
5 minutes. Drain, squeeze out any excess water and
add to the mushrooms. Add the egg, the Parmesan,
oregano and salt and pepper to taste and mix well.
Remove the heads from the sardines and discard. Slit
the sardines in half horizontally and remove any
bones. Spread the bread and mushroom mixture over
half the sardines, then cover the filling with the
remaining halves.
Brush a baking dish with half the oil and place the
sardines in the dish. Sprinkle with the dry
breadcrumbs and the rest of the oil. Cook in the oven
for about 15 minutes, or until slightly golden on top.
Serve very hot.

Serves 6

CODA DI ROSPO
AL GINEPRO
Monkfish with Juniper Berries

This is the time to find juniper berries, when they are
ripe and purple, but you have to use gloves because
the needles of the plant are unpleasant and the berries
have to be cleaned well before they can be stored in
pots for the winter. We use them for cooking with
wild boar, pheasant, different fish and
also spaghetti.

3 tbsp extra virgin olive oil
3 red onions, finely sliced
2 tbsp juniper berries
1.5kg/3lb monkfish, trimmed and skinned
1 glass dry white wine (about 120ml/4fl oz/¹/₂ cup)
Salt and pepper

Preheat the oven to 170°C/350°F/Gas 4.
Brush an oblong casserole dish with half the oil.
Cover the base of the dish with half the onions and
half the juniper berries. Add a little salt and pepper
and place the fish on top. Cover with the rest of the
onions, berries, remaining oil and more salt and
pepper. Pour over the wine, place in the oven and
cook for about 45 minutes.
Transfer the fish to a warmed serving platter,
surround with the onions, juniper berries and the
cooking juices and serve.

Serves 6

CINGHIALE AI MIRTILLI ROSSI
Wild Boar with Cranberries

Wild boars have always been popular in Tuscany, where they are cooked in many different ways. The most famous method is described in my book *The Renaissance of Italian Cooking*, and is called *Cinghiale in Dolceforte* as it is cooked in a sweet-and-sour sauce with garlic and chocolate. Here, it is accompanied by cranberries, which still grow in autumn if it is particularly warm. You could use the back legs of the boar for this dish.

1.5kg/3lb wild boar
½ bottle red wine
½ wine glass red wine vinegar (4 tbsp)
2 onions, sliced
3 carrots, sliced
3 celery stalks, sliced
1 tsp cloves
1 tsp juniper berries
1 tsp black peppercorns
1 tbsp unsalted butter
2 tbsp extra virgin olive oil
1 tbsp cornflour (cornstarch)
Grated zest of 1 organic orange
150g/5oz cranberries
Salt

Place the wild boar in a large bowl and pour over the wine and vinegar to cover the meat. Add 1 onion, 1 carrot, 1 celery stalk, the cloves, juniper berries and peppercorns. Cover and leave to marinate for 2 days in the refrigerator.
Drain the meat, reserving the marinade. Strain the marinade through a colander. Discard the vegetables and spices.
Dry the meat on a clean cloth. Heat the butter and oil in a large flameproof casserole. Add the meat and fry over a high heat, turning, until golden brown all over, about 10 minutes. Add the remaining onion, carrots and celery. Pour in the strained wine, cover and cook on the hob over a low heat for about 3 hours, adding water when necessary to prevent the cooking juices from drying out. Add salt to taste.
Drain the wild boar, reserving the cooking juices. Set aside and keep warm. Skim the fat from the surface of the cooking juices, then strain them through a fine sieve or a mouli into a clean pan. Add the cornflour (cornstarch) to the juices, whisking as you go, to avoid lumps. Add the orange zest, the cranberries and a little water to thin the sauce. Cook for about 10 minutes over a low heat until you have a smooth sauce.
Slice the boar, transfer to a warmed serving platter, cover with the sauce and serve.
Serves 6

TONNO AI FUNGHI
Tuna and Porcini Mushrooms

I like to use fresh tuna, but sometimes I use canned tuna, sprinkled at the last moment on top of mushrooms, which is really delicious.

3 tbsp extra virgin olive oil
300g/10oz fresh *porcini* or shiitake mushrooms
450g/1lb canned tomatoes, drained
1 tbsp dried marjoram
6 slices fresh tuna fillet, about 240g/6oz each
Salt and pepper

Preheat the oven to 200°C/400°F/Gas 6.
Brush a roasting tin (pan) with half the oil. Wipe the mushrooms clean and slice. Scatter the mushroom slices over the base of the roasting (tin) pan and cover with the tomatoes. Sprinkle with the marjoram and top with the tuna. Add salt and pepper to taste and the rest of the oil. Cook for about 15 minutes or until done. The flesh should become white and opaque.
Transfer to a warmed serving platter and serve.
Serves 6

POLPETTE ALLE MELE
Meatballs with Apples

Meatballs are very popular in Italy and we make many types. Usually we mix the meat with some breadcrumbs softened in milk, but this variation with apples gives a nice tartness.

2 eating apples, such as Golden Delicious
900g/2lb minced beef
1 tbsp fresh flat-leaf parsley, chopped
2 large eggs
120g/4oz/1 cup plain (all-purpose) flour
2 tbsp extra virgin olive oil
1 tbsp unsalted butter
1 glass dry white wine, about 120ml/4fl oz/$\frac{1}{2}$ cup
Salt and pepper

Peel the apples and grate the flesh.
Mix the grated apple with the minced beef, the parsley, the eggs and salt and pepper to taste.
Divide the mixture into 12 portions and form into meatballs using your hands. Flatten them slightly so they look like hamburgers. Coat lightly with flour.
Heat the oil and butter in a pan, add the meatballs and sauté over a high heat for about 3 minutes on one side and 2 minutes on the other. Add the wine to the pan and leave to evaporate almost completely.
Transfer the meatballs to a serving platter and serve.

Serves 6

CAPRIOLO AL MARSALA
Venison with Marsala

Since our woods have become inhabited by deer in recent years, this is more popular in the north-east of Italy. So we are just beginning to cook it in the south but in a different way. Marsala, with its strong taste, goes very well with the sweet taste of the meat.

1.5kg/3lb leg of venison, bone in
1 tbsp unsalted butter
2 tbsp extra virgin olive oil
1 handful fresh sage leaves
6 tbsp Marsala
Salt and pepper

Preheat the oven to 170°C/350°F/Gas 4.
Trim the venison leg and tie with kitchen string.
Sprinkle the meat with salt and pepper to taste. Heat the butter and oil in a roasting tin (pan), add the venison and sage and cook on the hob over a medium heat, turning, until golden brown on all sides, about 10 minutes.
Transfer the roasting tin (pan) to the oven and cook for another 45 minutes. Remove from the oven, transfer the meat to a warmed plate, cover with (aluminum) foil and leave to rest.
Pour the Marsala into the roasting tin (pan) and deglaze the cooking juices over a medium heat, stirring, until the Marsala has evaporated. Strain the sauce.
Untie the meat and cut into slices. Place the slices on a warmed serving platter, pour over the sauce and serve immediately.

Serves 6

PERNICI AI FUNGHI
Partridge with Mushrooms

It is not easy to buy partridges in Tuscany, but when I find them I like to cook them with a little pancetta which gives a tenderness to the meat and a lovely taste. In the end, I just remove the fat if there is too much, before adding the Cognac.

6 partridges, prepared for the oven
6 paper-thin pancetta slices
1 tbsp unsalted butter
5 tbsp extra virgin olive oil
4 tbsp Cognac
300g/10oz fresh *porcini* mushrooms
1 handful fresh mint
3 garlic cloves
Salt and pepper

Preheat the oven to 200°C/400°F/Gas 6.
Clean the partridges and sprinkle with a little salt. Wrap each partridge in a slice of pancetta, tie with kitchen string and place in a roasting tin (pan) with the butter and 2 tbsp of the oil. Cook in the oven for about 20 minutes, turning them once.
Remove the string from the partridges and place in a deep heatproof serving dish. Heat the Cognac in a saucepan and flame it (set fire to the surface with a match, standing well back as you do so). Pour the flaming Cognac over the partridges. Cover with (aluminum) foil and leave to rest.
Wipe the mushrooms clean and slice them. Heat the rest of the oil in a pan and sauté the mushrooms with the mint and garlic for about 5 minutes, stirring a couple of times. Discard the mint and garlic and add salt and pepper to taste.
Transfer the partridges to a warmed serving platter, surround with the mushrooms and serve.

Serves 6

LEPRE ALLE CILIEGIE
Hare with Cherries

As the hare has quite a strong flavour, the sweetness of the cherries is very appropriate and gives this dish a milder taste.

1.5kg/3lb hare, bone in, prepared for the oven
120g/4oz/1 cup plain (all-purpose) flour
1 tbsp unsalted butter
2 tbsp extra virgin olive oil
1 tbsp chopped shallots
1 tbsp chopped carrot
1 tbsp chopped celery
1 tbsp chopped fresh flat-leaf parsley
1/2 bottle dry white wine
1 bay leaf
1 tsp black peppercorns
3 fresh thyme sprigs
240g/8oz cherries in syrup, drained
Salt

Preheat the oven to 170°C/350°F/Gas 4.
Cut the hare into serving pieces and dredge in the flour.
Heat the butter and oil in a roasting tin (pan), add the hare and sauté for a few minutes until golden brown. Add the shallots, carrot, celery, parsley, wine, bay leaf, peppercorns and thyme. Sprinkle with salt to taste and cook in the oven, uncovered, for about 1 hour, turning the pieces a couple of times.
Transfer the hare pieces to a serving platter. Heat the cooking juices in the pan over a medium heat and simmer until thickened. Add the cherries and heat through.
Pour the sauce over the hare and serve.

Serves 6

VEGETABLES AND SALADS

BIETOLE IN PADELLA ALL'AGLIO
Beet Leaves Sautéed with Garlic

Beets can be easily substituted with the green part of Swiss chard or spinach, but they have a milder taste and are more tender. Sometimes I will add a few raisins to go with the anchovies.

1.5kg/3lb beet leaves
3 tbsp extra virgin olive oil
3 garlic cloves, chopped
3 anchovy fillets in oil, drained
Salt

Wash and trim the beet leaves, reserving the stems. Place a little water in a pan and bring to the boil. Add the leaves and blanch for a couple of minutes. Drain and pass under cold running water to stop the cooking process and to preserve their green colour. Squeeze out any excess water.
Heat the oil in a pan and add the garlic and anchovy fillets. Sauté over a medium heat until the garlic is translucent, about 3 minutes. Add the beet leaves and cook for about 5 minutes, stirring from time to time. Add salt to taste, transfer to a warmed serving platter and serve.

Serves 6

BARBABIETOLE AL RAFANO
Beetroots with Horseradish

Horseradish is a pest in the garden—the more you remove it, the more it grows. But I like to use it as an accompaniment to beetroots which have a sweet taste. I will often prepare a few pots to give as gifts to my friends at Christmas.

3 beetroots, about 150g/5oz each
1 small bottle of light beer or lager
240ml/8fl oz/1 cup double (heavy) cream
2 tbsp finely grated horseradish
Salt

Preheat the oven to 170°C/350°F/Gas 4.
Wash and trim the beetroots, and place in a casserole dish with the beer or lager. Cover and cook in the oven until tender, about 1½ hours, adding a little water if the liquid evaporates completely.
Peel and dice the cooked beetroot and transfer to a serving bowl. Leave to cool.
Place the cream and horseradish in a pan and reduce over a low heat for about 10 minutes. Add salt to taste and pour the sauce over the beetroot. Allow to cool to room temperature and serve.

Serves 6

INSALATA DI PATATE ALLA BIRRA
Potato Salad with Beer

The combination of potatoes and beer is delicious and very unique. At this time, the potatoes are new and I sometimes use the small ones that are similar in size. I do not even peel them, but just brush them well under water.

6 large boiling potatoes
240ml/8fl oz/1 cup beer
4 tbsp extra virgin olive oil
1 tsp finely grated horseradish
Salt

Boil the potatoes in their skins until tender, peel them and dice while still hot.
Transfer to a bowl and pour the beer over. Leave the potatoes to absorb the beer until completely cool, mixing them carefully from time to time.
Pour off the excess beer, add the oil and salt to taste and sprinkle over the horseradish.
Serve at room temperature.

Serves 6

CROSTONI AI FUNGHI

Toasts with Mushrooms

There are many variations of *bruschetta*, or toasted bread, but I like these particularly because they can easily substitute for the main dish for an evening meal. If that is the case, I will prepare a couple of toasts for each person intead of just one.

6 slices country bread
5 tbsp extra virgin olive oil
450g/1lb fresh *porcini* mushrooms
3 garlic cloves
1 handful fresh mint leaves
6 slices fontina cheese,
about the same size as the bread slices
Salt and pepper

Preheat the oven to 200°C/400°F/Gas 6.
Brush the bread slices on both sides with 2 tbsp of the oil and toast in the oven until lightly golden, turning once. Set aside.
Wipe the mushrooms clean and slice them. Sauté the garlic in the remaining oil for about 2 minutes over a medium heat. Add the mushrooms, salt and pepper to taste and cook for about 5 minutes, stirring a couple of times. Add the mint leaves and remove from the heat. Remove and discard the garlic.
Place 1 cheese slice on each piece of toast and put in the oven for a couple of minutes to reheat and melt the cheese slightly. Arrange on a serving platter and divide the mushroom mixture among the toasts.
Serve immediately.

Serves 6

CAVOLINI DI BRUXELLES ALLE CASTAGNE

Brussels Sprouts with Chestnuts

Chestnuts take a long time to prepare because they have to be peeled very well, but there is such a large quantity in our woods that I cook them quite often.

450g/1lb fresh chestnuts
450g/1lb Brussels sprouts
60g/2oz/4 tbsp unsalted butter
4 tbsp freshly grated fontina cheese
1 tsp grated nutmeg
Salt

Make an incision in the chestnuts with a sharp knife.
Place in a pan, cover with water and bring to the boil.
Cook until tender, about 20 minutes. Drain the chestnuts and peel them. Set aside and keep warm.
Cook the Brussels sprouts in boiling salted water for about 10 minutes, then drain. Mix the chestnuts and sprouts together in a serving bowl.
Melt the butter in a saucepan, but do not let it brown.
Sprinkle the sprouts and chestnuts with the cheese and the nutmeg and pour over the melted butter. Add salt to taste. Serve immediately.

Serves 6

SPIEDINI DI FUNGHI

Mushroom Skewers

As I use only the caps in this recipe, I will use the stems later sautéed in a risotto or sliced finely in a soup to give a special taste.

18 fresh *porcini* mushrooms with small caps, all roughly the same size
3 Italian pork sausages, each about 7.5cm/3in long
12 bay leaves
120ml/4fl oz/½ cup extra virgin olive oil
Juice of 1 lemon
2 tbsp finely chopped fresh flat-leaf parsley
Salt and pepper

Preheat the grill (broiler) to medium.
Slice the caps from the mushroom stems and wipe the caps clean. Cut each sausage into 4 pieces.
Take 6 metal skewers and thread each one with 3 mushroom caps, 2 sausage pieces and 2 bay leaves, alternating them along the skewer and beginning and ending with the mushroom caps.
Brush the skewers with a little of the oil and cook under the grill (broiler) for about 10 minutes, turning a few times, until the sausage is completely cooked.
Meanwhile, mix the remaining oil in a bowl with the lemon juice, the parsley and a little salt and pepper.
Arrange the skewers on a serving dish, and serve them with the parsley dressing.

Serves 6

PORRI ALLA CREMA DI FORMAGGIO

Leeks in Cheese Sauce

When I have guests, I often serve this dish as a main course in the evening or as a first course for lunch instead of pasta or rice. To be sure that the leeks are washed well, it is better to cut them partly lengthwise along the green stem so that it opens and and is easier to get rid of the dirt.

1kg/2¼ lb leeks
240ml/8fl oz/1 cup double (heavy) cream
120g/4oz/⅔ cup grated fontina cheese
Salt and pepper

Trim the leeks and clean very carefully under running water. Keep most of the green part. Cook them in boiling water until tender, 10–15 minutes, depending on their size.
Bring the cream to the boil in a pan, add the cheese and salt and pepper to taste. Mix until melted and reserve.
Drain the leeks and place in a warmed serving dish.
Pour the cream over the top and serve immediately.

Serves 6

BREADS AND DESSERTS

SCHIACCIATA CON L'UVA

Flatbread with Grapes

This dessert can be too much if it is has walnuts and raisins, but this more simple version is one of my favourites. I do it often for the grandchildren during harvest seasons, with dark or even white grapes.

30g/1oz/2 tbsp fresh yeast
360g/12oz/3 cups plain (all-purpose) flour,
plus extra for dusting
90g/3oz/6 tbsp granulated sugar
300g/10oz black seedless grapes

Dissolve the yeast in 210ml/7fl oz/⅞ cup lukewarm water, for about 10 minutes or until it starts foaming.
Sift the flour into a bowl and make a well at the centre. Add 2 tbsp sugar, then gradually add the water and the yeast mixture, stirring with fork in a circular motion to form a dough.
Transfer the dough to a lightly floured worksurface.
Work with the palms of your hands for about 3 minutes, until smooth. Form into a ball and put in a lightly floured bowl. Cover tightly with cling film (plastic wrap). Leave to rise until doubled in size, for 1 hour or more—the time it takes will depend on how warm the room is.
Knock back (punch down) the dough and roll out into a circle about 23cm/9in in diameter. Transfer to a floured baking sheet (cookie tray), dot with the grapes and sprinkle over the remaining sugar. Leave to rise for 20 minutes more.
Preheat the oven to 200°C/400°F/Gas 6.
Cook in the oven for about 30 minutes or until slightly golden on top. Allow to cool and serve.

Serves 6

PAN COI SANTI

All Saints' Day Bread

This is a very special Tuscan bread made with black pepper and is prepared for All Saints' day, but it is a must anytime during the autumn. You can buy it in almost every *panetteria*, or bakery, but this version by Betty from Gaiole is very special. We eat this for breakfast and for *merenda*, or teatime.

60g/2oz raisins
30g/1oz/2 tbsp fresh yeast
90g/3oz shelled walnuts, chopped
4 tbsp extra virgin olive oil
350g/12oz/3 cups wholemeal (wholewheat) flour
1 tbsp granulated sugar
1 tsp freshly ground black pepper
Salt

Soak the raisins in water for 30 minutes. Drain.
Dissolve the yeast in 210ml/7fl oz/⅞ cup lukewarm water for about 10 minutes or until it starts foaming.
Fry the walnuts in 3 tbsp of the oil for about 3 minutes, stirring. Set aside.
Sift the flour into a bowl and make a well in the centre. Gradually add the water and yeast mixture and stir in a circular motion with a fork to form a dough.
Transfer the dough to a lightly floured worksurface.
Work with the palms of your hands for about 3 minutes until smooth. Form into a ball and place in a lightly floured bowl. Cover tightly with cling film (plastic wrap). Leave to rise until doubled in size, for 1 hour or more—the time it takes will depend on how warm the room is.
Preheat the oven to 200°C/400°F/Gas 6.
Knock back (punch down) the dough and sprinkle over the walnuts and raisins, sugar and pepper and a little salt to taste. Form into a ball and flatten a little.
Transfer to a floured baking sheet (cookie tray). Leave to rise again for about 20 minutes. Cook in the oven for about 40 minutes.
Leave to cool and serve.

Serves 6

CROSTATA DI NOCI

Walnut Tart

When walnuts are still tender before San Giovanni on 24 June, I make a liqueur called *nocino* and when they are ready in autumn I prepare this delicious tart. When walnuts are fresh it is often easier to get rid of the inside skin.

FOR THE PASTRY:
300g/10oz/2 ½ cups plain (all-purpose) flour,
plus extra for dusting
120g/4oz/8 tbsp unsalted butter, chilled and cut into small
pieces, plus extra for greasing
120g/4oz/²⁄₃ cup granulated sugar
3 large egg yolks
FOR THE FILLING:
3 large eggs, separated
120g/4oz/²⁄₃ cup granulated sugar
120g/4oz shelled walnuts, finely chopped

To make the pastry, heap the flour on a worksurface, add the butter and work the mixture with your fingertips until it has the consistency of crumbs. Add the sugar and egg yolks and knead quickly to form a smooth dough. Shape the dough into a ball, cover with cling film (plastic wrap) and leave to rest in the refrigerator for about 1 hour.

Preheat the oven to 170°C/350°F/Gas 4. Prepare the filling by beating the egg yolks with the sugar in a bowl until foamy. Beat the whites separately until stiff. Add the walnuts to the yolks and sugar and gently fold in the whites.

Grease and flour a 25cm/10in tart tin (pan). Roll out the dough with a rolling pin on a floured surface to make a circle large enough to line the tin (pan). Trim the pastry, cover with the walnut mixture and cook for about 40 minutes or until golden. Remove the tart from the tin (pan), allow to cool on a wire rack and serve at room temperature.

Serves 6

CANNOLI DI MELE, PERE E MELOGRANO

Cannoli of Apples, Pears and Pomegranates

All the flavour of the season is in this dessert, which is very light and perfect for a lovely lunch. Pomegranates are becoming more and more popular in Italy and are often used to complement fish or meat also.

2 Golden Delicious apples
2 Bosch pears
2 pomegranates
30g/1oz/2 tbsp unsalted butter, plus extra for greasing
3 tbsp granulated sugar
1 large egg
300g/10oz puff pastry

Peel, core and dice the apples and pears. Halve the pomegranates and scoop out the seeds. Sauté the diced apples and pears with the butter and sugar over a low heat for a few minutes, until just tender. Add the pomegranate seeds and leave to cool completely. Beat the egg and mix with the fruit. Roll out the puff pastry on a lightly floured worksurface into a rectangle about 0.5cm/⅛in thick and divide into 6 squares each about 7.5cm/3in.

Preheat the oven to 200°C/400°F/Gas 6. Spread the fruit mixture over the squares and roll them up into cigar shapes, enclosing the fruit completely. Place on a lightly greased baking sheet (cookie tray) and cook in the oven for about 10 minutes or until golden and puffed up.

Leave to cool before serving.

Serves 6

BUDINO DI ARANCE
Orange Mould

This is one of the biggest successes of a very good friend of mine, Grazia Montesi, who is not only a wonderful cook but also an expert antique dealer. Her shop in Via Marsala in Milan is not only a nice place to find particular objects but to also exchange nice food ideas.

2 thin-skinned organic oranges
5 large eggs, separated
150g/5oz/1 cup less 2 tbsp granulated sugar, plus 180g/6oz/1 cup for caramelizing the mould
30g/1oz/2 tbsp plain (all-purpose) flour
4 tbsp Grand Marnier

Preheat the oven to 170°C/350°F/Gas 4.
Place the oranges in a pan, cover with water and bring to the boil. Simmer over a low heat for 15 minutes. Leave to cool, drain and chop very finely in a blender or a food processor.
Beat the egg whites with a fork to soft peaks. Beat the yolks separately. Fold the sugar, the flour and the Grand Marnier into the yolks. Gently fold in the egg whites and add the oranges.
Place the remaining sugar in a heavy-based saucepan and heat gently until golden brown and caramelized. Using a pastry brush, coat a 2 litre/4 pint/8 cup ring mould with the caramel. Leave to cool.
Pour in the orange cream, place the mould on a baking sheet and cook in the oven for about 1 hour, until set.
Invert on a serving platter, carefully remove the mould and serve lukewarm or at room temperature.

Serves 6

MONTEBIANCO
Chestnut Dessert

This is definitively one of the few desserts I love, because it reminds me of my childhood when it was prepared by my parents' home chef, Anna. The season for this dessert is short unfortunately, because chestnuts have a short life, like truffles. Also it is a dessert that is not really found in restaurants, but more in family cooking.

600g/1¼ lb fresh chestnuts
240ml/8fl oz/1 cup milk
6 tbsp icing (powdered) sugar
480ml/1 pint/2 cups double (heavy) cream
1 tbsp cocoa powder

Place the chestnuts in a pan, cover with water and bring to the boil. Cook until tender, about 20 minutes.
Drain and peel the chestnuts and place in a pan with the milk. Bring to the boil, breaking the chestnuts with a wooden spoon to let them absorb the milk evenly. Simmer gently, stirring constantly, until you have a purée. Remove from the heat, add the sugar and mix well.
Pass the mixture through a foodmill with large holes or a potato masher to form 'little worms', directly over a serving dish—try to shape the mixture into a mound or pyramid. Beat the cream to stiff peaks and spoon over the chestnut mound to cover.
Sift the cocoa powder over the cream. Serve at room temperature or chilled.

Serves 6

FEAST FOR THE GRAPE HARVEST

CROCCHETTE DI SPINACI E PROSCIUTTO
Spinach and Ham Croquettes

In Coltibuono, when we have almost finished the harvest, we prepare a feast for lunch with a menu consisting almost entirely of fingerfood. Only one dish will be generally served with a plate and fork. My grandchildren will join the harvesters and a few of them are allowed to help in cutting the grapes. These croquettes are a special treat for them.

1kg/2¼ lb fresh spinach
210g/7oz cooked ham
1 handful coarse fresh breadcrumbs
(from country bread, crusts removed)
1 glass of milk (120ml/4fl oz/½ cup)
3 large eggs
4 tbsp freshly grated Parmesan cheese
Pinch of grated nutmeg
360g/12oz/2 cups fine dry breadcrumbs
1 litre/1¾ pints/4 cups oil, for deep-frying
Salt and pepper

Wash the spinach, place in a pan with a little water and cook for a couple of minutes until soft. Drain, allow to cool slightly and squeeze out the excess water. Finely chop the spinach and the ham together. Soak the fresh breadcrumbs in the milk until soft, squeeze dry and mix in a bowl with the ham and spinach, 1 egg, the Parmesan cheese, the nutmeg and salt and pepper to taste. Using your hands, form into ovals about 5cm/2in long.
Beat the remaining eggs in a deep dish and put the dry breadcrumbs into another one. Dip the ovals in the egg and coat with the breadcrumbs.
Heat the oil in a deep frying pan until it reaches 170°C/350°F on a kitchen thermometer. Fry the croquettes in the oil, a few at a time, until lightly golden. Drain on paper towels and serve immediately.

Serves 6

PIZZETTE AI FUNGHI E MOZZARELLA
Mini Pizzas with Mushrooms and Mozzarella

Small pizzas are easier to serve than big ones, and then there is not a problem with the portions.

360g/12oz/3 cups plain (all-purpose) flour,
plus extra for dusting
30g/1oz/2 tbsp fresh yeast
300g/10oz fresh *porcini* mushrooms
2 tbsp extra virgin olive oil
300g/10oz buffalo mozzarella
1 tbsp dried oregano
Salt and pepper

Preheat the oven to 200°C/400°F/Gas 6.
Sift the flour into a bowl. Place the yeast in a cup or bowl with 240ml/8fl oz/1 cup lukewarm water and leave to dissolve for about 10 minutes.
Add the water and yeast to the flour, a little at a time, mixing with a fork in a circular motion until a dough is formed. Transfer the dough to a lightly floured worksurface and work with the palms of your hand to form a ball. Place the dough in a lightly floured bowl and cover tightly with cling film (plastic wrap). Leave to rise until doubled in size, 1 or 2 hours depending on the room temperature.
Wipe the mushrooms clean and slice them. Heat 2 tbsp of the oil in a pan and cook the mushrooms over a medium heat for about 5 minutes, stirring a couple of times. Add salt and pepper to taste.
Slice the mozzarella.
Knock back (punch down) the dough and divide into 6 portions the size of tennis balls. Flatten the balls with your hands to circles about 15cm/7in in diameter. Transfer to a lightly floured baking sheet (cookie tray). Leave to rise again for 20 minutes. Top the dough circles with the mushrooms and the mozzarella, sprinkle with the oregano and cook in the oven for about 10 minutes. Serve immediately.

Makes 6

FRITTATA DI SALSICCIA E PATATE
Potato and Sausage Frittata

Usually I prepare this *frittata* with dried *porcini* mushrooms that I always keep handy in my kitchen, but when I have time I also use sautéed fresh mushrooms for this dish, but not too many because the most important ingredient are the sausages that Vincenzo, the famous Gaiole butcher, prepares daily.

1 handful dried *porcini* mushrooms
300g/10oz Italian pork sausages
4 tbsp extra virgin olive oil
450g/1lb potatoes, peeled and diced
120g/4oz fontina cheese, diced
6 large eggs, separated
Salt and pepper

Cover the mushrooms with water and soak for about 30 minutes until soft, then drain and chop roughly, reserving the water. Filter the soaking water and freeze for use in another dish, such as risotto or soup.
Preheat the oven to 170°C/350°F/Gas 4.
Split the sausages, remove the meat from the casings and chop it finely.
Heat 3 tbsp of the oil in a pan, add the sausage meat and the potatoes. Sauté over a medium heat, shaking the pan often or stirring carefully, until the potatoes are soft and barely golden.
Brush a porcelain soufflé dish with the rest of the oil, distribute the potato and sausage meat mixture over the base and sprinkle over the cheese.
Beat the egg yolks with a little salt and pepper, then beat the whites separately until just stiff. Gently fold the yolks into the whites with a spoon, a little at a time, and pour the mixture over the potatoes and sausage meat then add the mushrooms. Mix everything together very gently. Cook in the oven for about 15 minutes or until the eggs puff up and the surface is lightly golden.
Serve immediately.

Serves 6

FUNGHI RIPIENI FRITTI
Deep-fried, Stuffed Porcini Mushrooms

One of the best Tuscan dishes is *fritto misto*, consisting mainly of vegetables and mushrooms from this region. In autumn, it is made with aubergines (eggplants), the first artichokes and potatoes.

12 fresh *porcini* mushrooms
3 garlic cloves, finely chopped
90g/3oz cooked ham, finely chopped
1 handful fresh flat-leaf parsley, finely chopped
1 handful fresh breadcrumbs
1 glass milk (120ml/4fl oz/½ cup)
3 tbsp freshly grated Parmesan cheese
120g/4oz/1 cup plain (all-purpose) flour
2 large eggs, beaten in a deep dish
300g/10oz/1²/₃ cup fine dry breadcrumbs
1 litre/2 pints/4 cups oil, for deep-frying
Salt and pepper

Separate the mushroom caps from the stems. Wipe the mushrooms clean, chop the stems and mix with the chopped garlic, ham and parsley.
Soak the fresh breadcrumbs in the milk for about 10 minutes, squeeze dry and add to the mushroom, ham and parsley mixture. Add the Parmesan cheese, mix well and add salt and pepper to taste.
Use the mixture to fill 6 of the mushroom caps. Cover with the remaining caps and press lightly to enclose the filling. Coat the stuffed mushrooms in the flour, dip them in the beaten eggs, then coat with the dry breadcrumbs.
Heat the oil in a pan until the temperature reaches 170°C/350°F on a kitchen thermometer. Deep-fry the mushroom caps for about 3 minutes on each side or until lightly golden. Drain on kitchen paper and serve immediately while very hot.

Serves 6

POLENTA CON IL COSTOLECCIO

Polenta (Yellow Cornmeal) with Spareribs

Spareribs, or *costoleccio*, is the most important dish in Tuscany and is very popular in autumn.

1.5kg/3lb 5oz pork spareribs
3 tbsp extra virgin olive oil
90g/3oz pancetta, finely chopped
1 onion, finely chopped
1 carrot, finely chopped
1 celery stalk, finely chopped
1 handful fresh flat-leaf parsley, finely chopped
450g/1lb canned tomatoes
300g/10oz/2 cups coarse polenta (yellow cornmeal)
4 tbsp freshly grated Parmesan cheese
Salt and pepper

Separate the spareribs. Put the oil in a pan, add the pancetta with the vegetables and parsley and fry over a low heat until translucent, stirring constantly, for about 5 minutes.
Add the spareribs and fry for a few minutes more. Add the tomatoes with their juice and salt and pepper to taste. Cover and simmer over a low heat for about 2 hours, adding a little water every now and then to prevent the cooking juices from drying out.
Bring 1.5 litres/3 pints/6 cups water to the boil in a heavy-based pan, add salt and the polenta (yellow cornmeal) in a stream, whisking constantly. Cover and cook over a low heat for about 30 minutes.
Pour the polenta (yellow cornmeal) into a warmed, deep serving dish and arrange the spareribs over the top. Sprinkle with the Parmesan cheese and serve immediately.

Serves 6

POLPETTE ALLA VERZA

Hamburgers with Savoy Cabbage

I like this particular version of hamburgers, which is very Italian, and we often eat it without the bread. Sometimes I would add to the meat instead some soft breadcrumbs that have been soaked in milk and squeezed. They create a lovely soft texture, but the meat has to be sautéed a little longer.

300g/10oz caul fat
900g/2lb minced beef
6 savoy cabbage leaves
3 tbsp grainy Dijon mustard
2 tbsp unsalted butter
1 tbsp extra virgin olive oil
Salt and pepper

Soak the caul fat in water for about 30 minutes. Drain and cut into 6 pieces.
Divide the meat into 6 portions and shape into 6 hamburgers.
Bring a saucepan of water to the boil. Blanch the cabbage leaves in the water, one at a time, for about 2 minutes each. Drain and place on top of the pieces of caul fat. Spread the mustard over the cabbage leaves and top with the hamburgers. Bring the cabbage leaves and caul fat up to enclose the meat like a parcel and secure with kitchen string.
Heat the butter and oil in a large pan, add the hamburgers and cook over a high heat for about 2 minutes on each side. Remove the string, sprinkle with salt and pepper to taste and serve immediately.

Serves 6

UVA ALLO CHAMPAGNE

Grapes with Champagne

For once for this harvest recipe, we use champagne instead of white wine—it will make a good accompaniment to the meal and create a lovely ending to a beautiful day.

1.2kg/3lb red and white grapes
6 tbsp granulated sugar
1 bottle champagne

Carefully peel the grapes and place in a serving bowl. Sprinkle with the sugar and refrigerate for about 2 hours. Keep the champagne well chilled. Before serving pour the champagne over the grapes.

Serves 6

INTRODUCTION

According to the farmer's almanac winter may not come until 22 December, but I always feel it upon us towards late November. By then the limpid light of autumn has dimmed and the days are dull. Darkness descends early and evenings turn cold. Overnight, or so it seems, the chill in the air has stripped the vineyards of their autumn colours and the landscape lies barren. Farmers hurry to pick the last of their olives before the frost gets to them first. Fires have long been burning in hearths and in the fields they are making bonfires with the leaves and cuttings from the vines. The smell of wood smoke is comforting. We usually have to wait until January and February for the return of brilliant days but they come with ice and snow.

In the market the cornucopia of autumnal plenty has perished but by no means are the stalls bare. In fact, right at this time one of Italy's great gastronomic delights, the prestigious and precious *tartufo bianco*, the white truffle, is coming into the fullness of its

short season. Its Latin name is *Tuber magnatum pico*, the Great Pico Tuber, named after the eighteenth-century botanist who first classified it. The colour of the white truffle actually varies from a yellowish grey to beige. It is called white because of the contrast it makes to the black truffle (*Tuber melanosporum*), which looks like a warty piece of coal. The black truffle, much valued in France, also grows in Italy, where it is called *tartufo di Norcia*, a city in Umbria, which is also their capital. We find white truffles superior both in aroma and taste and the international truffle trade seems to agree. A white truffle sells for many times more than its blander cousin. By the time it reaches the export market a kilo of white truffles will cost several thousand dollars.

Botanically speaking, a truffle is the fruiting body of a fungus, similar to a mushroom. It grows, however, entirely beneath the ground and only under particular trees, especially poplars and certain kinds of oak, from whose roots it takes nourishment. It also requires special types of soil, favouring a limestone base, and it is sensitive to climate, preferring humid areas. So choosy is the white truffle about its environment that it has yet to be successfully cultivated. White truffles can range from a

large hazelnut to a small orange in size. Prize-winning specimens have weighed in at as much as 2kg/4lb. An egg-sized truffle, perhaps about 30g/1oz, is perfectly satisfactory as well as being affordable. Depending on where it was dug up, a white truffle can be smooth and round if the soil where it took form was soft and loose, or knotty and irregular in shape if it had to struggle for space. Inside, the beige-coloured meat is compact and finely veined.

In the past female pigs were used to snout out this buried treasure. Those sows were wildly attracted to its musky aroma, which scientists recently discovered is similar to the sexual hormone of the male pig. Today, however, small, short-haired dogs are trained from puppyhood to track the scent. They are more agile than pigs and easier to dissuade from devouring their costly find. During the relatively brief season for white truffles, from about early November to late December, an experienced and energetic truffle hunter or *tartufaio* can, with the help of a good dog, make a quite handsome living.

Both the aroma and taste of a white truffle are unique. The fragrance is penetrating, pungent, musky and in a positive sense, faintly decadent. The taste is even more difficult to describe. 'The perfect marriage between a clove of garlic and a piece of the best Parmesan,' is how one connoisseur identifies it. If you are ever in Italy during the season you should splash out and try fresh white truffles.

Exported white truffles, even when properly handled, lose some of their aroma and taste, as they are normally washed before being shipped, which dries them out. Here we simply brush off the soil and maybe wipe the truffle clean with a damp cloth, so it remains moist and fragrant.

In medieval and Renaissance times, when, judging from ancient cookery books, truffles were plentiful and probably cheap to buy, they were cooked together with a variety of ingredients. Today white truffles are shaved raw and used sparingly over special dishes. The warmth of the food releases and intensifies their gastronomic qualities. The dish should be rich so it can stand up to the aroma and the taste of the truffle but uncomplicated so as not to distract your taste buds. One of the preferred ways of enjoying truffles in my family is simply to shave it generously over a couple of eggs, fried or scrambled in butter.

There are really two major white truffle centres in Italy—Alba, in the north-western region of Piedmont, and San Giovanni d'Asso in Tuscany, south of Siena. In both of these towns truffle fairs and festivals are held throughout this season. Truffle dealers, merchants, restaurateurs, connoisseurs and amateurs from all over the world come both to buy and feast on this unique food. The atmosphere is heady, both because of the pungent aroma that fills that air and the immense amount of money that changes hands. All the local restaurants feature a menu where truffles are celebrated with each course. You are most likely to begin with an *antipasto* of warm *crostini*—little toasts spread with truffle butter. If you are lucky these could be followed by a fennel salad dressed with lemon and olive oil and topped with shavings of Parmesan and truffles. The classic pasta for truffles are taglierini—thin, fresh egg noodles, tossed in butter and finished with a flurry of shaved truffles. A perfect and simple meat base for enjoying truffles is veal scallops sautéed in wine. Coming up with a decent dessert is more problematic. One solution in keeping with the theme is to serve chocolate truffles—cherry-sized balls of soft chocolate encased in a harder chocolate coating. Better yet, try sprinkling white truffles over any chocolate dessert. It is a decadent combination.

If the weather cooperates, the last of the season's truffles are available right before Christmas. The price usually goes sky-high but I try to corner a few for my Christmas dinner. I wrap them, soil and all, in kitchen paper, put them in a closed jar and store them in my pantry, where they will keep moist and fresh for a couple of weeks. My truffle philosophy is to use what you have generously in one dish, rather than sparingly in several. I also believe in serving them at the beginning of the meal where they will be fully appreciated, before your guests' taste buds are sated by wine and a myriad of other flavours. A rich and festive *antipasto* for holiday celebrations is pheasant pâté with white truffles.

After all those superb and sublime truffles, it seems salutary to consider next the most simple staple of the winter season, the humble dried bean. Actually Italians eat dried beans all year around, especially in Tuscany where I live. Tuscans are called, in a teasing way, *mangiafagioli* (or bean-eaters), by their fellow countrymen. Tuscany was a particularly poor region and protein-rich beans were the 'meat of the poor'. Tuscans are also considered 'full of beans' in the more poetic sense. I associate beans with winter food because they form the base of so many nourishing and hearty soups and go so well with meats grilled over the fire, like steak and sausage.

Beans are the seeds of legumes or seed-bearing pods. There are dozens of species, whose names are often confusing. In the course of the last century many regional or local varieties had become virtually extinct, in favour of national and international types. Recently there has been a laudable and successful effort in Italy to revive local types of beans. The *cannellini*, a medium-sized white bean, is perhaps the most popular national variety. Tuscans prefer their *toscanelli*. And now *zolfini*, which are smaller with a thinner skin and were once an endangered species, are enjoying a comeback.

These are the beans you will find in *ribollita*, that most hearty of *minestroni*, a thick vegetable soup made a couple of days in advance, then reheated or 'boiled again' which is what *ribollita* means. Any and every vegetable can go into the pot, but authentic *ribollita* requires, along with white beans, *cavolo nero*—a dark green, almost black-leaved variety of kale that thrives in the winter garden. The soup is thickened with stale bread and has the consistency of porridge. *Ribollita* originated in the rustic home kitchen as a way of using up leftovers. Today it is on the menu of practically every Tuscan restaurant. You taste the best *ribollita* in *trattorie* where mother or grandmother are still cooking in the kitchen.

Another Tuscan soup called *zuppa Lombarda*— although what it has to do with the Lombards nobody seems to know—is the quickest, simplest and most satisfying way to use leftover beans. All you need are cooked white beans and good bean broth, thick slices of country-style bread, garlic and quality extra virgin olive oil. Ladle some beans with their broth over the toasted bread rubbed with garlic and drizzle with extra virgin olive oil.

Il maiale, col suo ottimo fiuto, può essere utilizzato come buon ricercatore del prezioso e ghiotto tartufo

When my children were young one of their favourite winter suppers was pork sausages cooked over the fire and eaten right off the grill with *fagioli all'uccelletto*—'beans cooked like a little bird'. White beans are simmered in olive oil with garlic, sage and tomato pulp, the way small game birds are braised in Tuscany—hence the name of this dish.

The prettiest bean in the bag is the *lamon* from the Veneto. These beans are like cranberries, their pods pale pink with red speckles. Inside, the beans look like little speckled duck eggs. *Lamon* are difficult to find outside this area but the *borlotti* bean which resembles them makes a satisfactory substitute. The real *lamon* is used in the authentic Veneto version of *pasta e fagioli* soup. The beans are cooked with a ham bone and rosemary and then half of them are puréed to thicken the soup. The traditional pasta used is the Venetian *bigoli*, a thick spaghetti made with wholewheat flour, butter and eggs. In Siena they use *ceci*, chickpeas, as the 'bean' in their local version of *pasta e fagioli*. The pasta is tagliatelle. Chickpeas are a nutritious and delicious legume, both on their own and in combination with other flavours. A favourite bread of mine is *focaccia* made with chickpea flour and seasoned with sage.

Eating your way through Tuscany these days you will surely come across *zuppa di granfarro*, a rustic soup made of *borlotti* beans and *farro* (*triticum dicoccum durum*) or, in English, emmer or two-grained spelt. *Farro* is a grass of the wheat family, cultivated for millennia (it was the staple of the Roman legions) for its grain which is harvested for cereal. During more recent Italian history it was only grown in a small area near Lucca in Tuscany, the Garfagnana, where this soup originated. In Lucca's classic *trattoria*, Da Giulio, in Pelleria, they also make it with lentils instead of beans. I like it combined with barley and flavoured with dried *porcini* mushrooms. Recently *farro* has become available in speciality shops all over Italy and I have even come across it in New York and California.

When you prepare dried beans for cooking, the general wisdom is to soak them for at least eight hours, or overnight, and then to simmer them. Many Tuscan home cooks I know boil them for a couple of minutes instead and let them sit in the hot water for a while.

As tasty as these dishes are, fortunately Italians are not limited to dried beans for their winter diet. Staples such as yellow and red onions and white garlic, dried for the winter after summer and autumn harvesting, are indispensable in the Italian kitchen. If you know what to choose, there are plenty of seasonal fresh greens and vegetables available at the market. Here are some of the more interesting ones.

Walking through the Tuscan countryside you will see, sticking up in the midst of frost and snow in kitchen gardens, rows of large, long, dark green, almost black, curly leaves, like so many ostrich plumes. This is Tuscan kale, called *cavolo nero* (black cabbage). It is considered even better after the first frost, which softens its rather stiff leaves. As mentioned above, along with white beans, it is one of the essential ingredients for authentic *ribollita*. It also flavours winter stews. I particularly like to dress pasta with julienned black cabbage leaves that have been fried in garlic and olive oil.

Several other members of the cabbage family—broccoli, broccoli rabe and cauliflower—liven up winter market stalls with their colour and distinctive shapes, as well as adding welcome variety to cold seasonal dishes. In Italian *broccoli* means little buds and, horticulturally, it is the unopened sprout of a type of cabbage. Cauliflower is of the same species. In southern Italy broccoli is often called *cavolfiori*, which in other regions means cauliflower. Broccoli rabe is called *broccoletti* or *cima di rape*. You can use these three interchangeably in most recipes. Common Italian broccoli has small, dark green heads and small stalks. In the market they come with some of their leaves still attached and these will add flavour when it comes to cooking. You will see a rather startling species called *Romanesco*, which produces conical chartreuse heads with spiralling florets and a delicate flavour. Broccoli rabe is cultivated for its greens, which grow on thin stalks with budding heads and have a distinctive nutty and pleasantly bitter flavour. They are wonderfully tasty simply fried with olive oil and garlic. Besides the common white heads of cauliflower, pale yellow and green varieties add colour to a winter market. Fresh cauliflower is a perfect addition to *pinzimonio*, an *antipasto* of sliced raw vegetables dipped into fine extra virgin olive oil at the table. All these varieties are delicious sautéed and used as a pasta topping for family lunches. For guests I prepare broccoli in an elegant ring.

Another popular winter vegetable is *radicchio rosso* (red radicchio), a member of the large chicory family. In the Veneto region of northern Italy several towns cultivate their own particular variety of red radicchio. Most of these can now be found in markets throughout the peninsula. Radicchio from Chioggia, a fishing village on the south side of the Venetian lagoon and the region's produce centre, has tight, dark maroon leaves. The most prestigious variety is from Treviso. Its season lasts only a few weeks, beginning in December. The locals refer to their *rosso di Treviso* as '*un fiore che si mangia*'—an edible flower—and it is easy to see why. It has a long, white stalk and loose, spear-shaped, gorgeous ruby-red leaves with white veins.

I combine the crisp, crunchy, raw leaves of Chioggia in winter salads with apples, nuts and cheese, dressed with olive oil and balsamic vinegar. The traditional way to cook Treviso radicchio is simply to grill it in the oven or over a fire. If the heads are small you can leave them whole. Otherwise they should be halved or quartered. All you need do is brush them with extra virgin olive oil and turn them occasionally. The outer leaves will blacken and the heart should be soft and tender. It has a deliciously wild and pleasingly bitter taste. I fry it with pancetta as a topping for *crostini*, a perfect party appetizer. Chicory (Belgian endive) can be successfully substituted in most radicchio recipes.

I remember as a little girl driving with my family through the desolate winter countryside on the border between the regions of Veneto and Lombardy and stopping for a comforting roadside snack consisting of baked pumpkin slices sprinkled with sugar. This Italian variety of winter squash, *zucca invernale*, is not smooth and yellow like the American Hallowe'en pumpkin, but has a warty, green skin. Inside, the sweet and tasty flesh is deep yellow. Regional recipes use them in many delicious ways. Slices are deep-fried in olive oil and marinated in boiling hot vinegar for several hours before eating. They are often prepared as a dessert in the form of pumpkin fritters with sugar and raisins, pumpkin tarts and even pumpkin preserves. In Mantua they use the pulp as stuffing for *tortelli*. A favourite recipe of mine is pumpkin gnocchi.

In comparison with its northern neighbours, rural Italy was traditionally a poor country. Grazing land and, consequently, most meats were scarce and expensive. Pork was an exception, as every farming family annually singled out a piglet to fatten for slaughter. It would normally be the runt of the litter, which would have brought less money at market. For a year it would be treated like a king (in folk art it was often depicted with a crown on its head), fed on spring grass, autumn chestnuts and winter pumpkins. Then, during the period between Christmas and *Carnevale* in late February, when the rigidly cold days of deep winter provide the natural refrigeration necessary for the event, family and friends would gather for the 'communal sacrifice', shall we call it, of their pampered porker.

In country areas throughout Italy this ancient winter ritual is still enacted, although it has become increasingly rare and most likely someday soon will vanish altogether. A special butcher, called a *norcino*, after the town of Norcia in Umbria where this tradition was particularly prevalent, is the master of ceremonies. In my town the local butcher performs the feat for the few families who still carry on the

tradition. It is a two-day event. On the morning of the first day the pig is bled and left to hang for about forty-eight hours, until its flesh has firmed-up. Then, usually on a Sunday, the festivities begin.

The *norcino* arrives early in the morning and before dark he will have processed some 100kg /225lb of pig into numerous nourishing and tasty products that will replenish the family larder for another year. Some of the cuts are disposed of during the feast itself. The loin is roasted, seasoned with olive oil, garlic and fennel and the ribs are barbecued. From the two hind thighs he fashions prosciutto, rubbing them with a creamy paste of garlic and covering them with salt to cure for about two weeks, before they are hung in a well-ventilated room to age for at least eight months. The front shoulder is shaped and cured in much the same way and is called *spalla*. A prized little cut from the area between the head and shoulder, called *coppa* or *capocollo*, is cured in salt for just a few days and seasoned with coarsely ground pepper. Slabs of belly fat streaked with pink meat are cut into thick bacon-like strips to make the pancetta, which will be hung in the larder and used during the year to flavour innumerable dishes. Even the pig's jowl, called *guanciale*, is cured and used in the same way as pancetta.

Into a huge cauldron of boiling water go the head, ears, tongue, tail, trotter and other bits and pieces. After they have simmered for a good three hours, he transforms them into *soppressata*, similar to brawn. The cooked meat is chopped into small pieces and seasoned with spices and orange rind. Then it is tightly pressed into a linen cloth, tied and hung to cool. When it is unwrapped, *soppressata* looks like a large marbled salami.

Next come endless links of sausage and cylinders of salami, ground from selected lean cuttings, mixed to taste with a percentage of fat and seasoned with salt, peppercorns, garlic and a generous splash of wine. This mixture is kneaded to the desired consistency and, with the help of a machine, stuffed into its casing of pig's intestine. In Tuscany they add wild fennel seeds to make a regional salami called *finocchiona*. Lastly, the blood that had been saved at the time of slaughter is brought out to make *buristo* (blood sausage). It is mixed with pieces of pork skin and salt, pepper and garlic are added for seasoning. All these processed pork products are sliced and served in restaurants as an *antipasto*. They also make excellent fillers for delicious picnic sandwiches.

Traditional recipes for the main meat course of a winter meal are ones that take advantage of rural home fires burning, or in an urban setting, the welcome warmth that a lighted stove adds to the household-grilled steaks, pork sausages and chops, spit-roasted chickens and game birds, stewed meats of all kinds from wild boar to rabbit, and, especially, roasts that are cooked very slowly for a long period of time. This classic method of braising meat is called *brasato* in northern Italy and in Tuscany, *stracotto*, 'cooked for an extra long time'. In some recipes the meat is marinated overnight in wine and herbs. Before cooking, the piece of meat is sealed in its fat and then braised either over a very low heat on top of the stove or very slowly in the oven. One of my favourite recipes and one that brings my cooking classes to their feet in applause when it is presented on a meat trolley decorated with sprigs of flowers, I call 'veal shank in lemony sauce'. You use the same cut of meat as for *ossobuco*—the hindshank of a young calf, which is cooked for four hours. The meat will be juicy and so tender that it can be cut with a fork.

As dessert to end a hearty winter meal I prefer to serve fruit-based confections. The most colourful fruit this season provides is the blood orange. The first to show up at the market in November is the *Moro*, from southern Italy. It is a large orange with deep red flesh and a slight red blush on the rind. These are followed in December by the *Tarocco*, a little lighter in colour. The most beautiful variety, the *Sanguinello*, arrives last. It has intensely red flesh and red-flushed skin. Its name means 'lovely little blood-coloured' orange. When squeezed, it yields a splendid ruby-red juice.

The generous apple tree provides its fruit through the first weeks of winter. Of the many varieties you can find in the market, the *Gravenstein*, which is said to be of Italian origin, is the best apple for baking and using in desserts. Pears, of which Italy is the largest producer in Europe, also continue to ripen into early winter. They are particularly good at the end of meal combined with an aged cheese.

WINTER HOLIDAYS

In Italy the Christmas season traditionally begins on 8 December, the feast of the Immaculate Conception of The Blessed Virgin Mary, a national holiday as well as a Holy Day. For me the occasion is marked by the gala opening of the opera season at La Scala in Milan the evening before. In Rome the Pope and various civic and business leaders ceremoniously place flowers at the foot of a statue of the Virgin just off Piazza di Spagna. Shepherds from the nearby region of Abruzzi, dressed in traditional leather leggings and sheepskin vests, stroll the streets playing carols on their primitive bagpipes. Their favourite piece, which could be considered the Italian national Christmas carol—what *Jingle Bells* and *Silent Night* are to other parts of the world—is a song written by Saint Alfonso Liguri in the eighteenth century, *Tu Scendi Dalle Stelle*, 'You come down from the stars'. Even Luciano Pavarotti has recorded a version. Vendors roast chestnuts on practically every corner. Churches set up their elaborate *presepi*, Nativity scenes, in competition with each other for dramatic effects. And once again the scents and sounds and spirit of Christmas warm the crisp atmosphere.

Culturally and gastronomically, there is no single traditional way in which Christmas is celebrated in Italy. Regional customs still prevail. For some families, Christmas Eve is the occasion for the principal feast. For others it is Christmas Day. For many it is both. Fortunately for all, 26 December, Saint Stephen's Day, is a national holiday, a day to rest and recover from all the celebrations. Everyone eats leftovers or goes to their favourite local restaurant so that the home cook can have a holiday, too.

We have our family feast and exchange of gifts, now a gathering of three generations, on Christmas Eve. I prepare *cappone*, capon, a young, castrated cock, fatter and tastier than any macho cockerel, for the main course of our meal. Eating capon on Christmas Eve is an ancient custom in Italy. In former times in Catholic countries one abstained from meat on the eve of major Holy Days—fasting before feasting, still a good idea, I think. Capon was not classified as meat according to the law of the church, perhaps because it was a 'virgin'. In any case, it provided a tasty way around the law. I boil it together with onion, carrot, celery and several bay leaves. For the first course I serve *cappelletti*, a small pasta stuffed with a mixture of ground meats and shaped liked little caps with a turned-up brim, in the hot capon broth. If there is any capon left over, I use it to make capon meatballs or in a salad as a light meal after the feasting.

Another traditional delicacy served on Christmas Eve, particularly in Rome, is *capitone*, a very long and fat female eel—up to 1m/3ft long and weighing nearly 5kg/11lb—not only bigger but more flavourful than the male of the species. It is cut into pieces, which can be grilled, seasoned with olive oil, vinegar, garlic and salt or stewed with white wine. On Christmas Eve day special fish markets in Milan and Rome feature big basins of wriggling eel.

On Christmas Day it is traditional all over the country to serve turkey (*tacchino*) stuffed and roasted, as the main course of the meal. Turkeys, of course, are native to North America, but they had arrived in Europe by the mid-sixteenth century and were popular as a table bird a good half century before the first Thanksgiving in the New World. Caterina de'Medici, sixteenth-century queen of France and daughter of Florentine ruler Lorenzo de'Medici, was said to be fond of them and she is credited by some as having brought them to France, along with lots of other good things. At a feast in her honour in 1549, sixty-six turkeys were served. The great Italian Renaissance writer on gastronomy, Bartolomeo Scappi, included several recipes for cooking turkey in his works, spit-roasted, stuffed, baked in a crust (with the head exposed) or made into dumplings. The capon recipe I have chosen for my Christmas menu is also ideal for a classic turkey dish, with its sweet-and-sour Renaissance flavour. The bird is stuffed with apples and prunes and the sauce is seasoned with sugar, raisins and balsamic vinegar.

Another festive bird, esteemed in Italy since Roman times, is pheasant (*fagiano*). In Tuscany you frequently come across them in the wild and large populations are encouraged in game reserves. Tuscan hunters will chase any bird that lets out a peep, while cooks seek out the female of the species, which is plumper and more tasty and tender. A young hen can be roasted, whereas the cock, leaner and drier of flesh, is usually braised. In any case it is usual to wrap the bird in prosciutto to add moisture to the cooking juices. As an elegant *antipasto* for Christmas dinner, I prepare pheasant pâté enriched with white truffle butter. This dish combines well with the other *antipasto* on my menu—little toasts spread with fresh goats' cheese and topped with sautéed red radicchio as well as paper-thin slices of pancetta.

Traditionally, for formal meals with guests we would not serve a bowl of pasta or rice as a first course, which does not mean you have to renounce these delicious staples when you entertain. Instead I transform them into elegant timbales or moulds. For this particular occasion, I coat little cups with lasagne and fill them with a mixture of ricotta and cream. I present my rice dish in a ring mould with sautéed artichokes.

As you will see from the menu, I have chosen two dishes each for the first and second courses of my dinner, in keeping with the spirit of holiday abundance. As help is hard to come by on Christmas Day, I serve both dishes at the same time and let my family and friends help themselves to whichever takes their fancy first.

Throughout all of Italy the Christmas cake *par excellence* is *panettone*, a dome-shaped, butter-enriched yeast cake. During the holidays families eat a slice with their morning coffee, serve it for dessert with a festive bottle of *spumante* and in the afternoon with a cup of tea or a glass of Vin Santo. *Panettone* originated in Milan and the traditional form was a squat-shaped dome. Commercial bakeries began making them more cylindrical. Nowadays you can buy them plain or studded with raisins and little bits of candied citrus fruit. The traditional Christmas cake of Verona, which has also become omnipresent during the holidays, is *pandoro*, 'golden bread', a light, soft cake made with flour, eggs, butter and yeast. It is baked in a star-shaped mould and sprinkled with icing sugar (powdered sugar). Another version of this classic cake, which has remained more regional, is *pandolce* from the city of Genoa in Liguria. The basic recipe is the same but more flavours are added—pine nuts, fennel seeds, various spices, as well as candied fruits.

The celebrated *panforte* from Siena was originally a Christmas cake, although now it is produced and eaten all year around. Its name, which means 'pungent bread', describes its spicy aroma and taste. It is made with honey, sugar, crystallized melon, citron, orange and lemon rinds (peels), walnuts, hazelnuts, almonds, coriander (cilantro), cinnamon, cloves, nutmeg, mace, flour and water. Each producer keeps the exact number and proportion of ingredients a well-guarded secret. The oldest recipe, dating from medieval times, includes pepper, which was one of the rarest and most exotic of all spices brought back by the crusaders from the Middle East. This is called *panpepato*, 'pepper bread', and is still made today. A sweeter version called *panforte* was created in 1879, on the occasion of the visit of Queen Margherita of Savoy to Siena—it is less spicy than *panpepato*, lighter in colour, texture and taste, and is covered with a veil of icing (powdered) sugar.

All of these special holiday cakes are far too difficult to make at home. Everyone buys their favourite commercial brand, packaged in colourful Christmas wrappings. Most Italians have strong opinions regarding which is best. For Christmas dinner I dress up *panettone* as an elaborate (but easy) dessert with Vin Santo and melted chocolate and bake it in individual moulds.

In Italian there is a rhyming couplet that says, not without a bit of irony, '*Natale con i tuoi, Capodanno con chi vuoi*', 'Christmas with the family and New Year's with whom you want.' For some this is a ticket to take off for warmer climes, North Africa or the Caribbean. For many who stay behind, the traditional way to celebrate New Year's Eve is to reserve, well in advance, a table with friends in a special restaurant. The *Cenone*, or 'Big Bash', begins around 10 p.m., with music, dancing and champagne at midnight.

For those who eat at home the traditional dish is *zampone*, stuffed pig's foot. *Zampone* is really a huge sausage, invented in Modena during the sixteenth century when, or so the story goes, the city was under siege and butchers ran out of sausage casing. Choice bits and pieces of pork, seasoned with cinnamon, cloves, nutmeg, salt and pepper are finely minced together and pushed into a boned foot, which is then securely tied at the end. Before cooking it is wrapped in cheesecloth to prevent the skin from splitting and the stuffing escaping, and simmered for at least three hours. During the season you can buy pre-cooked *zampone* at the supermarket which only need to be heated up, but the flavour is not nearly as good. The classic accompaniment for *zampone* is stewed lentils, whose shape symbolizes a pile of coins promising prosperity in the New Year.

Italians stretch their Christmas holidays over a two-week period, from 24 December until 6 January, the Feast of the Epiphany or, as it is more popularly known, the feast of the Three Kings, the Magi, who brought their gifts of gold, frankincense and myrrh to the Christ Child. In the past, in southern Italy especially, the Epiphany was a more important Holy Day celebration than Christmas itself. A few years ago when the government eliminated it from the calendar of national holidays, the popular outcry was so unanimous that the politicians quickly reinstated it, out of fear of losing their jobs. Nowadays the Magi take a back seat to an even more ancient figure, the *Befana*, a usually benevolent old woman, who personifies Winter. She is a kind of white witch who arrives on the eve of 6 January, riding a broomstick. She enters homes via the chimney and fills the children's stockings either with sweets or, theoretically, if they have been naughty, with charcoal. Most find a perfect compromise corresponding to their conduct— lumps of candy charcoal, along with other little gifts.

Another popular saying has it that, '*L'Epifania, tutte le feste porta via*', which means that after the Epiphany it is back to work for a few, long, dark weeks until the final winter feast, *Carnevale* (Carnival). This literally means 'good-bye to meat' and traditionally it was the day or days before the beginning of Lent, a period of fast and abstinence. It seems I hardly get the Christmas decorations packed away before I see youngsters out on the street in their Carnival costumes.

The largest *Carnevale* celebration in Europe is held in the Tuscan seaside town of Viareggio. On every weekend a month before the beginning of Lent, the city hosts a huge parade with elaborate floats, most of them satirizing the prominent political figures of the year. On the final day, the Tuesday before Ash Wednesday, there is a fantastic fireworks display out over the sea. Venice celebrates *Carnevale* with elaborate costume balls, parades and competitions.

Most of the contemporary Carnival treats are sweets, as they are what one traditionally 'gives up' for Lent. All over Italy during this period you will find strips of sweetened fried dough that go by different regional names. Here in Tuscany they are called *cenci*, rags, because of their uneven shape, and as a playful, gastronomic reminder of the penitential 'sackcloth and ashes' which characterized more ancient Lenten observations. Ideally the fried dough should be crisp, light and puffy. When golden they are sprinkled with icing (powdered) sugar. Sometimes they are enriched with sweet wine, Vin Santo, and flavoured with vanilla and orange zest. *Frittelle*, fritters, are another popular Carnival treat. These are small pieces of deep-fried batter with a filling whose ingredients depend on where they are being made. Apple and rice fritters are popular throughout Italy. Originally these sweets were simple street food, fried, sold and eaten on the spot. Today you will also find them on sale in fancy pastry shops. Seasonal street vendors still set up shop on main piazzas during the days of *Carnevale* and their sweets always taste best, providing quick energy food to warm and fuel the celebrations.

THE PANTRY

OLIO AL LIMONE
Lemon Oil

Scented oils are very useful for many recipes such as salads and I always keep some in my store room. To prevent the possibility of mould forming, it is better to strain the oil after about fifteen days, to remove the herb which gives it its flavour.

2 organic lemons
480ml/16fl oz/2 cups extra virgin olive oil
Salt

Wash the lemons carefully, dry them on a cloth and slice paper-thin.
Place the lemon slices in a deep dish, sprinkle with salt and leave for about 20 minutes.
Transfer the contents of the dish to a large sterilized screw-top jar, add the oil and seal. Leave for 1 month in a cupboard or dark place.
Filter through a paper filter into a sterilized bottle or bottles. Use in dressings or in a cooked vegetable salad. The oil will keep for several months.

Makes 480ml/16fl oz/2 cups

MARMELLATA DI MELE E LIMONI
Lemon and Apple Jam

I have many grandsons with a sweet tooth so I often make jam for them. When combined with bottles of scented oil or vinegar, I find these also make perfect and very personal Christmas gifts.

1kg/2 ¼ lb cooking apples
6 organic lemons
1kg/2 ¼ lb/4 ¼ cups granulated sugar

Quarter, peel and core the apples, reserving some of the skins. Slice the apples thinly.
Wash the lemons carefully, dry them on a cloth and slice paper-thin. In a large, heavy stainless steel saucepan or preserving pan make a layer of lemons, followed by a layer of apples and a layer of sugar.
Continue until all the ingredients are used. Add the reserved skins.
Cook over a low heat, stirring occasionally and skimming the scum from the surface every now and then, until the syrup becomes quite thick and reaches setting point. This should take about 1 hour. To test for set, drop a spoonful of jam on to a cold saucer. If the surface wrinkles when you push it with your finger, setting point has been reached.
The jam is now ready to be spooned into sterilized jars.
To sterilize jars, place them in a pan and pour in water to come about 3cm/1in up the sides of the jars. Bring to the boil, boil for 20 minutes and leave to cool in the pan. Remove and dry the jars.
The jam can be stored for up to 1 year in a cupboard or dark place. Once opened, keep in the refrigerator and eat within 3 weeks.

Makes about 900g/2lb/4 cups

LIMONCELLO
Lemon Liqueur

Limoncello has become very popular in recent years and as we have a few lemon trees in the garden, I make this liqueur myself. Sometimes I will add a few sage leaves to the lemon zest, for a slightly bitter taste. The pure alcohol content is 95% and is sold in drug stores, or *drogherie*, in Italy. Some recipes give instructions for making a syrup with hot water and sugar, a method which results in an opaque *limoncello*. This recipe will give you a transparent liquid.

12 organic lemons
750g/1lb 10oz/4 cups granulated sugar
1 litre/1 ³/₄ pints/4 cups alcohol (90–95%)
1 litre/1 ³/₄ pints/4 cups water

Remove the zest from the lemons with a zester, making sure you don't cut through to the white pith. Divide the zest between 3 sterilized wine bottles adding the sugar, alcohol and water. Seal with a cork. Put the bottles in a dark cupboard and turn the bottles every day for a couple of months, until the sugar has completely dissolved.
Filter the liquid through a paper filter into clean bottles and serve at room temperature or chilled. This liqueur will keep for a long time.

Makes 2.2 litres/3³/4 pints

SCIROPPO DI VINO
Wine Syrup

After a wine tasting in our winery at Badia a Coltibuono, there are often many unfinished bottles of wine left open, so I always make this syrup to use them up. It keeps for many months at room temperature, does not have to be stored in special places and is good on fruit salads, with strawberries or berries, as well as with ice-cream and as a glaze for fruit tarts.

1 litre/1 ³/₄ pints/4 cups red wine
Juice of 6 lemons and grated zest of 1
450g/1lb/2 ¹/₄ cups granulated sugar
1 stick cinnamon
8 cloves

Boil the wine with the rest of the ingredients in a large stainless steel pan or preserving pan, for 20 minutes. Allow to completely cool, then strain through a fine colander. Decant into a sterilized bottle and store in a cupboard or dark place.
This is delicious with fresh fruit, ice-cream and soft cakes.

Makes about 1 litre/1³/4 pints/4 cups

SUGO DI CARNE
Meat Sauce

Although I do not like meat juices generally, I always keep some in the refrigerator because they can be useful if any last-minute guests arrive, to finish a risotto, a polenta dish or refresh leftover meats.

2kg/4lb beef bones, roughly chopped (ask your butcher)
1kg/2 1/4 lb beef shank, bone in, roughly chopped
450g/1lb skin and fat of prosciutto, roughly chopped
1kg/2 1/4 lb chicken bones and cooked leftover chicken meat, roughly chopped
3 carrots, roughly chopped
2 celery stalks, roughly chopped
2 onions, roughly chopped
1 fresh rosemary sprig
1 handful fresh sage leaves
3 bay leaves
240ml/8fl oz/1 cup Marsala wine

Preheat the oven to 180°C/375°F/Gas 5.
Place all the ingredients in a large roasting tray. Cook for about 1 hour or until the bones become very dark in colour. Transfer the contents of the tray to a big pan and cover with water (about 6 litres/12 pints). Bring to the boil and simmer for 10 hours, over a low heat, skimming the foam off the surface at regular intervals.
Strain the broth, allow it to cool slightly, then place in the refrigerator.
Once cool, skim the fat from the surface and discard. Transfer the broth to a clean pan and bring again to the boil. Simmer gently until reduced to 2 litres/ 3 1/2 pints/8 cups. This should take about 2 hours. As the liquid reduces, add the Marsala from time to time. Allow to cool completely and keep in the refrigerator for up to 1 month. The sauce is delicious served with meat, or used as a base for soups and sauces.

Makes 2 litres/3 1/4 /8 cups

GELATINA
Meat Gelatine

Gelatine is the perfect finish for an elegant dinner, making it particularly useful during Christmas or New Year's Eve when I have many friends coming to visit me in Coltibuono. At that time we indulge in making pâté or terrines as appetizers but I find them especially good for a buffet. I will often pour the gelatine to set on a platter about 1 cm/1/4 inch thick, which I will then dice and garnish when well set.

2 litres/3 1/2 pints/8 cups meat stock
1 veal foot
1 pork shank
10 gelatine leaves
1 bay leaf
1 celery stalk, finely chopped
Half an organic lemon, finely chopped
1 handful fresh flat-leaf parsley, finely chopped
1 carrot, finely chopped
1 tbsp fresh thyme leaves
1 large egg white, beaten
90g/3oz brisket beef, roughly chopped
Salt

Bring the stock to the boil in a large pan with the veal foot and pork shank, then simmer over a low heat for about 2 hours.
Meanwhile soak the gelatine leaves in cold water, drain and squeeze.
Remove the veal and pork from the pan, add the gelatine leaves, the bay leaf, celery, lemon, parsley, carrot, thyme and egg white. Add salt to taste. Bring to the boil again, add the beef and simmer for about 10 minutes. Leave to cool for about 15 minutes, strain into a container and transfer to the refrigerator. The gelatine will keep for up to 8 days.

Makes about 1 litre/1 3/4 pints/4 cups

APPETIZERS, PASTA AND SOUPS

FOGLIE D'INSALATA BELGA RIPIENE
Stuffed Chicory (Belgian Endive) Leaves

The bitter taste of chicory (Belgian endive) goes very well with many ingredients. I often make a simple salad, mixing the sliced chicory with sliced fennel bulbs, Granny Smith apples, a little olive oil and salt, or I will fill the leaves with Gorgonzola and chopped walnuts.

6 chicory (Belgian endive) leaves
120g/4oz/½ cup ricotta cheese
120g/4oz fresh goats' cheese
1 tsp powdered sweet paprika

Trim, wash and dry the leaves.
Cream the ricotta and the goats' cheese together in a bowl and spoon into a piping bag fitted with fluted nozzle.
Pipe the mixture into the rounded part of the leaves and sprinkle with the paprika. Arrange on a platter and serve.

Serves 6

CARCIOFI IN PINZIMONIO
Artichokes Dipped in Oil

One of the best ways to eat artichokes is to serve them raw in *pinzimonio*, which is an oil, pepper and salt dip. You can add some celery stalks and carrots to the artichokes too. In Italy it is so popular (once it was strictly Tuscan) that it is served in special bowls.

Juice of 1 lemon
6 artichokes
6 tbsp extra virgin olive oil
Salt and pepper

Have ready a bowl of water mixed with lemon juice. Clean the artichokes, and discard the tough outer leaves and the stem. Cut them in half lengthwise and remove the furry inner choke with a paring knife. Drop the prepared artichokes in the water to prevent them from discolouring. Pat dry on paper towels and arrange on a serving dish.
Put the oil in a small serving bowl, add salt and pepper to taste and eat the artichokes by dipping the leaves one by one in the oil.

Serves 6

SPIEDINI DI PECORINO E MELA VERDE
Pecorino (Romano) and Apple Skewers

Pecorino (Romano) cheese in winter becomes more dry and strong in taste so it is a good idea to mix it with diced apples, as shown in this lovely appetizer. I usually serve the skewers in grapefruit to make a colourful porcupine.

300g/10oz pecorino (Romano) cheese
3 tbsp extra virgin olive oil
2 Granny Smith apples
Pepper

Remove the rind from the cheese and discard. Dice the cheese and place in a shallow bowl. Sprinkle with the oil and pepper. Place in the refrigerator and leave to marinate for about 2 hours, mixing from time to time to coat with the oil.
Peel and dice the apples.
Take 6 wooden skewers and alternate the pecorino (Romano) with the apple, using 3 pecorino dice and 2 apple dice per skewer.
Arrange on a platter and serve.

Serves 6

GNOCCHI DI ZUCCA
Pumpkin Gnocchi

This is another speciality from Mantua that recalls the pumpkin ravioli again. Sometimes I will also sprinkle some amaretti on top with the cheese, for a stronger taste.

1.5kg/3 ½ lb pumpkin with peel and seeds
3 large eggs
120g/4oz/1 cup plain (all-purpose) flour
120g/4oz/1 cup fine fresh breadcrumbs
2 amaretto biscuits (cookies)
60g/2oz/4 tbsp unsalted butter
4 tbsp freshly grated Parmesan cheese
Salt and pepper

Preheat the oven to 170°C/350°F/Gas 4.
Prepare the pumpkin, discarding the seeds and the skin. Cut the flesh into pieces, place on a baking sheet (cookie tray) and cook for about 30 minutes in the oven or until soft. Keep the oven on for the final cooking stage.
Tip the pumpkin into a bowl and mash with a fork. Add the eggs, the flour, breadcrumbs and amaretto biscuits (cookies) and mix until well blended. Sprinkle with salt and pepper and mix well.
With the help of a spoon shape the mixture into small dumplings each about the size of a walnut. Bring a pan of water to the boil, add salt, then add the dumplings a few at a time. They are cooked when they rise to the surface. As they are ready, lift them out with a slotted spoon and arrange in a baking dish. Meanwhile melt the butter in a saucepan over a low heat. Sprinkle the dumplings with the Parmesan, pour over the melted butter and cook in the oven for about 20 minutes. Serve immediately while very hot.

Serves 6

SPAGHETTI ALLA PANCETTA E ROSMARINO
Spaghetti with Pancetta and Rosemary

This hearty dish is a speciality of a Sardinian friend of mine, Nanni Guiso, the founder of the first Museum of the Year 2000. The museum is in his house in Orosei and there you can see his collection of puppet theatres, drawings and even richly embroidered evening dresses from Valentino, Capucci and others, presented to his museum by his numerous elegant friends.

600g/1 ¼ lb spaghetti
120g/4oz pancetta
2 fresh rosemary sprigs
3 garlic cloves
4 tbsp extra virgin olive oil
Salt and pepper

Bring a large pan of water to the boil, add the spaghetti and salt. Cook until just *al dente* (a couple of minutes less than stated on the package is a good rule). Meanwhile roll the pancetta into tubes and slice thinly.
On a chopping board, finely chop the rosemary with the garlic, then add salt and pepper to taste.
Heat the oil in a large non-stick pan over a medium heat and add the pancetta and the rosemary and garlic mixture. Fry for about 3 minutes, stirring constantly.
Drain the pasta and add it to the pan with the pancetta and rosemary. Mix for a couple of minutes over a low heat, tip into a warmed serving bowl and serve immediately, while still very hot.

Serves 6

PENNE AL CAVOLO NERO
Penne with Black Cabbage

Black cabbage is a speciality of Tuscany. It is very dark and tall, and I once saw it during a trip to Burgundy planted in gardens and mixed with flowers and artichokes, making a very unusual decoration.

6 black cabbage or kale leaves
6 tbsp extra virgin olive oil
3 garlic cloves, finely chopped
600g/1¼ lb penne
Salt and pepper

Cut out the central stem from each cabbage leaf and discard. Finely slice the remaining leaf. Heat half the oil in a saucepan and fry the garlic for about 2 minutes. Do not let it become golden. Add the sliced leaves, lower the heat, add salt and pepper and cover. Cook for about 30 minutes, until the cabbage becomes very soft. If necessary, add a little water to keep the leaves moist.
Meanwhile bring a large pan of water to the boil. Add salt and the penne and cook until just *al dente* (a couple of minutes less than stated on the package). Drain, add to the cabbage and cook, stirring, over a medium heat for 2 minutes. Add the rest of the oil, mix and tip into a warmed serving bowl.
Serve immediately, while still very hot.

Serves 6

CROSTINI AL RADICCHIO ROSSO E PANCETTA
Toasts with Red Radicchio and Pancetta

Pancetta and bacon can be used in this recipe to give it a smoky taste. The best red radicchio is the long one, almost white with red tips, from Treviso, or the round one from Chioggia, a lovely little harbour near the Po river, which is like a miniature Venice.

10 slices Italian country-style bread, about 0.5cm/¼ in thick
2 heads red radicchio
2 tbsp extra virgin olive oil
10 paper-thin slices pancetta or bacon
1 small onion, thinly sliced
120g/4oz fresh goats' cheese
Salt and pepper

Toast the bread slices lightly in a toaster or in the oven. Slice each radicchio head lengthways into 5 parts. Heat the oil in a pan, add the pancetta and cook until crispy. Remove the pancetta from the pan and reserve. In the same oil cook the onion, covered, until translucent—about 3 minutes. Add the radicchio, cover and cook for 5 minutes more, turning once. Sprinkle with salt and pepper.
On each slice of bread spread some cheese, then place 1 piece of radicchio on top with some onion and finish with the pancetta.
Just before serving preheat the oven to 200°C/400°F/Gas 6, and place the *crostini* in the oven for just a couple of minutes. Arrange on a serving platter.

Serves 10

CREMA DI SEDANO
Cream of Celery Soup

Around Chistmas, I try to eat all of the remaining celery in the garden, because in January it might snow and the celery will be destroyed.

1kg/2 1/4 lb celery
1 head celeriac
3 tbsp extra virgin olive oil
1 small white onion, chopped
1.5 litres/3 pints/6 cups vegetable stock
3 tbsp unsalted butter
3 slices coarse country bread, crusts removed, diced into
1.5cm/3/4 in cubes
2 large egg yolks
120ml/4fl oz/1/2 cup double (heavy) cream
4 tbsp grated fontina or Emmenthal cheese
Salt and pepper

Peel the celery stalks, using a vegetable peeler or sharp knife to remove the strings. Reserve the pale inner green leaves. Cut the celery into pieces. Peel the celeriac and slice thinly. Heat the oil in a saucepan, add the onion, celery, it's reserved green leaves and the celeriac, cover and cook for about 10 minutes over a low heat, stirring once.
Pour in the stock, bring to the boil and cook for about 30 minutes. Pass the mixture through a mouli or fine sieve and reheat. Check the salt and add pepper to taste.
Melt the butter in a pan, add the bread cubes and sauté over a medium heat, stirring constantly, until lightly golden. Remove from the pan, place on kitchen paper and allow to cool.
Beat the yolks with the cream in a bowl, add the cheese and pour into the soup, whisking as you go.
Remove from the heat, pour into a warmed soup tureen and serve, passing the croûtons round separately.

Serves 6

MINESTRONE D'ORZO E FARRO
Barley and Spelt Soup

Farro, or spelt, was once a speciality from Umbria but it is now becoming very popular, along with other grains that have previously been seldom used.

1 handful dry *porcini* mushrooms
2 leeks
8 tbsp extra virgin olive oil
1 litre/1 3/4 pints/4 cups light meat stock
150g/5oz/about 1 cup barley
150g/5oz/about 1 cup spelt (a type of grain)
Salt and pepper

Soak the *porcini* for about 30 minutes in a bowl of water. Drain the mushrooms, keeping the soaking water. Squeeze out any excess water from the *porcini* and chop. Strain the soaking water and reserve—you can freeze it and keep for a risotto, substituting it for part of the stock.
Thinly slice the white and green parts of the leeks. Heat 2 tbsp of the oil in a saucepan and sauté the leeks for about 3 minutes over a low heat, stirring constantly, until translucent. Add the stock, chopped *porcini*, the barley and the spelt and cook, covered, for about 1 hour. Add salt and pepper to taste and pour into warmed soup dishes, adding 1 tbsp oil per person before serving.

Serves 6

MINESTRONE DI RISO E BROCCOLI

Rice and Broccoli Soup

Minestrone is, in Italy, as popular as spaghetti and there are endless variations of it. The more important thing to remember when making a *minestrone* is to use seasonal vegetables that will make a tastier and better stock.

1 handful dark raisins
1kg/2 ¼ lb broccoli
3 tbsp extra virgin olive oil
6 garlic cloves, chopped
300g/10oz canned chopped Italian tomatoes, with their juice
1.5 litres/3 pints/6 cups vegetable stock
6 handfuls rice (any type)
1 handful toasted pine nuts
1 small red chilli, chopped
Salt

Soak the raisins in water for about 30 minutes or until soft. Drain and reserve.
Trim the broccoli and cut into florets, reserving the tough stalks. Set aside. Peel the stalks and dice.
Heat the oil in a pan and fry the garlic over a medium heat for about 3 minutes, stirring constantly, until barely golden. Add the tomatoes, their juice and the stock and bring to the boil. Add the rice, the broccoli florets and diced stalks and cook until the rice is *al dente*—the timing will depend on the quality of the rice.
Add the raisins, the pine nuts, the chilli and salt to taste.
Pour in a warmed soup tureen and serve immediately.

Serves 6

POLPETTINE DI CAPPONE IN BRODO

Capon Balls in Stock

Capon is the most typical dish at Christmas, more popular than turkey. It is usually served boiled with freshly pressed oil, and the stock in which the capon is cooked is used for *tortellini in brodo*.

1 capon, about 2kg/4lb
1 small onion
1 carrot
1 celery stalk
3 bay leaves
2 large eggs
90g/3oz/¾ cup coarse fresh breadcrumbs
2 tbsp chopped fresh flat-leaf parsley
2 tbsp plain (all-purpose) flour
Salt and pepper

Using a sharp knife, separate the breasts from the capon and reserve.
Put the capon in a large flameproof casserole, add the onion, carrot, celery and bay leaves. Add 3 litres/6 pints/12 cups water, a little salt and bring to the boil. Cook, covered, over a low heat for about 1 hour. Strain the liquid from the casserole into a heatproof bowl, allow to cool a little, and then put in the refrigerator.
In a food processor process the capon breast into small pieces, add the eggs, breadcrumbs, parsley, flour and a little salt and pepper to taste. Process again until well blended. Using your hands, form the mixture into small balls the size of a cherry.
When the fat on the surface of the stock has solidified, remove it carefully and discard. Reheat the remaining stock in a pan. When the stock is boiling add the capon balls and cook for about 5 minutes.
Pour the soup and capon balls into a warmed tureen and serve immediately. The leftover cooked capon flesh is wonderful in salads.

Serves 6

COPPETTE DI LASAGNE ALLA RICOTTA
Lasagne Cups with Ricotta

These lasagne cups make another perfect buffet dish because you can prepare the lasagne and cream ahead of time, fill the lasagne just before serving and heat them in the oven. Of course I make many variations adding different things to the ricotta, like sautéed prawn (shrimp) tails, diced and sautéed vegetables such as broccoli, beet leaves or spinach, or simply add some chopped thyme, rosemary or parsley.

10 sheets fresh or dried lasagne, about 15cm/7in square
1 tbsp unsalted butter
600g/1¼ lb/2 cups fresh ricotta cheese
6 tbsp freshly grated Parmesan cheese
2 large egg yolks
Grated zest of 1 organic lemon
240ml/8fl oz/1 cup double (heavy) cream
Salt and pepper

Preheat the oven to 200°C/400°F/Gas 6.
If you are using dried lasagne, soak it according to the instructions on the packet. Butter 10 ovenproof moulds, about the size of teacups, and line each one with 1 lasagne square. You will have to fold it in places to fit the mould. Place on a baking sheet (cookie tray) in the oven for about 5 minutes.
Remove from the oven, leaving it on for the final cooking stage. Carefully unmould the lasagne so you have 10 pasta cups, and reserve.
Cream the ricotta with the Parmesan, the egg yolks, the lemon zest, and salt and pepper to taste. Beat the cream to stiff peaks and fold into the ricotta mixture.
Spoon the mixture into a piping bag fitted with a large fluted nozzle and pipe the ricotta cream into the lasagne cups. Cook for 5 minutes more in the oven until warm and slightly golden. Serve immediately.

Serves 10

RISOTTO AL FOIS GRAS
Risotto with Foie Gras

Once in a while I like to indulge in more rich foods, such as foie gras, together with my two grandsons who are capable of eating half a pound of foie gras each, on top of toast with butter. They love it so much, Emanuele and Giacomo, that I try to get it from friends who are coming from France, because they only like the fresh version, which is half cooked, and not the tinned one.

2 litres/3½ pints/8 cups chicken or meat stock, both very light
½ small white onion, finely chopped
60g/2oz/4 tbsp unsalted butter
12 handfuls arborio rice (or vialone nano)
120ml/4fl oz/½ cup Sauternes wine
180g/6oz foie gras, diced
120g/4oz/1 cup finely grated Emmenthal cheese
Salt

Heat the stock in a pan and keep on a slow boil.
In a large saucepan fry the onion in half the butter over a medium heat for about 3 minutes or until translucent. Add the rice and cook over a high heat until the rice is very hot, stirring constantly with a wooden spoon.
Add the Sauternes and allow to evaporate. Add a ladleful of hot stock or enough to ensure that the rice is covered with a veil of liquid. Keep adding the stock, a ladleful at a time, about once every minute.
About 14 minutes after the rice first started boiling, add the foie gras, stir and remove from the heat. Add the cheese, the rest of the butter, taste for seasoning and cover. Leave to stand for 2 minutes.
Stir well, transfer to a warmed bowl and serve immediately. The rice should have a soupy consistency.

Serves 6

TIMBALLO DI RIGATONI
Rigatoni Timbale

Pasta moulds are popular in the south of Italy, especially in Naples. One of the more famous ones has a sweet crust around it, as described in one of my books, *The Villa Table*.

600g/1¼ lb rigatoni
150g/5oz/10 tbsp unsalted butter
plus 1 tbsp for buttering the mould
6 tbsp freshly grated Parmesan cheese
1kg/2¼ lb fresh spinach
60g/2oz/4 tbsp plain (all-purpose) flour
480ml/16fl oz/2 cups milk
Pinch of grated nutmeg
2 large eggs
120g/4oz/½ cup fine dry breadcrumbs
1kg/2¼ lb canned plum tomatoes
3 tbsp extra virgin olive oil
Salt and pepper

Preheat the oven to 170°C/350°F/Gas 4.
Bring a large pan of water to the boil, add salt and the rigatoni. Cook until just *al dente* (about 2 minutes less than stated on the package), drain and tip into a bowl with 60g/2oz/4 tbsp of the butter. Stir until the butter has melted and coated the pasta. Stir in the cheese, add salt and pepper to taste and set aside.
Cook the spinach in a little boiling water for about 2 minutes. Drain well and squeeze out any excess water. Sauté briefly with 30g/1oz/2 tbsp of the butter. Add salt and pepper to taste, and tip on to a chopping board. Allow to cool, chop very finely, and reserve.
Make a béchamel sauce by melting the remaining butter in a saucepan and gradually adding the flour. Cook over a medium heat, stirring all the time, for a couple of minutes or until well combined. Add the milk a little at a time, stirring constantly. Finally, add the nutmeg. Cook for a few minutes until the béchamel is smooth. Add salt to taste.
Beat the eggs with a little salt. Butter a 30cm/11in ring mould and add half the breadcrumbs, tipping the mould from side to side to distribute them evenly. Pour in the beaten eggs and turn the mould from side to side to coat the breadcrumbs with the eggs. Pour away any excess. Repeat with the remaining breadcrumbs to make a solid crust.
Layer the base of the mould with half the rigatoni, add half the spinach and top with half the béchamel. Make a second layer of everything, finishing with the béchamel. Cook in the oven for about 30 minutes. Meanwhile drain the tomatoes and crush them in a bowl with a fork, then cook in a saucepan with the oil for about 30 minutes until well reduced.
Add salt to taste.
Hold a round serving plate over the top of the ringmould and invert it gently, leaving the mould on top for a few minutes to allow the contents to settle. Carefully remove the mould, then spoon the tomato sauce into the centre of the mould and all around.
Serve very hot.

Serves 10

TAGLIERINI COI CARCIOFI

Taglierini with Artichokes

If you pre-cook the artichokes, you can prepare this dish at the last moment, reheating the artichokes while the taglierini are boiling, which only takes a few minutes.

Juice of 1 lemon
6 artichokes
6 tbsp extra virgin olive oil
3 garlic cloves, chopped
450g/1lb taglierini
2 tbsp chopped fresh flat-leaf parsley
Salt and pepper

Have ready a bowl of water mixed with lemon juice. Clean the artichokes, discard the tough outer leaves and the stem. Cut them in half lengthwise and remove the furry inner choke with a paring knife. Slice vertically, quite thinly, and place the slices in the water and lemon juice as you go, to prevent them from discolouring. Drain and dry on paper towels.
Heat the oil in a pan, add the garlic and the artichokes, cover the pan and cook over a low heat for about 20 minutes, stirring from time to time. Meanwhile bring a pan of water to the boil, add the taglierini and cook until *al dente*. Drain and add to the artichokes.
Sprinkle over the parsley and salt and pepper to taste, stir for 2 minutes over a low heat and serve immediately.

Serves 6

TORTINI DI RISO

Rice Pancakes

This is another recipe that I like because I can cook the risotto ahead of time, prepare the pancakes and in a moment, sauté them just before serving.

2 litres/3 ¼ pints/8 cups light meat stock
1 small white onion
120g/4oz/8 tbsp unsalted butter
12 handfuls arborio or vialone nano rice
120ml/4fl oz/½ cup dry white wine
Pinch saffron powder, or 1 tsp saffron threads
4 tbsp freshly grated Parmesan cheese
White truffle, to garnish (optional)
Salt and pepper

Heat the stock in a pan and keep at a slow boil.
In a large saucepan fry the onion in 30g/1oz/2 tbsp of the butter over a medium heat for about 3 minutes until translucent, stirring constantly. Add the rice, and cook over a high heat until very hot, stirring constantly with a wooden spoon. Add a ladleful of stock or enough to ensure that the rice is always covered with a veil of liquid.
Keep adding the stock, a ladleful at a time, about once every minute, alternating it with the wine. After 10 minutes add the saffron and 14 minutes from the time the rice first started boiling, remove from the heat.
Add another 30g/1oz/2 tbsp of the butter, the Parmesan and salt and pepper to taste. Mix well and spread the rice out on a large cold surface to stop the cooking and to cool it as quickly as possible. Leave to cool completely. The rice should be quite dry at this point. Divide the rice into 6 equal portions.
Heat one-sixth of the remaining butter in a non-stick pan over a low heat. Add 1 portion of the rice and flatten into a disk with a spoon until quite thin—about 0.5cm/¼ in. Cover and cook for about 10 minutes or until the rice is golden.
Turn the rice *tortino* over with the help of a lid or spatula and cook on the other side for about 10 minutes more. Slide the *tortino* on to a dish, cover and keep warm while you make the others.
Serve sprinkled with more Parmesan, if liked, and perhaps some paper-thin slices of white truffle.

Serves 6

MEAT AND FISH

FILETTO DI MAIALE ALLA MOSTARDA
Pork Fillet with Mustard

This very succesful recipe is the speciality of Cesarina d'Elci, a friend of mine from Siena, who is noted for the most beautiful private palace in town, overlooking the famous Piazza del Campo where Palio is held twice a year. Cesarina likes to have many friends around and feed them beautifully, sometimes using seventeenth-century Ginori dishes.

180g/6oz caul fat
4 savoy cabbage leaves
700g/1½ lb pork fillet
4 tbsp seeded French mustard
2 tbsp extra virgin olive oil
1 tbsp unsalted butter
Salt

Preheat the oven to 200°C/400°F/Gas 6.
Soak the caul fat in a bowl of water for about 30 minutes. Bring a large saucepan of water to the boil, add salt and the cabbage leaves. Blanch for 2 minutes, drain and lay on a clean cloth to dry. Discard the central tough stem from each leaf.
Coat the pork fillet carefully with the mustard. Lay the caul fat on a clean surface, arrange the cabbage leaves on top and put the pork fillet in the centre. Roll up the leaves and the fat to enclose the fillet completely, tucking in the ends, and tie with kitchen string.
Heat the oil and butter in a flameproof roasting tin (pan) over a medium heat. Once the butter has melted add the fillet and transfer to the oven—do not cover. Cook for 10 minutes, then open and immediately close the oven door, switch off the heat and leave the fillet in the oven for 10 more minutes. Slice the fillet, arrange on a warmed serving platter and serve immediately.

Serves 4

CONIGLIO ALL'ACETO BALSAMICO
Rabbit in Balsamic Vinegar Sauce

Balsamic vinegar is a very special produce of Modena and Reggio Emilia, where it once was only sold through auctions at very high prices. Now it is produced more commercially and I think it makes a nice sauce for meats or cheeses, although I very seldom use it in salads.

1 tbsp fennel seeds
1 rabbit, about 2kg/4lb, prepared for the oven
150g/5oz pancetta, sliced paper-thin
2 tbsp extra virgin olive oil
1 tbsp unsalted butter
150g/5oz green olives, pitted
120ml/4fl oz/½ cup dry white wine
3 tbsp balsamic vinegar
Salt and pepper

Preheat the oven to 170°C/350°F/Gas 4.
Place the fennel seeds in a shallow dish with salt and pepper and turn the rabbit in the seeds and seasoning to coat. Lay the pancetta slices over the rabbit and secure with kitchen string.
Heat the oil and butter in a flameproof roasting tin (pan), add the rabbit, cover and cook in the oven for about 30 minutes. Add the olives. Cook for 30 more minutes, uncovered, adding the wine a little at a time and turning the rabbit a couple of times. Remove the rabbit and place on a warmed serving dish.
Transfer the roasting tin (pan) to the hob and, over a medium heat, deglaze the cooking juices with the balsamic vinegar. Pour over the rabbit together with the olives and serve.

Serves 6

STINCO AL LIMONE
Veal Shank in Lemon Sauce

This is a favourite recipe for the graduation dinner of my cooking classes in Coltibuono. The shank is mouth-melting and delicious, easy to cook and beautifully presented by Hadtidza, my help and home chef, who decorates the shanks with plenty of bay leaves.

1 whole veal shank, about 1.2kg/2½ lb, bone in
1 tbsp unsalted butter
2 tbsp extra virgin olive oil
1 carrot, halved
1 onion, halved
1 celery stalk, halved
A few bay leaves
½ bottle dry white wine
Grated zest of 1 organic lemon
Salt and pepper

Preheat the oven to 170°C/350°F/Gas 4.
Rub the shank all over with salt and pepper and tie up tightly with kitchen string.
Heat the butter and oil in a large flameproof casserole, add the shank and brown on all sides for about 10 minutes over a medium heat. Add the vegetables and bay leaves, cover and cook for about 4 hours in the oven, adding wine from time to time to prevent the cooking juices from drying out. Place the shank on a serving platter and keep warm.
Add the lemon zest to the juices in the casserole and deglaze over a medium heat, scraping the bottom of the dish well.
Pass the cooking juices and the vegetables through a food mill or fine sieve, into a saucepan. Reheat, pour the sauce over the shank and serve.

Serves 4

POLLO ARROSTO ALLE ERBE
Roasted Herbed Chicken

This is a very tasty way of cooking chicken, so that in the end it is tender and brown. In summertime I substitute rosemary and sage with herbs such as basil, parsley, chives or tarragon.

2 fresh rosemary sprigs, finely chopped
1 handful fresh sage leaves, finely chopped
1 tbsp dried mint
3 garlic cloves, finely chopped
1 chicken, about 1.2kg/2lb, prepared for the oven
2 tbsp extra virgin olive oil
1 tbsp unsalted butter
120ml/4fl oz/½ cup dry white wine
Salt and pepper

Preheat the oven to 170°C/350°F/Gas 4.
Mix the herbs and garlic with some salt and pepper to taste. Carefully ease the skin away from the chicken at the breasts and at the top of the legs and push the herb mixture between the skin and the flesh. Truss the chicken with kitchen string.
Put the oil and butter in a large flameproof casserole, place the chicken on top and cover the dish. Cook in the oven for about 1½ hours. Remove the lid and cook for 1 more hour, adding wine from time to time and turning the chicken a couple of times to brown it completely, until it is quite dark. Transfer the chicken to a serving platter and keep warm.
Over a medium heat, deglaze the cooking juices in the dish with a little water, scraping the bottom of the dish well. Pass the juices through a sieve into a pan and reheat. Pour over the chicken and serve.

Serves 4

INVOLTINI DI VITELLO ALLA PANCETTA
Veal Rolls with Pancetta

We take the students from our cooking classes out for dinner in the evening to private grand homes and this is the recipe my friend Franchina Parisi used to cook for them when they went to her house. She served them with the best potato purée one can dream of.

30 round, thinly sliced veal *scaloppine* (thin slices of silverside of veal)
10 paper-thin slices pancetta
30 small fresh sage leaves
1 handful coarse fresh breadcrumbs
120ml/4fl oz/½ cup milk
150g/5½ oz minced pork
1 large egg yolk
2 tbsp freshly grated Parmesan cheese
2 tbsp unsalted butter
2 tbsp extra virgin olive oil
120ml/4fl oz/½ cup dry white wine
Salt and pepper

Pound the *scaloppine* with a meat pounder, making sure you keep the round shape. Divide each slice of pancetta into 3 and place 1 piece on top of each piece of veal, followed by 1 sage leaf.
Soak the bread briefly in the milk and squeeze out the excess milk. In a bowl, mix the soaked bread with the pork, the egg yolk, the cheese, and salt and pepper to taste. Place a teaspoon of this mixture on top of each of the *scaloppine* and roll up carefully to enclose the filling. Secure with toothpicks.
Heat the butter and oil in a large pan, add the *scaloppine* and sauté for about 10 minutes over a medium heat until golden all over. Add the wine, cover and lower the heat. Cook for 10 minutes more, adding a little water if necessary to prevent the cooking juices from drying out. Arrange on a warmed serving platter and serve with the cooking juices, discarding the toothpicks.

Serves 6

BACCALÀ AI CARCIOFI
Salt Cod with Artichokes

Salted cod is very popular all over Italy and is easy to prepare. In Italy, you can buy the cod already soaked, but it is sufficient to keep it under water for about 24 hours, changing the water a few times.

600g/1¼ lb salt cod fillet
Juice of 1 lemon
8 artichokes
2 garlic cloves, chopped
6 tbsp extra virgin olive oil
1 tbsp finely chopped fresh flat-leaf parsley

Soak the salt cod in water for 24 hours, changing the water at least 4 times. Drain. Remove the bones and divide the fish into 6 portions.
Have ready a bowl of water mixed with lemon juice. Clean the artichokes, discard the tough outer leaves and the stem. Cut them in half lengthwise and remove the inner furry choke with a paring knife. Slice the artichokes into quarters and place in the water and lemon juice as you go, to prevent them from discolouring. Drain and pat dry on paper towels.
Heat half the oil in a pan over a low heat and sauté the garlic until translucent, about 3 minutes. Add the artichokes, the salt cod and the parsley, cover and cook until the artichokes are tender, about 10 minutes. Set aside the cod and artichokes and keep warm.
In a blender, blend 8 of the artichoke quarters with the remaining oil and a little water to thin the sauce. Heat the sauce gently in a pan. Arrange the salt cod and remaining artichoke quarters on a warmed serving platter, pour over the sauce and serve.

Serves 6

BRANZINO AL CARTOCCIO
Sea Bass Cooked in a Parcel

Any fish that can be cooked in the oven is good for this recipe. Sometimes I use tuna fillets slices, and if so, will just cover them with the lemon slices.

1 sea bass, about 2kg/4lb
120ml/4fl oz/½ cup extra virgin olive oil
1 organic lemon, halved
90g/3oz canned tuna in oil, drained
1 handful fresh flat-leaf parsley
1 anchovy fillet in oil, drained
30g/1oz capers in vinegar, drained
1 large hard boiled egg
1 tbsp red wine vinegar
Salt and pepper

Preheat the oven to 170°C/350°F/Gas 5.
Clean the sea bass, wash and pat dry. Brush with a little of the oil inside and out, then stuff the cavity with one half of the lemon. Cut the other lemon half into thin slices. Put the sea bass on a sheet of baking parchment large enough to wrap it up, cover with the lemon slices and sprinkle with salt and pepper. Wrap the fish in the paper so it is completely enclosed.
Cook in the oven for about 40 minutes.
Put the tuna, parsley, anchovy fillet, capers, hard-boiled egg, vinegar, some pepper and the rest of the oil in a blender. Blend until creamy.
Arrange the fish on a warmed serving platter and serve immediately with the sauce.

Serves 6

SOGLIOLE AL FINOCCHIO E ARANCIA
Sole with Fennel and Orange

Oranges and fennel are a reminder of the medieval times when the Arabs navigated the Italian waters and introduced these ingredients to Italy. They have been adopted, particularly by Sicilians, into many recipes.

6 sole, filleted (24 pieces)
3 fennel bulbs
3 tbsp extra virgin olive oil
Zest of 1 organic orange
Salt and pepper

Preheat the oven to 180°C/375°F/Gas 5.
Carefully roll up each sole fillet and secure with a toothpick.
Clean the fennel bulbs, cut them in half vertically, wash them carefully and slice thinly. Brush a baking dish with half of the oil, arrange the fennel slices in the dish, and add salt and pepper to taste. Cover and cook in the oven for about 20 minutes, adding a little water if necessary to prevent the fennel from drying out.
Arrange the sole fillets in one layer over the fennel and sprinkle with the orange zest, the remaining oil and a little salt. Cover again and cook for 10 minutes more. Uncover and serve.

Serves 6

BOVE AL CUCCHIALIO
Beef Stewed in Red Wine

My father used to love this recipe and his home chef Anna tought me how to cook it. It takes a long time, but you do not even have to cut the meat—just serve it with a crown of risotto or polenta for the most successful dinner.

About 2.5kg/5lb 8oz stewing beef, in one piece
2 carrots, halved
2 onions, halved
2 celery stalks, halved
3 bay leaves
1 tbsp juniper berries
1 tsp peppercorns
1 small fennel bulb
2 bottles good aged Chianti or Barolo wine
2 tbsp extra virgin olive oil
1 tbsp unsalted butter
Salt and pepper

Two days before serving, tie the meat with kitchen string and place in a large, deep casserole dish. Add the carrots, onions, celery, bay leaves, juniper berries and peppercorns. Slice the fennel in half, wash carefully and add to the meat. Add the wine. Cover the dish and place in the refrigerator for 24 hours.

The day before serving, lift the beef out of the marinade, pat dry with paper towels and sauté with the oil and butter in a large flameproof casserole over a medium heat until brown all over—about 10 minutes.

Meanwhile preheat the oven to 170°C/350°F/Gas 4. Strain the vegetables from the marinade, reserving the wine. Add the vegetables to the meat in the casserole with half of the wine from the marinade. Reserve the rest of the wine. Cover and cook in the oven for about 6 hours, turning the meat from time to time. Remove from the oven, allow to cool completely, then refrigerate overnight.

The next day, skim the fat from the surface, and preheat the oven to 170°C/350°F/Gas 4. Add some of the reserved wine if necessary, so that the meat is partially submerged. Cover and cook in the oven for a further 8 hours turning it very carefully from time to time.

Untie the meat and place in a deep serving dish. Pass the cooking liquid and the vegetables through a food mill or fine sieve into a saucepan and reheat. If necessary reduce the liquid to thicken. The sauce should be neither too thick nor too thin. Season. Pour the sauce around the meat and serve using a spoon and a fork.

Serves 8-10

SEPPIE CON PATATE E CIPOLLE
Squid with Potatoes and Onions

This is a very hearty recipe for cold winter lunches. I like to serve it followed simply by a fruit salad.

600g/1¼ lb squid
3 tbsp extra virgin olive oil
1 large onion, finely sliced
3 large potatoes, peeled and diced
1 tbsp chopped fresh flat-leaf parsley
Salt and pepper

Clean the squid and cut into large pieces.
Heat the olive oil in a large pan and sauté the onion over a medium heat, stirring constantly, until translucent—about 3 minutes.
Add the squid and sauté for a few more minutes. Add the potatoes and salt and pepper to taste. Cover and cook for about 10 minutes or until the potatoes are tender. If necessary add a little water to prevent the cooking juices from drying out.
Sprinkle with the parsley, arrange on a warmed serving platter and serve.

Serves 6

WINTER VEGETABLES

SFORMATO DI BROCCOLI
Broccoli Mould

Not too long ago, it was very popular to serve a vegetable mould between the soup and the main course for a family dinner. It was often accompanied by fried sweetbreads in a lemon sauce, cock combs or a mixture of the two. Now these make up a perfect dinner main course or a an elegant starter.

1kg/2 ¼ lb broccoli
2 tbsp extra virgin olive oil
60g/2oz smoked pancetta or bacon, thinly sliced
3 large eggs
4 tbsp grated provolone cheese
120ml/4fl oz/½ cup double (heavy) cream
1 tbsp unsalted butter, softened
120g/4oz/½ cup fine dry breadcrumbs
Salt and pepper

Preheat the oven to 170°C/350°F/Gas 4.
Clean the broccoli, divide into florets and set aside, reserving the tough stalks. Peel the stalks and cut into pieces. Bring a pan of water to the boil, add the chopped broccoli stalks and cook for about 5 minutes. Add the florets and cook for 2 more minutes. Drain. Heat the oil in a pan, add the pancetta and sauté until it becomes crisp. Add the chopped broccoli stems and florets and sauté over a medium heat for a couple of minutes. Add salt and pepper to taste. Pass the contents of the pan through a foodmill or fine sieve to make a purée.

In a bowl beat the eggs, cheese and cream with a whisk until well blended. Add the broccoli purée and mix well. Grease a 23cm/9in ring mould with the butter, add the breadcrumbs and tip from side to side to coat. Fill the mould with the mixture. Place the mould on a baking sheet (cookie tray), place on a shelf in the oven, then pour in water to come about 3cm/1in up the sides. Cook in the oven for 1 hour. Remove from the oven and run a knife round the inside of the mould to loosen. Invert on to a serving dish, carefully remove the mould and serve very hot.

Serves 6

FRITTELLE DI CIPOLLE
Fried Onion Pancakes

On the first day of the cooking classes at Coltibuono, we often present these onions as an accompaniment to an aperitif. They are very crisp and must be served very hot.

1 large egg
60g/2oz/4 tbsp plain (all-purpose) flour for the batter, plus 120g/4oz/1 cup for deep-frying
150ml/5fl oz/⅔ cup water
1 litre/1 ¾ pints/4 cups vegetable oil for deep-frying
3 onions, peeled and sliced into rings
Salt

Beat the egg in a bowl, then add the flour for the batter a little at a time, beating between each addition, to avoid lumps. Incorporate the water, beating to avoid lumps, and a little salt.
Heat the oil in a frying pan until it reaches 170°C/350°F on a kitchen thermometer. Coat the onions in the rest of the flour and shake off any excess. Dip them in the batter and deep-fry for few minutes, until golden. Drain on paper towels, sprinkle with salt and serve immediately, piping hot.

Serves 6

INSALATA DI SPINACI AL GORGONZOLA

Spinach Salad with Gorgonzola Dressing

If the spinach leaves are really small and tender you could also keep the stems for this salad. Otherwise just discard them and keep only the leaves. You can substitute Gorgonzola with a little milder cheese like Taleggio or the French version, Camembert.

600g/1¼ lb baby spinach
90g/3oz Gorgonzola cheese
120ml/4fl oz/½ cup extra virgin olive oil
Juice and zest of 1 organic lemon
Salt and pepper

Clean the spinach, wash carefully and dry.
Arrange the spinach in a salad bowl.
Put the Gorgonzola, oil, lemon juice and pepper in a blender and blend until creamy and runny. Sprinkle the spinach with a little salt and the lemon zest, pour the dressing over the top, toss and serve.

Serves 6

LENTICCHIE AL CORIANDOLO

Lentils with Coriander (Cilantro)

This is an Italian adaptation from recipes found during my many travels to India, a place I cherish above all the eastern countries for its architectural treasures, the beauty of the sky and the elegance and colour of the people.

420g/14oz green lentils
1 handful fresh coriander (cilantro)
3 tbsp extra virgin olive oil
Grated zest of 1 organic lemon
Salt and pepper

Place the lentils in a large bowl, cover with water and soak overnight.
Drain, transfer to a large saucepan, cover with fresh water and bring to a low boil. Cook for about 1 hour. Meanwhile finely chop the coriander (cilantro). Drain the lentils and tip into a serving bowl. Sprinkle with salt and pepper, add the coriander (cilantro), the oil and the lemon zest. Mix well and serve warm.

Serves 6

SCAROLE RIPIENE

Stuffed Chicory

This is a very Neapolitan dish that I enjoy when I visit my friends in Naples. Very seldom cooked in restaurants, it is a typical regional recipe.

30g/1oz black raisins
3 heads chicory
60g/2oz black (ripe) olives, Gaeta or Kalamata, pitted
30g/1oz capers in vinegar, drained
30g/1oz pine nuts
2 tbsp grated pecorino (Romano) cheese
3 canned anchovy fillets, drained and chopped
1 handful fresh coarse breadcrumbs, soaked in water and squeezed dry
3 garlic cloves, finely chopped
3 tbsp extra virgin olive oil
Salt and pepper

Preheat the oven to 170°C/350°F/Gas 4.
Soak the raisins in water for about 30 minutes, then drain.
Bring a pan of water to the boil. Clean and trim the chicory heads, then blanch in the water for about 2 minutes. Drain and arrange on a cloth, then open up the leaves to make a hollow at the centre for the stuffing.
Cut the olives in half and mix in a bowl with the capers, pine nuts, pecorino (Romano) cheese, anchovies, breadcrumbs and garlic. Season to taste. Divide the mixture into 3 and fill the chicory. Bring the leaves together to enclose the filling and secure with kitchen string.
Brush a baking dish with the oil and place the stuffed chicory heads in the dish. Cover and cook in the oven for about 30 minutes. Serve immediately.

Serves 6

CROCCHETTE DI SPINACI
Spinach Croquettes

Serve these with deep fried fish and other vegetables, but also as an appetizer with a glass of our very special Trappoline white, or even as a first course in summertime, accompanied by a tomato coulis.

1kg/2 1/4 lb fresh spinach
300g/10oz/1 1/4 cups ricotta cheese
2 large eggs
4 tbsp freshly grated Parmesan cheese
120g/4oz/1 cup plain (all-purpose) flour
120g/4oz/1 cup fine dry breadcrumbs
1 litre/1 3/4 pints/4 cups vegetable oil, for deep frying
Salt

Clean the spinach, leaving the stems intact. Bring a little water to the boil, add the spinach and cook for a few minutes until wilted. Drain, allow to cool slightly and squeeze out any excess water. Chop finely and mix in a bowl with the ricotta, 1 egg and the Parmesan cheese. Add salt to taste.
With floured hands, shape the mixture into ovals the size of small eggs. Coat with the rest of the flour. Beat the other egg with a fork in a deep dish and place the breadcrumbs in another wide, shallow dish. Dip the spinach ovals in the egg and then roll them in the breadcrumbs to coat.
Heat the oil in a frying pan until it reaches 170°C/350°F. Deep-fry the spinach croquettes until golden, a few at a time. Drain on absorbent paper and serve immediately while very hot.

Serves 6

FRITTATA DI PATATE ALL'ORIGANO
Potato Omelette with Oregano

There is a rule that I observe for my *frittate* whereby I only make them if mixed with vegetables of my choice, from potatoes, artichokes, onions, spinach and broccoli to courgette (zucchini). The other rule is to mix the vegetables with only half an egg per person. Never cook a *frittata* in the oven as it will become too dry—we say that it should be *bavosa*, a little liquid.

6 tbsp extra virgin olive oil
1kg/2 1/4 lb boiling potatoes, peeled and thinly sliced
3 large eggs
1 tbsp dried oregano
6 tbsp freshly grated Parmesan cheese
Salt and pepper

Heat half the oil in a non-stick pan, add the potatoes and salt and pepper to taste, cover and cook over a low heat for about 10 minutes. With the help of a spatula, turn the potatoes and cook on the other side for a few more minutes or until tender.
Beat the eggs in a large bowl with a little salt and pepper, the oregano and the cheese. Break up the potatoes in the pan slightly with a fork and pour the egg mixture over. Shaking the pan, cook over a medium heat until the eggs have started to set. Slide the *frittata* out of the pan on to a plate, then carefully turn over and slide back into the pan. Cook this side for a few more minutes. Transfer to a warmed serving platter and serve immediately.

Serves 6

DESSERTS AND BREADS

SOUFFLÉ FREDDO DI MELE

Cold Apple Soufflé

This sort of cold soufflé is not complicated and is very tasty. You could also substitute the apples with strawberries in summertime.

1kg/2 ¼ lb cooking apples
1 tbsp powdered cinnamon
180g/6oz/1 cup granulated sugar
3 large egg whites
400g/13oz/1 ¾ cup double (heavy) cream
Salt

Peel, quarter and core the apples. Place in a pan, add a little water, cover and cook over a low heat for about 10 minutes or until soft. Pass through a foodmill or fine sieve, add the cinnamon and set aside.
Put the sugar with a little water in a heavy saucepan. Prepare a basin of cold water large enough to hold the saucepan. Heat the sugar and water gently until the temperature reaches 100°C/210°F exactly on a kitchen thermometer. Transfer the saucepan to the cold water to stop the cooking.
Beat the egg whites with a pinch of salt until stiff, then fold in the warmed sugar a little at a time with a metal spoon. Beat the cream in a separate bowl until stiff.
Fold the apple purée into the egg whites, then fold in the cream.
Line a soufflé mould with baking parchment and fill with the apple cream. Chill in the refrigerator for a minimum of 8 hours. Unmould the soufflé, carefully remove the paper and serve.

Serves 8

MOUSSE DI PANETTONE AL CIOCCOLATO

Chocolate and Panettone Mousse

Being born in Milan *panettone* is the dessert I would serve for Christmas even in Tuscany, but a little transformed, of course, to make it more festive. Sometimes I just scoop a bit out from under the *panettone* and fill at the last minute with chocolate ice-cream.

300g/10oz *panettone*
4 tbsp Vin Santo or other white dessert wine
90g/3oz bitter chocolate
60g/2oz/4 tbsp unsalted butter, plus
1 tbsp for coating the moulds
3 large eggs
90g/3oz/6 tbsp granulated sugar,
plus 1 tbsp for coating the moulds
2 tbsp icing (powdered) sugar

Preheat the oven to 170°C/350°F/Gas 4.
Dice the *panettone*, place in a bowl and sprinkle with the Vin Santo.
Melt the chocolate and butter in the top half of a double boiler, or in a heatproof bowl that fits snugly over a pan of barely simmering water. Remove from the heat and leave to cool.
Beat the eggs with the sugar, fold in the chocolate mixture and the *panettone*. Mix until well blended. Butter and sprinkle 10 small individual moulds with the rest of the sugar and fill with the *panettone* mixture. Cook in the oven for about 15 minutes, until still a little creamy in the centre. Let cool completely, then carefully unmould on to individual dishes. Sprinkle with the icing (powdered) sugar and serve.

Serves 10

TORTA DI PINOLI AL LIMONE

Lemon and Pine Nut Tart

My friend Sandra Bianchi Bandinelli has one of the most beautiful seventeenth-century houses near Siena, full of frescoes and nice furniture. We go there with the students for a very lovely evening dinner and often she presents this dessert at the end of the meal.

FOR THE PASTRY:
180g/6oz/1½ cups plain (all-purpose) flour
60g/2oz/4 tbsp semolina
120g/4oz/8 tbsp unsalted butter, cut in small pieces,
plus 1 tbsp for the tart shell
60g/2oz/4 tbsp granulated sugar
1 large egg, plus 1 large egg yolk
FOR THE FILLING:
1 egg, plus 1 yolk
240g/8oz/1 cup ricotta cheese
60g/2oz/4 tbsp icing (powdered) sugar
Grated zest of 1 organic lemon
10 drops lemon extract
120ml/4fl oz/½ cup double (heavy) cream
120g/4oz pine nuts

Preheat the oven to 170°C/350°F/Gas 4.
To make the pastry, place the flour, semolina, butter, sugar, egg and yolk in a food processor fitted with metal blades. Process until the mixture forms a ball. Wrap in cling film (plastic wrap) and refrigerate for about 1 hour.
Butter a 23cm/9in loose-bottomed tart tin (pan). Roll out the dough on a lightly floured surface and line the tart tin (pan). Prick the base with a fork. Bake in the oven for about 20 minutes until barely golden. If the pastry pops up in places during cooking, flatten it again with the palm of your hand, protected with a cloth, then return to the oven. Remove the tart from the oven and set aside to cool.
For the filling, beat the egg and yolk with the ricotta, icing (powdered) sugar, lemon zest and extract until well blended. Beat the cream to soft peaks and fold into the ricotta mixture. Spoon the filling into the tart shell, smooth the top and sprinkle with the pine nuts. Cook in the oven for 20 minutes more or until golden on top. Carefully remove the tart from the tin (pan) and leave to cool on a wire rack before serving.

Serves 8

PANELLO CON UVETTE E NOCI

Bread with Raisins and Walnuts

In wintertime when the grapes are no longer so good, raisins and walnuts make a wonderful substitute for *schiacciata*, the Tuscan version of this bread.

30g/2oz/2 tbsp fresh yeast
240ml/8fl oz/1 cup lukewarm water
300g/10oz walnuts (unshelled weight),
or 120g/4oz shelled walnuts
2 tbsp extra virgin olive oil
1 fresh rosemary sprig, chopped
360g/12oz/3 cups plain (all-purpose) flour,
plus some for working
60g/2oz/4 tbsp granulated sugar
Grated zest of 1 organic lemon
120g/4oz raisins
120ml/4fl oz/½ cup Vin Santo or other dessert wine
1 tsp aniseeds
Salt

Place the yeast in the lukewarm water and leave to dissolve for about 10 minutes. Shell the walnuts, if necessary, and halve them.
Heat the oil in a pan, add the walnuts and rosemary and sauté for about 3 minutes over a medium heat, stirring often. Remove the pan from the heat and leave to cool.
Put the flour in a bowl, add half the sugar, the lemon zest, a pinch of salt, from the walnuts and the water and yeast. Mix with a fork until a soft dough is formed. Turn the dough out on to a floured work surface and knead for a few minutes to form a ball.
Place the ball in a floured bowl, cover with cling film (plastic wrap) and leave to rise for about 1 hour or until doubled in size.
Meanwhile soak the raisins in the wine for about 1 hour. Drain.
Place the dough on a floured surface and punch back. Flatten into a disc of about 23cm/9in in diameter. Transfer the disc to a floured baking sheet, dot with the raisins and walnuts and sprinkle with the aniseeds. Leave to rise again for about 20 minutes. Preheat the oven to 200°C/400°F/Gas 6.
Bake for about 30 minutes. Leave to cool on a wire rack and serve.

Serves 6

ARANCE AL COCCO

Blood Oranges with Coconut

Blood oranges come from Sicily from January onwards for about three months and make wonderful desserts. You can use dry coconut instead of fresh, and soak for a while in the little orange juice that you will lose from cutting the slices to make them moist, but the coconut is also delicious when dry.

6 blood oranges
2 large egg whites
120g/4oz/1 cup icing (powdered) sugar
120g/4oz/1 cup fresh coconut (prepared weight),
or 60g/2oz dessiccated coconut
120g/4oz peeled and chopped hazelnuts

Peel the oranges, and remove any white pith. Slice them and arrange in a shallow baking dish, discarding any juices.
Preheat the grill (broiler) to high.
Beat the egg whites until quite stiff, then carefully fold the icing (powdered) sugar in with a spoon
Grate the coconut, if using fresh. Add the coconut to the egg whites, folding it in carefully.
Spoon the meringue mixture over the sliced oranges, then sprinkle over the chopped hazelnuts.
Put under the grill (broiler) and cook for a few minutes until slightly golden. Serve immediately.

Serves 6

AVOCADO AL PORTO

Avocado Pear with Port Wine

I am not very fond of desserts, as I do not have the sweet tooth of most Italians. So I try to use as much fruit as possible in desserts, treated in many ways. This is a wonderful advocado dish I learned in Spain.

6 very ripe avocados
Juice of 1 lemon
90g/3oz/6 tbsp granulated sugar
6 tbsp double (heavy) cream
6 small glasses of Port, 60ml/2fl oz/¼ cup each

Peel and stone the avocados. Blend the avocado flesh in a blender with the lemon juice, sugar and double (heavy) cream. Divide among 6 champagne glasses, pour over the Port and serve.

Serves 6

FOCACCIA DI CECI ALLA SALVIA

Chickpea and Sage Focaccia

Chickpea flour can be found at health stores, although in Italy it is quite popular and you can buy it in supermarkets.

30g/1oz/2 tbsp fresh yeast
240ml/6fl oz/1 cup lukewarm water
240g/8oz/2 cups plain (all-purpose) flour,
plus extra for working
120g/4oz/1 cup chickpea flour
6 tbsp extra virgin olive oil
1 handful fresh sage leaves
Sea salt

Stir the yeast into the lukewarm water and leave to dissolve for about 10 minutes.
Place both types of flour in a large bowl, add half the oil and the water and dissolved yeast. Stir with a fork in a circular motion until you have a soft dough.
Knead the dough on a lightly floured surface to make a ball, then transfer to a floured bowl. Cover with cling film (plastic wrap). Leave to rise for about 1 hour, until doubled in size.
Brush a 25cm/10in circular tart tin (pan) or flat baking tray (sheet) with 1 tbsp of the remaining oil. On a floured surface, punch down the dough and roll into a circle the same size diameter as the tin (pan). Brush with the rest of the oil, sprinkle with the sage leaves and the sea salt. Leave to rise again for 20 minutes more.
Preheat the oven to 200°C/400°F/Gas 6.
Transfer the dough to the baking tray (cookie sheet) and bake for about 30 minutes. Remove from the oven, leave to cool on a wire rack and serve.

Serves 6

THE WINTER FEAST

P TÉ DI FAGIANO AI TARTUFI

Pheasant Pâté with White Truffles

This pâté has been a must for many years in my parents' home. Anna, their home chef, decorated it with small birds made from butter. All these Christmas recipes serve 10 people.

1 whole pheasant, about 1.5kg/3lb, prepared for the oven
90g/3oz prosciutto, thinly sliced
1 tbsp unsalted butter for cooking, plus 90g/3oz/6 tbsp for the truffle cream
2 tbsp extra virgin olive oil
120ml/4fl oz/½ cup dry Marsala wine
1 small carrot
1 small onion
1 celery stalk
6 juniper berries
2 fresh sage leaves
1 bay leaf
2 slices stale white bread, crusts removed
1 small white truffle (depending on your generosity)
Salt and pepper

Preheat the oven to 170°C/350°F/Gas 4.
Remove the skin from the pheasant, starting from the legs. Cover the bird with the prosciutto slices and secure the slices in place with kitchen string.
Heat 1 tbsp butter and the oil in a large flameproof oval casserole dish, add the pheasant and cook on a high heat on the stove for about 5 minutes, turning occasionally, until barely golden all over. Add the Marsala and salt and pepper to taste, let the liquid evaporate and add the vegetables, juniper berries and herbs. Cover and cook in the oven for about 2 hours, adding a little water from time to time to prevent the cooking juices from drying out.
Remove the pheasant from the oven, add the bread to the dish and leave it to soak up the juices. Leave the pheasant to cool, then strip the meat from the bones, reserving the prosciutto, and roughly chop the meat.
Put the pheasant meat in a blender with the soaked bread, prosciutto, juices and vegetables, until creamy.

Slice the truffle paper-thin and blend thoroughly in a cup with the rest of the butter. Add this to the pheasant mixture and pass through a sieve. Mix well. Line the inside of a 23 x 6cm/9 x 2½ in rectangular mould with baking parchment and fill with the pheasant pâté. Place in the refrigerator for about 10 hours before serving with slices of hot toast.

Serves 10

TACCHINO RIPIENO

Turkey Roll

A delicious alternative to the classic Christmas turkey.

3 fresh rosemary sprigs, finely chopped
3 garlic cloves, finely chopped
1 turkey, about 3kg/6lb
300g/10oz ricotta cheese
300g/10oz fresh sweet sausages, peeled and crumbled
2 large eggs
150g/5oz fresh breadcrumbs, soaked in milk and squeezed dry
1 tbsp unsalted butter
2 tbsp extra virgin olive oil
120ml/4fl oz/½ cup dry white wine
Salt and pepper

Preheat the oven to 170°C/350°F/Gas 4.
In a shallow dish, mix the rosemary, garlic, salt and pepper. Debone the turkey or ask your butcher. Top with the rosemary mixture and cover well.
Place the ricotta, sausages, eggs and breadcrumbs in a bowl and mix well. Add a little salt and fill the turkey with the mixture. Make a roll and secure with string. Spread the butter and oil over the base of a large roasting tin (pan) and place the turkey roll on top. Cook in the oven covered for about 2 hours, adding the wine from time to time to keep the meat moist.
Cook uncovered for 1 more hour to brown, occasionally adding a little water.
Discard the string, arrange on a platter and keep warm. Deglaze the cooking juices with more water, pour on top of the turkey and serve.

Serves 10

RAVIOLI DI ANATRA
Duck Ravioli

This is a special ravioli which was taught to me from a home chef in Mantua, one of the more beautiful towns in northern Italy, where I like to go so I can eat the famous *agnolotti con la zucca* (pumpkin ravioli), as well as to admire the frescoes of Andrea Mantegna in the Palazzo Ducale.

1 duck breast, skin removed
90g/3oz/6 tbsp unsalted butter
120g/4oz spinach
1 large egg
1 tbsp fresh thyme leaves
1 tbsp chopped fresh flat-leaf parsley
1 large peeled boiled potato
Salt and pepper
FOR THE PASTA:
300g/10oz/2 ½ cups plain (all-purpose) flour
3 large eggs

Thinly slice the duck breast and sauté in a pan with 1 tbsp of the butter for a few minutes, until still pink. Remove from the pan and reserve.
Blanch the spinach in a little boiling water, drain well and reserve. When the spinach is cool enough, squeeze out any excess water.
Put the sautéed duck breast, the spinach, egg, thyme, parsley and the potato in a food processor and pulse until well blended. Add salt and pepper to taste.
Prepare the pasta. Set aside a couple of tablespoons of the measured flour. Heap the rest of the flour in a mound in a large mixing bowl. Make a deep well in the centre and break the eggs into it. Beat the eggs lightly with a fork until yolks and whites are well blended. Gradually draw in the flour from the lower inside of the well, using a circular movement. When the egg and flour are well amalgamated, transfer the dough to a floured work surface and start kneading. Knead the dough for at least 10 minutes, turning the dough always in the same direction. When it seems ready, wash and dry your hands. Poke a finger into the middle and, if it comes out clean, you require no more flour. If your finger is sticky, work in a little of the flour you have set aside. If the dough seems hard and too dry, add a little moisture by working it a little with wet hands. When the dough is neither too sticky nor too dry, cover it with a bowl. Carefully scrape the worksurface to get rid of any loose flour or scraps of dough and immediately roll out the dough.
Roll the pasta through the machine until very thin (about 0.5mm/¼ in thick). Cut into long strips 5cm/2in wide and put small spoonfuls of the duck and spinach filling along the strips at regular intervals about 5cm/2in apart.
Moisten the edges of the pasta and between the fillings with a damp pastry brush. Place another strip on top and press with the tip of your fingers round each mound of filling to seal well. Cut into squares with a fluted roller.
Bring a large pan of water to the boil, add salt and the ravioli. Cook for about 2 minutes after the water returns to the boil. Meanwhile, melt the remaining butter in the same pan in which you sautéed the duck breast.
Drain the ravioli, arrange on a platter, pour the butter over and serve immediately while still very hot.

Serves 10

SFORMATO DI RISO AI CARCIOFI
Rice Mould with Artichokes

Moulds are very useful for parties because they can be prepared in advance and reheated just before serving. In winter artichokes can be substituted with spinach, broccoli florets (cook them very briefly) or fennel bulbs.

Juice of half an organic lemon
12 artichokes
3 tbsp extra virgin olive oil
2 garlic cloves, whole
2 1/4 litres/3 3/4 pints/10 cups chicken stock
1 small white onion, finely chopped
90g/3oz/6 tbsp unsalted butter,
plus 1 tbsp for greasing the mould
800g/1lb 12oz arborio or vialone nano rice
120ml/4fl oz/1/2 cup dry white wine
90g/3oz/3/4 cup freshly grated Parmesan cheese
2 tbsp finely chopped fresh flat-leaf parsley
Salt and pepper

Have ready a bowl of water mixed with lemon juice. Clean the artichokes, discard the tough outer leaves and the stem. Cut them in half lengthwise and remove the furry inner choke with a paring knife. Slice them and place the slices in the water and lemon juice as you go, to prevent them from discolouring.
Drain the artichokes and stew in a covered pan with the oil, the garlic and a little salt for about 10 minutes. Discard the garlic and reserve the artichokes.
Heat the stock in a large pan and keep on a slow boil. In a large saucepan fry the onion in half the butter over a medium heat for about 3 minutes or until translucent. Add the rice and cook over a high heat until the rice is very hot, stirring constantly with a wooden spoon. Add the wine and allow to evaporate. Add a ladleful of stock or enough to ensure that the rice is always covered with a veil of liquid. Keep adding the stock, a ladleful at a time, about once every minute and cook for 12 minutes in total from the moment when the rice starts boiling.
Remove from the heat, add the rest of the butter, the Parmesan, half the artichokes and half the parsley, and mix to blend the flavours. Add salt and pepper to taste and spread the rice out on a large cold surface to stop the cooking and to cool it as quickly as possible. Grease a ring mould of about 30cm/11in with butter and fill with the rice. You can keep the filled mould in the refrigerator for up to 12 hours.

Before serving, preheat the oven to 170°C/350°F/Gas 4. Cover the rice with foil and place in the oven on a baking sheet. Cook for about 30 minutes. Turn the mould on a warmed serving platter and leave to rest for about 5 minutes without removing the mould. Meanwhile heat the rest of the artichokes over a medium heat, and add the rest of the parsley. Carefully remove the mould from the rice and arrange the artichokes in the hole in the middle of the rice and around the edges. Serve immediately.
Serves 10

CESTINI DI PATATE AL FORMAGGIO
Potato Baskets with Cheese

I love this recipe because I can change the filling as much as I like, adding different cheeses, or some chopped ham or even salted cod boiled and puréed in a blender, which is one of my favourites.

10 large unpeeled baking potatoes, all about the same size
210g/7oz/3/4 cup ricotta cheese
90g/3oz fontina cheese
2 large egg yolks
Large pinch of grated nutmeg
Salt and pepper

Preheat the oven to 170°C/350°F/Gas 5.
Wrap the potatoes in foil and cook in the oven for about 1 hour. Leave the oven on for the next stage of cooking.
Cut a large horizontal slice off the length of the potato and discard. Remove about one-third of the inner pulp with a spoon and discard. Keep the rest of the potato in the (aluminum) foil.
In a bowl beat the ricotta with a fork until creamy. Grate the fontina and add to the ricotta with the egg yolks, nutmeg, salt and pepper to taste.
Fill a piping bag with a large fluted nozzle with the ricotta mixture. Pipe the mixture into the potato cavities and cook for 15 minutes in the oven. Arrange on a warmed platter and serve.
Serves 10

CAPPONE AL BALSAMICO
Capon in Balsamic Sauce

Capon is a must in our family for Christmas and this is another speciality from my parents' chef that I still make, remembering always the lovely evening in Milan that was very special because it was also the birthday of my grandfather and this is one of the dishes he most loved.

1 handful fresh sage leaves, finely chopped
2 garlic cloves, finely chopped
1 capon, about 4kg/8lb, prepared for the oven
300g/10oz pitted soft prunes
2 Golden Delicious apples, peeled and diced
2 tbsp unsalted butter
2 tbsp extra virgin olive oil
300g/10oz shallots
60g/2oz raisins soaked in water for about 30 minutes and drained
2 tbsp granulated sugar
4 tbsp balsamic vinegar
Salt and pepper

Preheat the oven to 170°C/350°F/Gas 4.
In a large shallow dish, mix the sage with the garlic and salt and pepper to taste. Pat the mixture over the capon to coat well.
Stuff the capon with the prunes and the apples and truss.
Spread 1 tbsp of the butter with the oil over the base of a large roasting tin (pan) and place the capon on top. Cook in the oven for about 2 hours, basting at intervals to keep the meat juicy.
Meanwhile melt the rest of the butter in a saucepan, add the shallots and cook for about 5 minutes. Add the raisins, the sugar and the balsamic vinegar, cover and cook for 10 minutes more, shaking the pan from time to time. If necessary add a little water to prevent the liquid from drying out. Add salt and pepper to taste.
Transfer the capon to a serving platter, surround with the sauce and serve immediately.
Serves 10

CROSTATA DI MELE CARAMELLATE
Caramelized Apple Tart

A delicious treat at Christmas, although the chocolate and *panettone* mousse is particularly festive.

FOR THE PASTRY:
180g/6oz/1½ cups plain (all-purpose) flour
60g/2oz/½ cup coarse semolina flour
120g/4oz/8 tbsp unsalted butter, at room temperature
60g/2oz/4 tbsp granulated sugar
1 large egg, plus 1 large yolk
FOR THE FILLING:
60g/2oz/4 tbsp unsalted butter
90g/3oz/6 tbsp granulated sugar
5 Golden Delicious apples
1 fresh rosemary sprig, very finely chopped

Heat the oven to 170°C/350°F/Gas 4.
In a food processor fitted with metal blades put the flour, the semolina, butter, sugar, egg and egg yolk and process until a ball is formed. Wrap the dough in cling film (plastic wrap) and put in the refrigerator for a maximum of 2 hours.
Butter a 26cm/10in tart tin (pan) with removable base. Roll out the dough on a lightly floured surface and line the tart tin (pan). Bake in the oven until barely golden, about 20 minutes. If the pastry pops up in places, remove it from the oven and flatten again with the palm of your hand, protected with a cloth. When the pastry is ready, remove from the oven and set aside to cool.
For the filling, heat the butter and the sugar for about 10 minutes in a large, heavy-based non-stick pan. Meanwhile peel, core and dice the apples. Add the apples to the butter and sugar mixture and cook for 3 minutes more until lightly caramelized.
Tip the apples into the pastry shell, and cook for 10 more minutes in the oven. Sprinkle with the chopped rosemary and allow to cool slightly. Carefully unmould the tart from the tart tin (pan), transfer to a serving platter and serve at room temperature.
Serves 10

WINE

I have the good fortune to live on an ancient and prestigious wine estate, located in Chianti, an area whose name is synonymous with Italian wine. The property, Badia a Coltibuono, has been in my husband's family for almost two hundred years. Now my daughter manages the estate and my son, Roberto, is the winemaker. Happily this simplifies my decision about what wine to select for a meal. I serve our own wines exclusively. Not only are they excellent and varied, I know that if I were a guest at another vineyard, I would want to taste the estate wine. Here are a few of my Coltibuono favourites.

I like to greet my guests with a glass of Trappoline, a white wine named after one of Coltibuono's vineyards, a blend of Pinot Blanc, Chardonnay, Trebbiano and Malvasia grapes. Fresh and fruity when young, Trappoline makes the perfect aperitif and also goes well with fish or vegetable-based first courses. With some bottle ageing it develops more complex aromas. At that stage I combine it with mushrooms, white meat and shellfish. For summer meals, especially, I often serve our Cetamura Rosato. This rosé has a brilliant and vivacious strawberry pink colour. Its aroma is reminiscent of fresh fruit and berries. I find it very satisfying to serve chilled as a warm weather aperitif, as well as an accompaniment to salads and fresh cheeses.

A few years ago my son, Roberto, first began experimenting with Chardonnay grapes in our vineyards, a varietal that adapts very well to Chianti's climate and soil. The result is Sella del Boscone, made from a hundred per cent Chardonnay grapes, carefully selected and hand-picked and fermented in oak barrels. This wine has an elegant and intense fruity aroma with a spicy accent from the wood. I serve it with first courses, pasta and risotto. Because it has well-balanced acidity and body, it is delicious on its own, as an aperitif for a more formal occasion or while lingering at the table after an alfresco meal.

Another relatively recent wine in the Coltibuono collection is Chianti Classico RS. RS, I am proud to say, stands for Robert Stucchi, my son, who created his signature wine to pay homage to the noble Sangiovese grape, native to the Chianti Classico area. It is made from pure, hand-picked Sangioveto grapes, selected from the best growing areas in the Chianti Classico region. It is deep ruby red in colour with aromas of blackberry, cherry and vanilla and tastes to me of wild berries and spice. As it is full-bodied yet very smooth and elegant, it is virtually a perfect match to any substantial dish, from roasts to cheese.

Badia a Coltibuono's Chianti Classico Riserva is our most renowned wine. The grapes are carefully selected from Sangioveto and Canaiolo vines which are all twenty to forty years old. It is aged in oak casks for two years and in bottle for at least one more year. When young, it has a deep ruby red colour, a flowery nose and fruity taste. With maturity it develops brick hues, an aroma with hints of truffles and moss and is more complex on the palate. For meals with guests I usually serve one of our younger Riserva—hopefully a bottle of 1997, perhaps the best vintage of the twentieth century, if I can nip one from the cellar. It goes best with dishes with a pronounced flavour. For special or formal occasions, I choose an older Riserva to serve with red meats. I would suggest uncorking it a couple of hours before serving at room temperature, in order to let it breathe.

Sangioveto is the ancient name used in this area of Tuscany for the Sangiovese grape and it is the name we chose to call a very special wine, made only when the vintage is extraordinarily good, from Sangiovese grapes selected from the oldest estate vineyards. It is aged for several years in wood and in bottle. Sangioveto is a wine of great body, deep ruby red colour and intense aroma. It is the perfect match for game, roasts and spicy stews. I often serve it as the second red wine at a more formal meal. That way my guests can enjoy it while they relax at the finish of a hopefully delicious dinner. I usually decant Sangioveto to allow the wine to open to its fullness. A crystal decanter full of rubies also adds beauty to your table.

With dessert I serve Coltibuono's Vin Santo, the ancient Tuscan sweet white wine, which we produce in small quantities according to traditional methods. It is made from a blend of Trebbiano and Malvasia grapes, which are hung in bunches to dry for several months before being pressed and placed in small oak casks for a period of about five years. Coltibuono Vin Santo is golden yellow with amber hues. It has the rich aroma and taste of apricots, honey and vanilla. Try serving it slightly chilled as an aperitif, and also with pâté or sharp cheese.

After dinner, when my guests retire to the drawing room for coffee it is time to bring out the grappa, a distilled liquor produced from the lightly pressed skins of the same selected grapes used in making our red wines. The result is a crystal clear spirit with forty per cent alcohol content. Grappa is definitely 'fire water', but fine grappa such as Coltibuono's does not have the rough edges associated with more rustic distillations. Once you have acquired the taste, it goes down perhaps all too smoothly.